An Introduction to AutoCAD Designer

An Introduction to AutoCAD Designer

A. Yarwood

Autodesk.
Registered Developer

LONGMAN

Addison Wesley Longman Limited
Edinburgh Gate, Harlow
Essex CM20 2JE, England
and Associated Companies throughout the world

First published 1996

British Library Cataloguing in Publication Data
A catalogue entry for this title is available from the British Library

ISBN 0-582-28874-6

Set by 24 in 10/13pt Melior
Produced by Longman Singapore Publishers (Pte) Ltd
Printed in Singapore

Contents

List of plates

Plates are placed between pages 82 and 83.

Preface

AutoCAD Designer is a computer-aided design (CAD) 3D modelling software package, which works within AutoCAD. At the time of writing AutoCAD Designer is available in two versions – AutoCAD Designer Release 1.1 which works within the MS-DOS version of AutoCAD Release 12 and AutoCAD Designer Release 1.2 which works within AutoCAD Release 13. Both of the Designer versions function in a similar manner, so that if one can construct 3D models in Release 1.1, the same methods of working can be used when working with Release 1.2. Methods of working with both versions are described in this book.

But Designer is far more than a CAD 3D modelling package. Any 3D model constructed with the aid of the software can be produced as a series of views in orthographic projection by calling a single command and setting check boxes within a dialogue box. In addition, if the parametric functions of the software are employed, 3D models can be immediately changed parametrically to models of different scales with the changes reflected in the accompanying orthographic projections. The changes are effected by using a single Designer command (tool) to change any one parametric dimension in the model. The single change is reflected in all the parametric dimensions throughout the model. Dimensions are carried between model and views in orthographic projection, with all parametric dimensions appearing in the orthographic views. Orthographic views can be re-dimensioned and notes added if required. A series of models with accompanying orthographic views for a whole series of components of different sizes can be created using the parametric functions of Designer.

Any model created with Designer can be rendered in a variety of colours and materials and with any suitable lighting effects either with the set of AutoCAD Render commands (tools) or in Autodesk AutoVision. The files of Designer models can be loaded into Autodesk 3D Studio for rendering if required. A number of examples of rendered Designer models, both in black and white and in colour, are given in this book.

The contents of the book are designed for the beginner new to Designer and is suitable for students in Further and Higher Education as well as those in industry who wish to learn how to use the software. A basic knowledge of how to use AutoCAD itself is assumed, because some of the methods of working – such as the drawing of sketches – is carried out with AutoCAD command systems. Although not essential for following the methods of working explained in the book, it is also best if the reader understands 3D coordinate systems to some extent and is able to think in terms of 3D coordinate geometry – i.e. in terms of *x,y,z* when constructing models on screen.

All the illustrations throughout the book were constructed in either AutoCAD Release 12 for MS-DOS or in AutoCAD Release 13 for Windows. One of the colour plates was constructed in AutoCAD for Windows (Release 12) to illustrate that Designer models can be carried into AutoCAD for Windows to be rendered with AutoVision. It must however be remembered that Designer will not work in AutoCAD for Windows. Both illustrations and accompanying text were worked on a PC (personal computer), equipped with a 486 DX2 operating chip.

As this book was about to be published, Autodesk released a new version of Designer (Release 2) designed to work within AutoCAD Release 13 for Windows 95. All the methods of working described in this book are as applicable to readers using Release 2 of Designer as they are to readers using Release 1.

A. Yarwood
Salisbury 1996

Acknowledgements

The author wishes to acknowledge with grateful thanks the help given to him by members of the staff at Autodesk Ltd.

Registered trademarks

The following are registered trademarks of Autodesk Inc.:

Autodesk®, AutoCAD®, Advanced Modelling Extension (AME)®, AutoCAD® Designer.

AutoVision™ is a trademark of Autodesk Inc.

IBM® is a registered trademark of the International Business Machines Corporation.

MS-DOS® is a registered trademark, and Windows™ is a trademark of the Microsoft Corporation.

A. Yarwood is a Registered Developer with Autodesk Ltd.

Autodesk.

Registered Developer

CHAPTER 1

Introduction

System requirements for Designer

AutoCAD Designer Release 1.1 is an extension program which can only be run when loaded into the DOS version of AutoCAD Release 12.

Hardware requirements

The software will only function if the following computer hardware requirements are met, as shown in Fig. 1.1:

PC (personal computer) with 386, 486 or Pentium operating chip.

16 Mbytes of RAM.

Hard disk with at least 9 Mbytes free space over and above the space used for AutoCAD R12.

A VGA (video graphics array) monitor, or better.

Notes

1. Designer Release 1.1 will not run in the Windows version of AutoCAD Release 12 (AutoCAD for Windows).
2. Throughout this book all illustrations of screens were taken from a VGA monitor.

Software requirements

In addition to the above hardware requirements, Designer 1 requires the following software to be loaded.

AutoCAD Release 12 (DOS version).

MS-DOS 3.3 or better.

The Designer 1.1 software, pre-loaded into AutoCAD R12.

With the Designer files pre-loaded into the AutoCAD R12 directory setup, upon starting up AutoCAD, followed by a *left-click* on **Designer** in the menu bar, the resulting AutoCAD drawing editor will be as shown in Fig. 1.2.

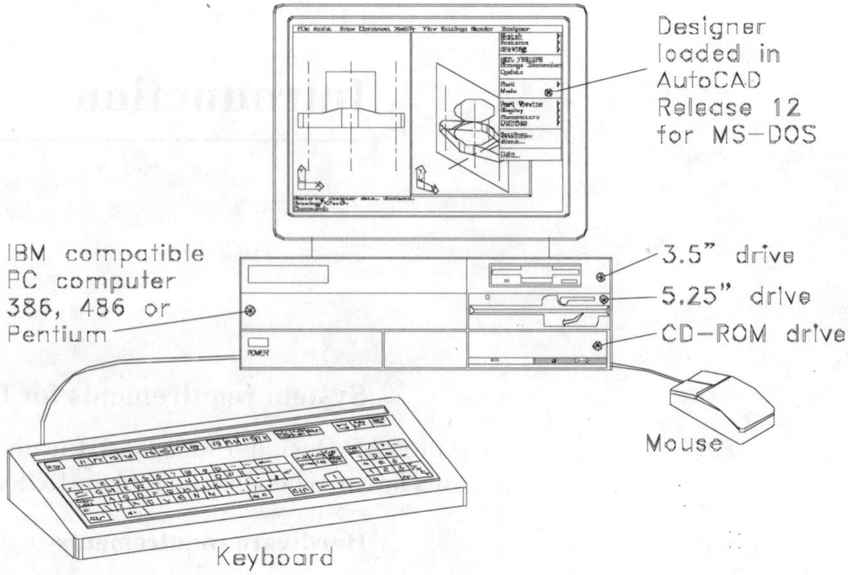

Fig. 1.1 A typical hardware setup for running Designer Release 1.1

What is AutoCAD Designer?

AutoCAD Designer is a feature-based, parametric 3D solid modelling software tool. This means that:

Any solid model constructed in AutoCAD Designer will consist of a number of features:

Extrusions;

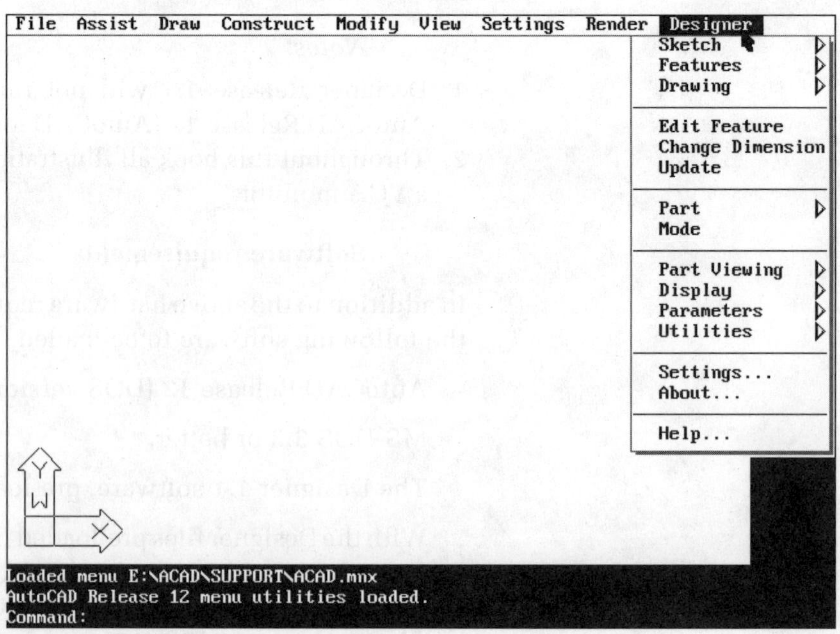

Fig. 1.2 The AutoCAD drawing editor showing the **Designer** pull-down menu

Revolved surfaces;
Sweeps;
Holes;
Fillets;
Chamfers.

Designer solid models are three-dimensional (3D).

Designer solid models can be amended parametrically. Any change in dimension or shape of any part of a Designer 3D model will be automatically reflected in all those parts of the solid model which are affected by the change.

It is the parametric facility of Designer which make it such a good software design tool.

Part Mode and Drawing Mode

There are two *modes* available in Designer – **Part Mode**, displaying the 3D solid model, and a **Drawing Mode** producing an orthographic projection of the model. When the operator is satisfied with his/her construction of a 3D model in **Part Mode**, it can then be viewed in **Drawing Mode** as an orthographic projection. **Part Mode** relies upon

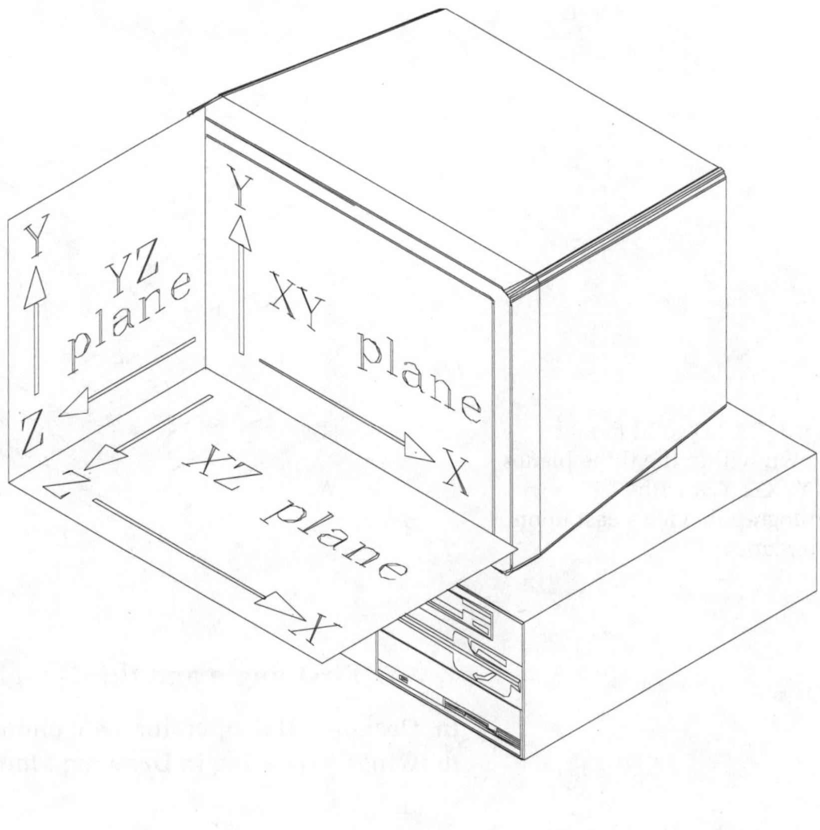

Fig. 1.3 The XY, XZ and YZ planes upon which 3D solids are constructed

constructions in three dimensions – using X, Y and Z axes. **Drawing Mode** is two-dimensional – based upon only X and Y axes.

When working in **Part Mode** a construction proceeds in three planes – the XY plane – the surface of the monitor screen, together with an XZ and a YZ plane – each perpendicular to the surface of the monitor screen. These three **Part Mode** planes (XY, XZ, YZ) are illustrated in Fig. 1.3. To fully understand the positions of the XZ and YZ planes, it must be remembered that they must be envisaged as being perpendicular to the monitor screen surface. According to how the operator is working when constructing a model, the XZ and YZ planes may be in any position relative to the screen surface. Thus in Fig. 1.3 the XZ plane is shown at the bottom of the monitor screen. In Fig. 1.4 a 3D model is shown placed within the three planes XY, XZ and YZ. Figure 1.4 shows how an orthographic projection appears within the three planes. Note that whereas in Fig. 1.3 the XZ plane is shown at the bottom of the monitor screen, in Fig. 1.4 it is shown at the top. However in both Fig. 1.3 and Fig. 1.4 the XZ and the YZ planes are perpendicular to the surface of the monitor screen.

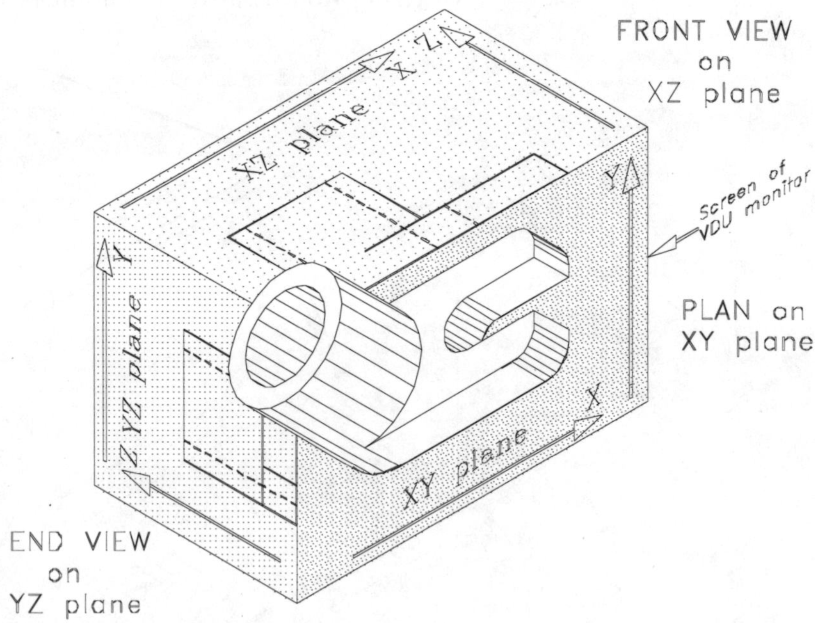

Fig. 1.4 A 3D solid model shown within the three planes (XY, XZ, YZ) with orthographic views cast upon the planes

First-angle and third-angle orthographic projection

In Designer the operator can choose whether the orthographic drawings appearing in **Drawing Mode** are in first- or in third-angle

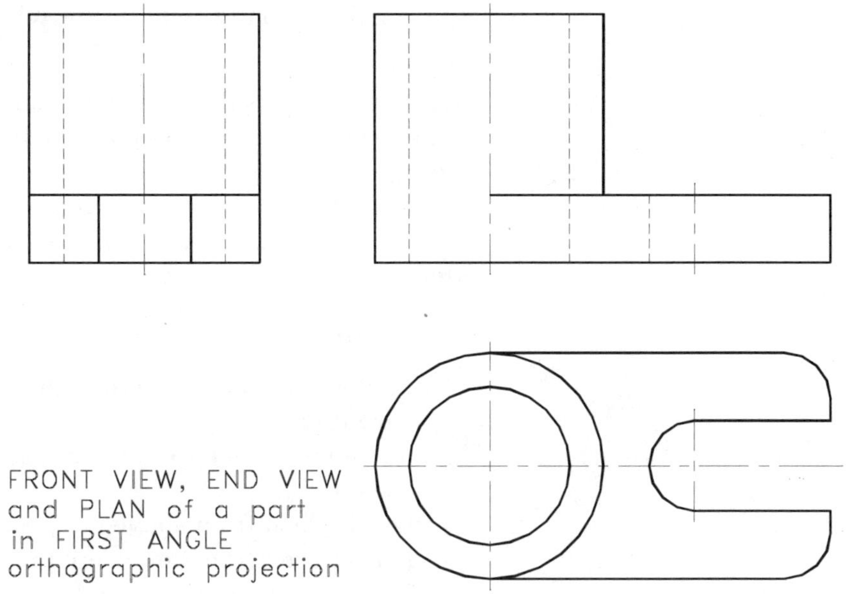

Fig. 1.5 The 3D solid model of Fig. 1.4 in first-angle orthographic drawing

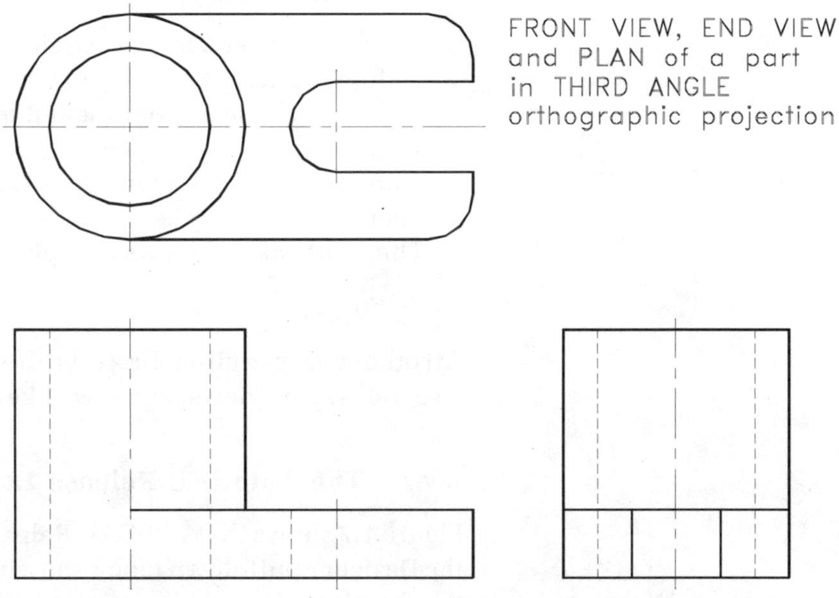

Fig. 1.6 The 3D solid model of Fig. 1.4 in third-angle orthographic projection

projection. Taking the example of the 3D solid model shown in Fig. 1.4 within three planes (XY, XZ, YZ), Fig. 1.5 shows a three-view first-angle orthographic projection of the model and Fig. 1.6 a three-view third-angle orthographic projection of the model.

Comparing first angle with third angle

Orthographic projections may contain any number of views from one, to as many as the designer wishes. As an example, a thin metal plate to be worked in one plane will probably only require a single view. Other 3D models may require more. It is fairly common to see drawings with three views, but some may contain many more. However the following applies to views as seen in the **Drawing Mode** of AutoCAD Designer:

First-angle projection

End views as seen from the right are positioned to the left of the front view.
End views as seen from the left are positioned to the right of the front view.
Plans as seen from above are positioned below the front view.
Plans as seen from below are positioned above the front view.
The fronts of end views and plans face outwards from the front view.

Third-angle projection

End views as seen from the right are positioned to the right of the front view.
End views as seen from the left are positioned to the left of the front view.
Plans as seen from above are positioned above the front view.
Plans as seen from below are positioned below the front view.
The fronts of end views and plans face towards the front view.

Note

All other views in either first- or third-angle orthographic projection – sections, part views, etc. – will be based upon these rules.

The AutoCAD Release 12 drawing editor for DOS

Figure 1.7 shows the AutoCAD Release 12 DOS drawing editor with the **Designer** pull-down menu showing and the names of the parts of the drawing editor.

Methods of working

Throughout this book it will be assumed that the operator is working with a two-button mouse as a selection device, although AutoCAD

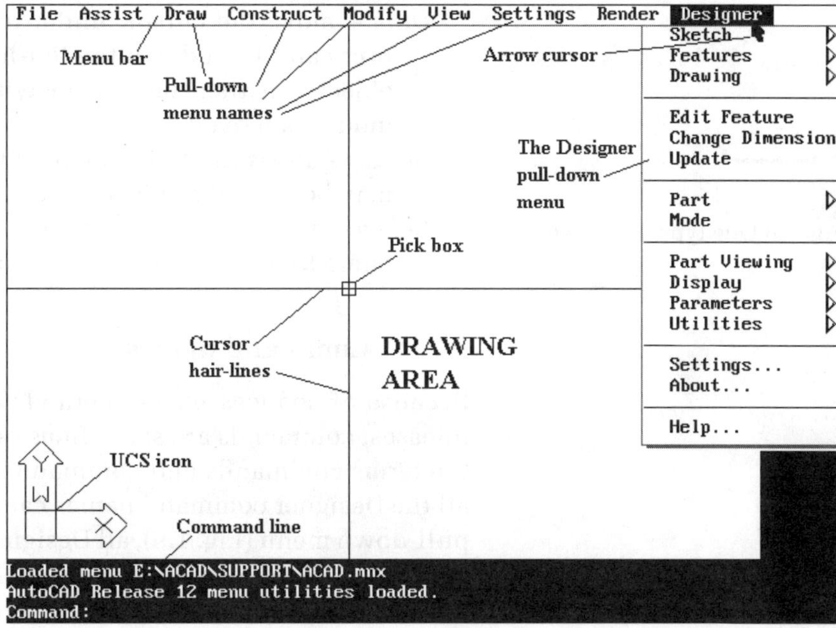

Fig. 1.7 The parts of the AutoCAD Release 12 DOS drawing editor

R12 can be controlled with other types of selection device. The following describes the actions involved in using the mouse:

Move the mouse over the surface of the desk on which the computer stands. A cursor in the form of an arrow (when it is within the area of the menu bar or of a pull-down menu), a cross or cursor lines (when in the drawing area) moves in response to movement of the mouse.

Moving the mouse over a menu name or a command name in a menu causes the name and its background to *highlight* – the name changes colour and appears against a contrasting background colour.

Enter – type the word, figures or names following *enter* at the keyboard.

Left-click – press and release the left-hand button of the mouse. A *left-click* usually (but not always) has the same result as pressing the **Return** key of the keyboard (see below).

Right-click – press and release the right-hand button of the mouse.

Double-click – press and release the left-hand button of the mouse twice in quick succession.

Pick – move the cursor under mouse control until it is over the name or object to be selected followed by a *left-click*.

Call or calling – *picking, entering* or selecting a command name.

Drag – move the cursor, under mouse control, onto an object, press and hold down the left-hand button of the mouse. The object can then be moved within the drawing area as the mouse is moved.

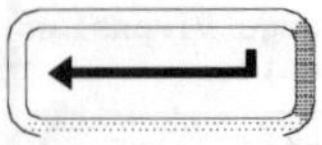

Fig. 1.8 One type of **Return** key

Return – press the **Return** key of the keyboard. The **Return** key may be named **Enter** or may show an arrow as in Fig. 1.8.

Select – move the cursor under mouse control over the object or name to be used, followed by a *left-click*.

Command names

Because of changes in the methods of working AutoCAD in later releases, commands are sometimes referred to as *tools*. In this book the terms commands and command names will be used. Although all the Designer command names can be selected from the **Designer** pull-down menu (Fig. 1.9), all Designer commands will be shown in the text as being *entered* in full at the keyboard, followed by the options which appear at the Command Line when a command name is *entered* from the keyboard. If the command name is selected from the **Designer** pull-down menu (Fig. 1.9), the same options appear at the Command Line. The only difference is that the command name appears preceded by a dash. Examples are:

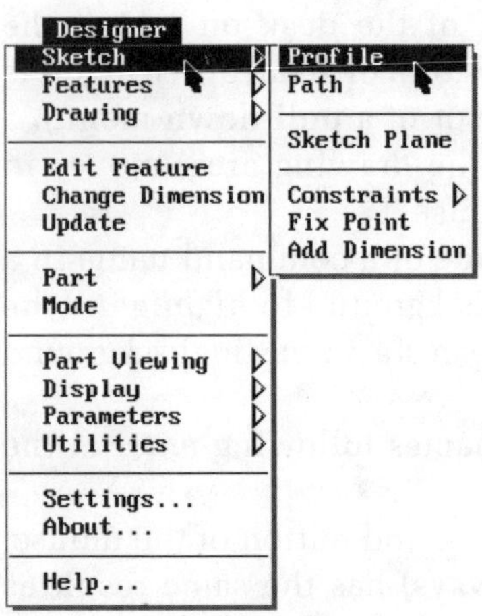

Fig. 1.9 Selecting **Profile** from the **Designer** pull-down menu

Entering the command name at the keyboard

Command: *enter* adprofile *right-click*
Select objects to sketch: *pick* the object **1 found.**
Select objects: *right-click*
Solved under constrained sketch requiring 3 dimensions/restraints.
Command:

Selecting the command name from the pull-down menu

Command: _adprofile
Select objects to sketch: *pick* the object **1 found.**
Select objects: *right-click*
Solved under constrained sketch requiring 3 dimensions/restraints.
Command:

CHAPTER 2

Basic principles of construction

Prototype drawings for Designer

Two prototype drawing files for use when constructing Designer drawings will be found in the *acad\support* directory. These are **adesign.dwg** for working in Imperial measurements – inches, feet, etc. and **adiso.dwg** for working is ISO measurements – mm, cm, etc. For my own purposes I formed my own Designer prototype and gave it the filename of **admine.dwg**. More about my Designer prototype drawing file later.

Starting a Designer drawing

It is advisable when wishing to construct a drawing with the aid of the Designer software, to call a New prototype drawing to the AutoCAD editor. This can be carried out in one of two ways:

1. *Left-click* on **File** in the menu bar, followed by another *left-click* on **New...** in the **File** pull-down menu. This brings the **Create New Drawing** dialogue box on screen (Fig. 2.1). *Left-click* on the **Prototype...** Button in the dialogue box, bringing the **Prototype Drawing File** dialogue box to screen. Either *double-click* on the

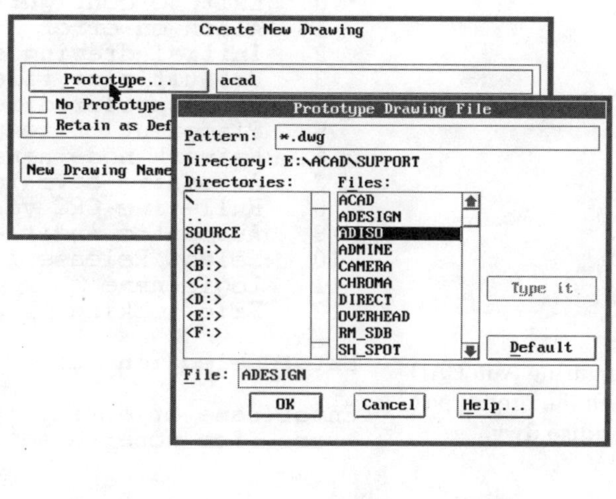

Fig. 2.1 Selecting a New Prototype file for constructing Designer drawings

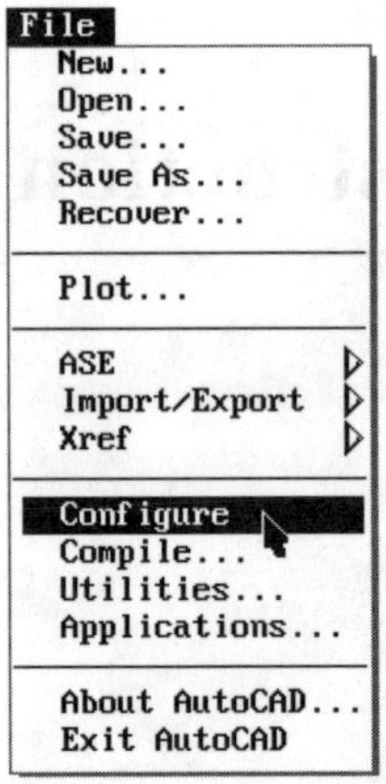

Fig. 2.2 Selecting **Configure** from the **File** pull-down menu

required drawing filename – in Fig. 2.1 **ADISO** has been selected, or *left-click* on the desired filename, followed by another *left-click* on the **OK** button of the dialogue box.

2. Select **Configure** from the **File** pull-down menu (Fig. 2.2). An AutoCAD text screen appears. Press **Return** twice as requested and follow the instructions as in Fig. 2.3. One disadvantage of this method is that if one wishes to use AutoCAD without Designer, configuration of the **Initial drawing setup** must be repeated to call **acad.dwg** or **acadiso.dwg** upon AutoCAD startup. However if you are using AutoCAD for a series of Designer drawings, you may find it better to set **Initial drawing setup** to a Designer prototype drawing.

The AutoCAD Designer screens

When the New prototype drawing **adiso.dwg** is called, the screen appears as in Fig. 2.4. *Left-click* on **Designer** in the menu bar, followed by another on **Mode** in the pull-down menu which appears.

```
Configuration menu

  0.  Exit to drawing editor
  1.  Show current configuration
  2.  Allow detailed configuration

  3.  Configure video display
  4.  Configure digitizer
  5.  Configure plotter
  6.  Configure system console
  7.  Configure operating parameters

Enter selection <0>: 7

Configure operating parameters

  0.  Exit to configuration menu
  1.  Alarm on error
  2.  Initial drawing setup
  3.  Default plot file name
  4.  Plot spooler directory
  5.  Placement of temporary files
  6.  Network node name
  7.  Automatic-save feature
  8.  Full-time CRC validation
  9.  Automatic Audit after IGESIN, DXFIN, or DXBIN
 10.  Select Release 11 hidden line removal algorithm
 11.  Login name
 12.  File locking

Enter selection <0>: 2 .

Enter name of default prototype file for new drawings
  or . for none <acad>: adiso
```

Fig. 2.3 Configuring AutoCAD to startup with the prototype drawing file **adiso.dwg**

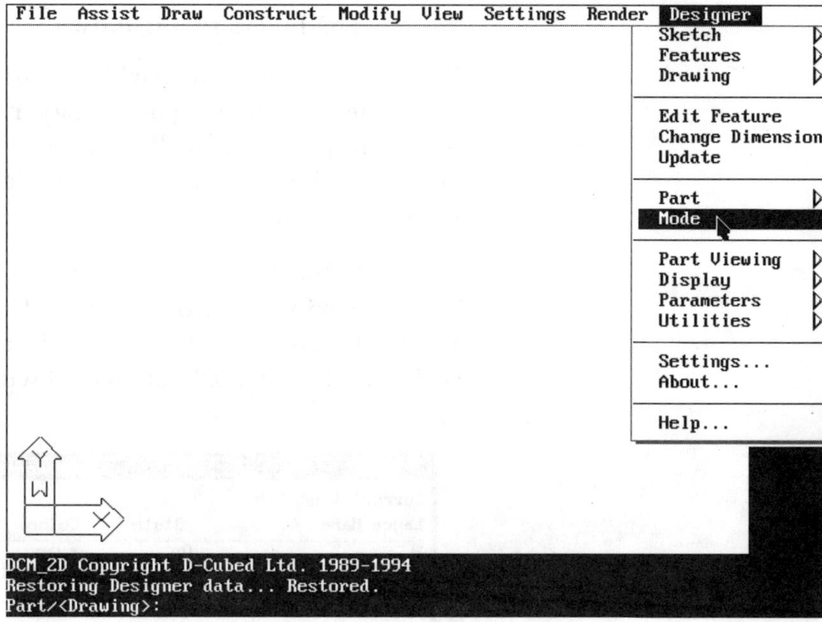

Fig. 2.4 Selecting **Mode** from the **Designer** pull-down menu in the prototype drawing **adiso.dwg**

Right-click and the second Designer screen replaces the first as in Fig. 2.5. This screen, which is in **Paper Space** (PSpace), contains an A2 sheet layout, complete with a title block (shown enlarged in Fig. 2.5). This sheet layout is a block which has been inserted in the PSpace drawing editor.

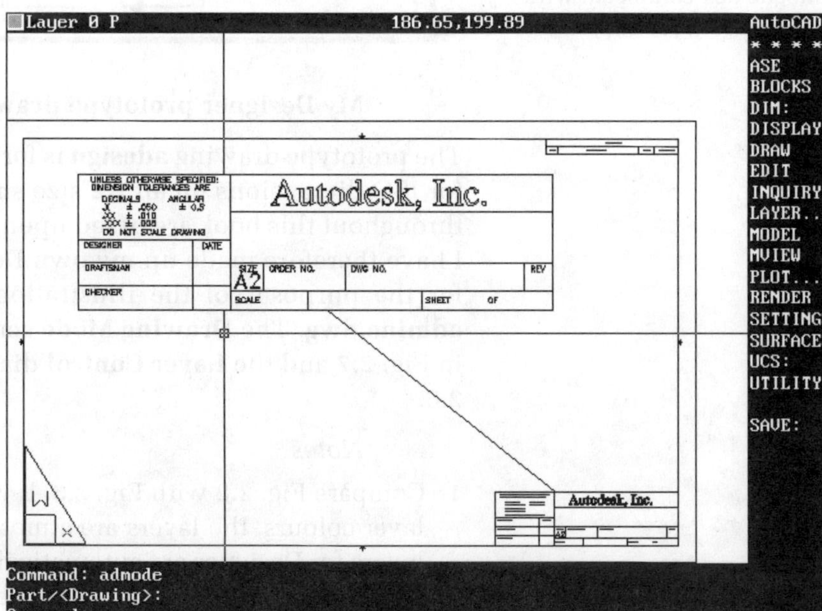

Fig. 2.5 The drawing sheet in **Drawing Mode** from the **adiso.dwg** prototype file showing the title block enlarged

The layers in adiso.dwg

Go back to the **Part** screen while in **adiso.dwg**. *Left-click* on **Settings...** in the menu bar and again on **Layer...** in the menu which appears. As the **Layer Control** dialogue box appears (Fig. 2.6) note that a number of layers have been automatically formed. Note also that some layers have colours other than **white**.

Warning

While working in Designer, do not attempt editing the contents of any of the Designer layers. To do so will result in loss of detail without which your Designer drawings cannot be formed.

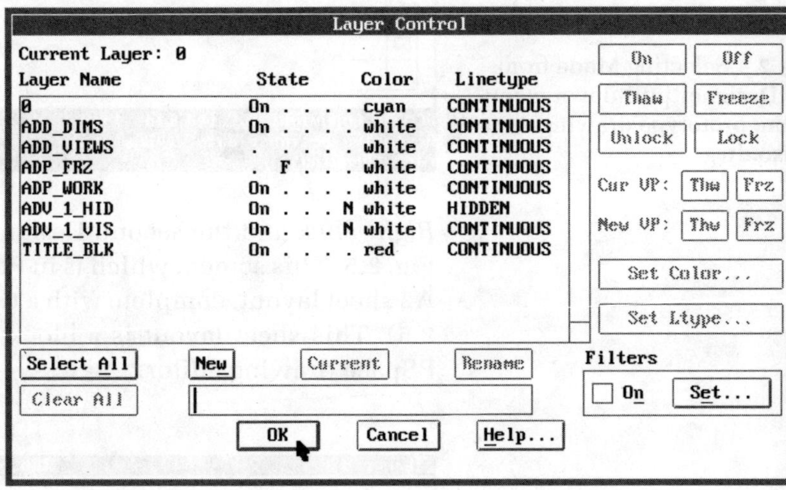

Fig. 2.6 The **Layer Control** dialogue box connected with the **adiso.dwg** prototype

My Designer prototype drawing

The prototype drawing **adesign** is for Imperial dimensions. **Adiso** is for ISO dimensions on an A2 size sheet. The majority of drawings throughout this book are based upon drawings for an A3 size sheet. I have therefore made up my own Designer prototype drawing file for the purposes of the illustrations shown here and named it **admine.dwg**. The **Drawing Mode** screen for this drawing is shown in Fig. 2.7 and the **Layer Control** dialogue box is illustrated in Fig. 2.8.

Notes

1. Compare Fig. 2.8 with Fig. 2.6. It will be seen that, apart from the layer colours, the layers are almost identical. This is because the layers for Designer are automatically formed when any command is called from the Designer command set.

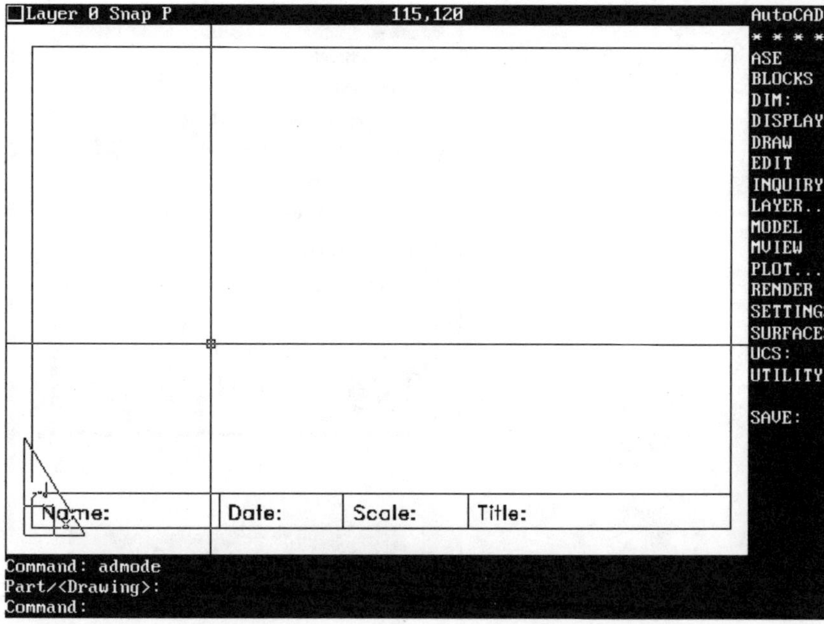

Fig. 2.7 The drawing sheet in **Drawing Mode** from the **admine.dwg** prototype file

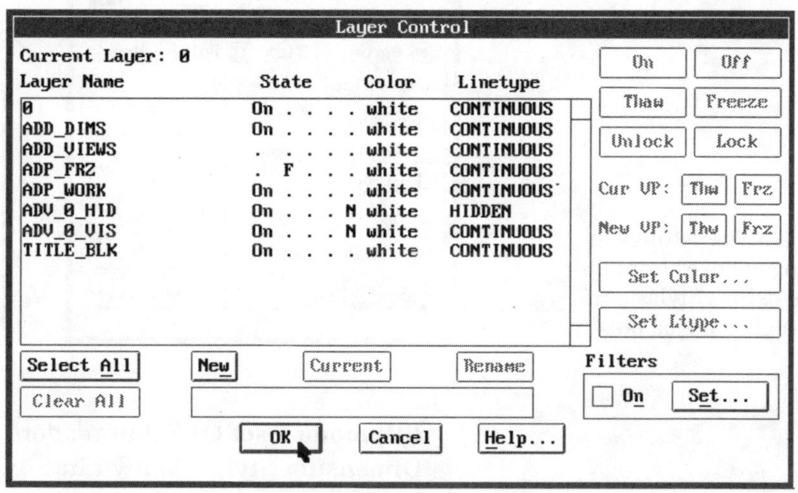

Fig. 2.8 The **Layer Control** dialogue box associated with my prototype drawing file **admine.dwg**

2. The drawing sheet shown in Fig. 2.7 was drawn in AutoCAD and saved as an AutoCAD drawing. It was then inserted into the **Drawing Mode** screen of my **admine** drawing as a block on the layer **TITLE_BLK**.
3. The following settings were made for my **admine** prototype:

   Limits – 420,300
   Units – no figures after the decimal point
   Snap – set to 5 and **ON**
   Grid – set to 10, but **OFF**

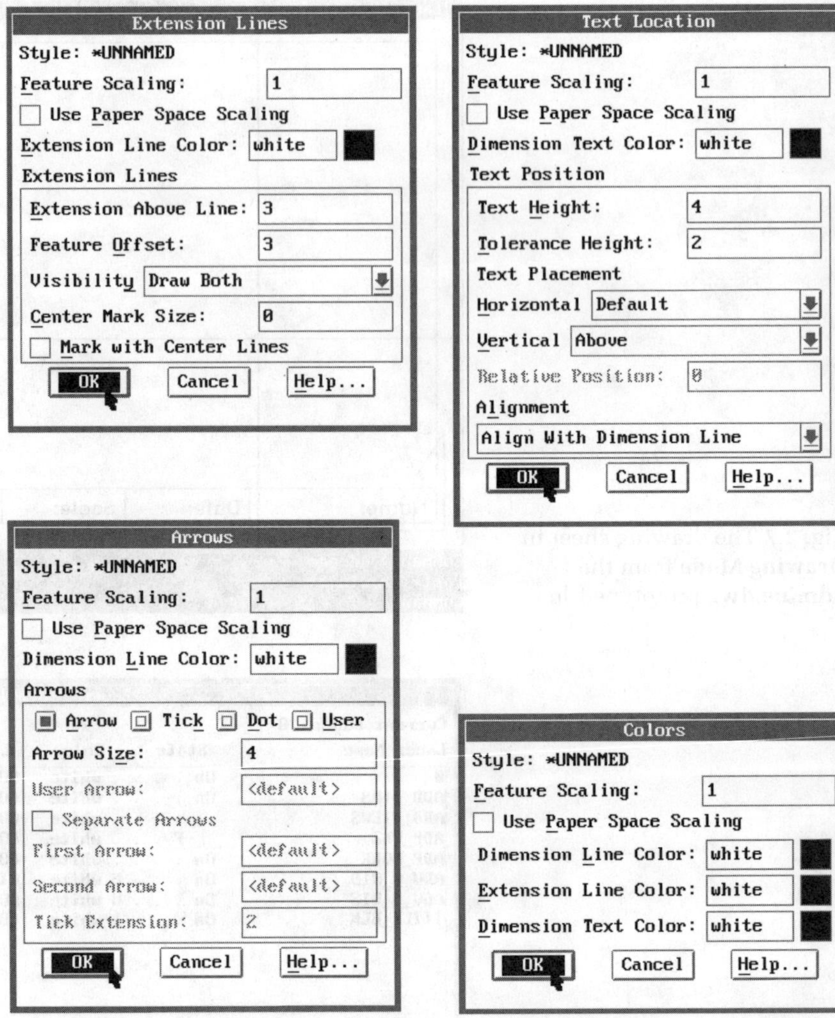

Fig. 2.9 The settings in dialogue boxes from the **Dimensions Styles and Settings** dialogue box

Blipmode – set **OFF**, but readers may prefer it to be **ON**
Dimension Style – shown in Fig. 2.9.

4. There is no need to include a title block in one's own Designer prototype drawing file. If required, sheet margins, a title block and other notes can be added to the drawing when construction of a Designer solid model and its orthographic projection have been completed.
5. My title block in **admine.dwg** includes a simple title block area designed for student use or for those learning how to use AutoCAD Designer.

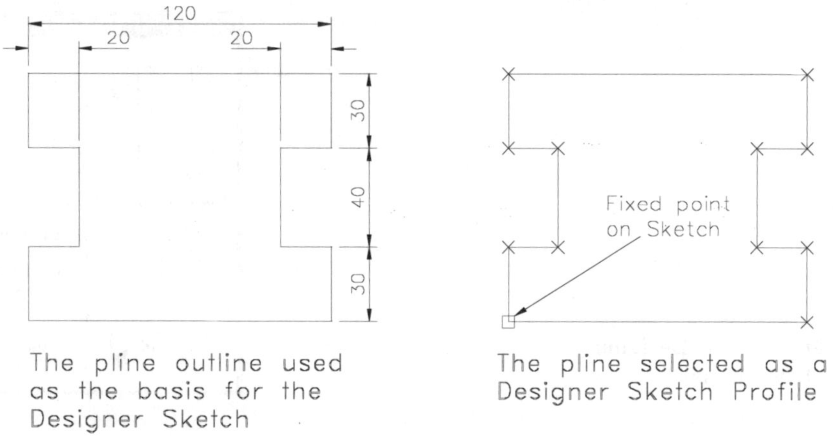

Fig. 2.10 The pline outline and the **Sketch Profile** from the outline

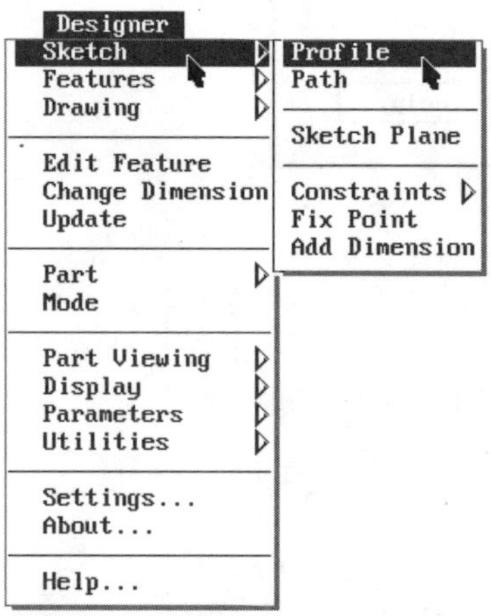

Fig. 2.11 Select from the **Designer** pull-down menu instead of *entering* adprofile

Examples

A first example to show use of basic commands

This first example does not include dimensions added from the Designer dimensioning commands. The dimensions given with Fig. 2.10 are only included to allow the reader to work this first, very simple example. The stages in constructing this example are:

1. Draw the pline outline as given in the left-hand drawing of Fig. 2.10.
2. At the Command Line:

   Command: *enter* adprofile *right-click* (see Fig. 2.11)
   Select objects for sketch.
   Select objects: *pick* the pline outline
   Select objects: *right-click*
   Solved under constrained sketch requiring 6 dimensions/constraints
   Command:

   A fixed point rectangle and crosses appear at the corners of the sketch outline – right-hand drawing of Fig. 2.10.
3. At the Command Line:

   Command: *enter* adextrude *right-click* (see Fig. 2.12)

   The **Designer Extrusion** dialogue box (Fig. 2.13) appears. *Enter* 40 in the **Distance** box, followed by a *left-click* on the **OK** button of the dialogue box. The sketch outline extrudes.
4. At the Command Line:

   Command: *enter* vpoint *right-click*
   VPOINT/Rotate/<View point> <0,0,0>: *enter* –1,–1,1 *right-click*
   Command: *enter* z (Zoom) *right-click*

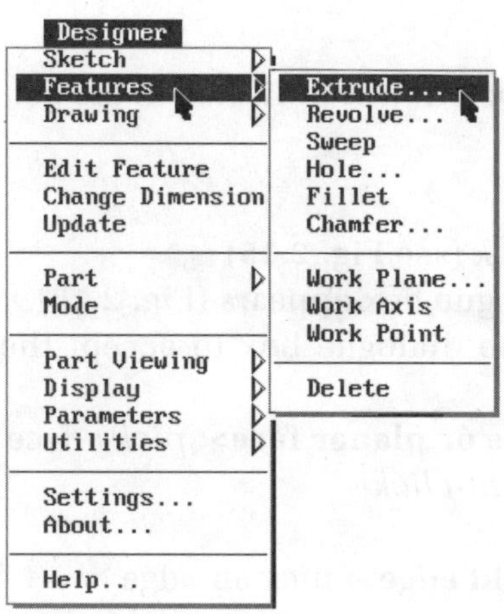

Fig. 2.12 Select from the **Designer** pull-down menu instead of *entering* adextrude

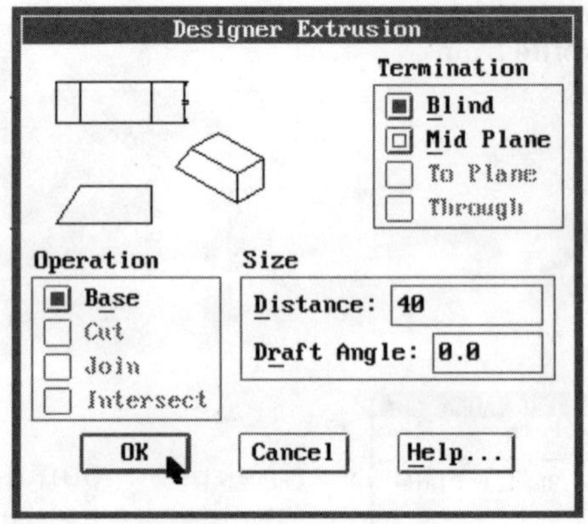

Fig. 2.13 The **Designer Extrusion** dialogue box

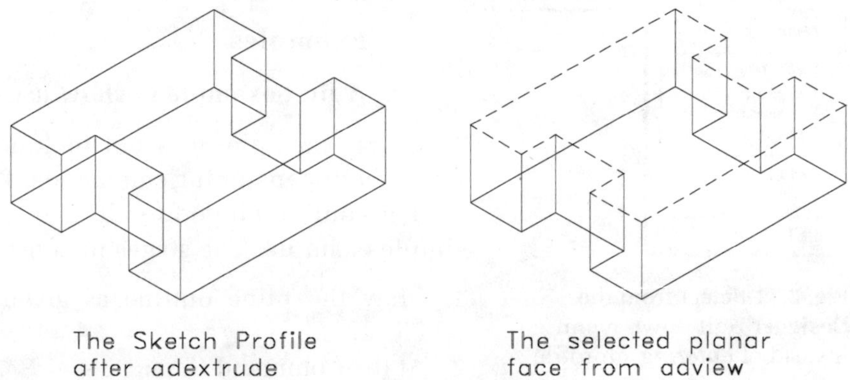

Fig. 2.14 The extruded profile

All/Center/Dynamic/Extents/Left/Previous/Vmax/Window/ <Scale(X/XP)>: *enter* 1 *right-click*

Command:

The extrusion assumes a pictorial position as indicated in the left-hand drawing of Fig. 2.14.

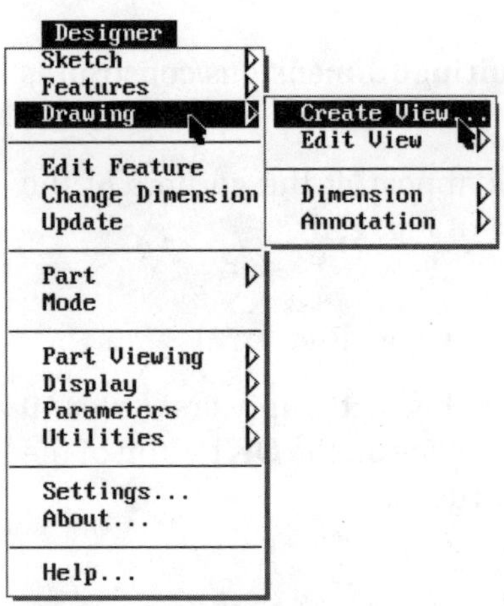

Fig. 2.15 Select from the **Designer** pull-down menu instead of *entering* adview

5. At the Command Line:

Command: *enter* adview *right-click* (see Fig. 2.15)

The **Designer Drawing View** dialogue box appears (Fig. 2.16).

Left-click on the **OK** button of the dialogue box to accept the current settings.

Xy/Yz/Zx/UCS/<Select work plane or planar face>: *pick* a face

Next/<Accept>: *enter* N (Next) *right-click*

Next/<Accept>: *right-click*

X/Y/Z/<Select work axis or straight edge>: *pick* an edge

Rotate/<Accept>: *right-click*

The screen switches to PSpace (**Designer Drawing Mode**).

View center: *pick* a position for the view centre

Command:

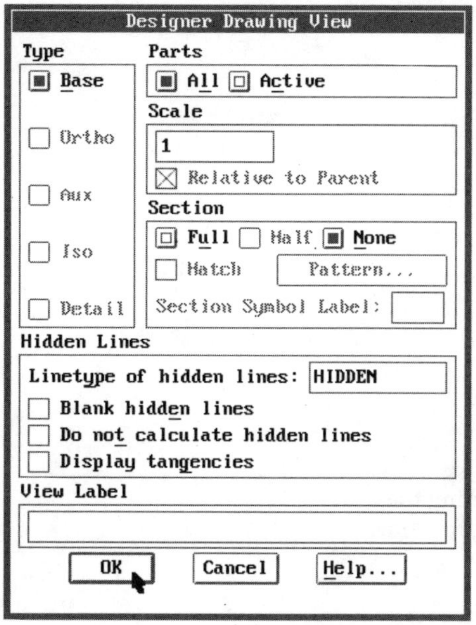

Fig. 2.16 The **Designer Drawing View** dialogue box

The required view appears in the **Designer Drawing Mode** screen as shown in Fig. 2.17. The *picked* point is in the centre of the view.

6. At the Command Line:

Command: *enter* adview *right-click*

In the **Designer Drawing View** dialogue box, *left-click* in the **Ortho** button, followed by another *left-click* in the **OK** button of the dialogue box.

Select parent view: *pick* the view already in the **Drawing Mode** screen

Location for orthographic view: *pick* the required location along the rubber band which is attached to the centre of the parent view

Command:

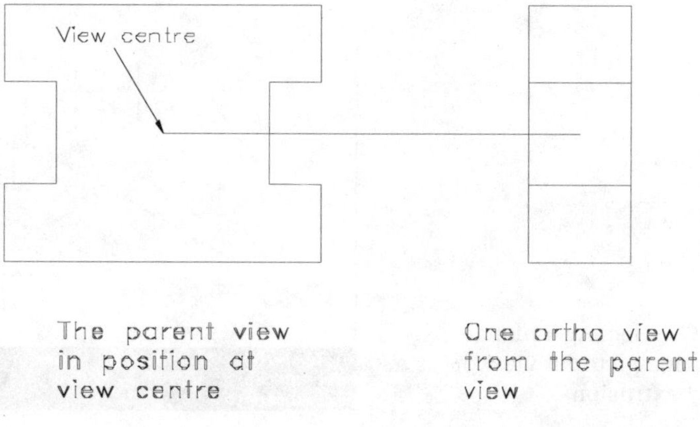

Fig. 2.17 Views as they appear in the **Drawing Mode** screen

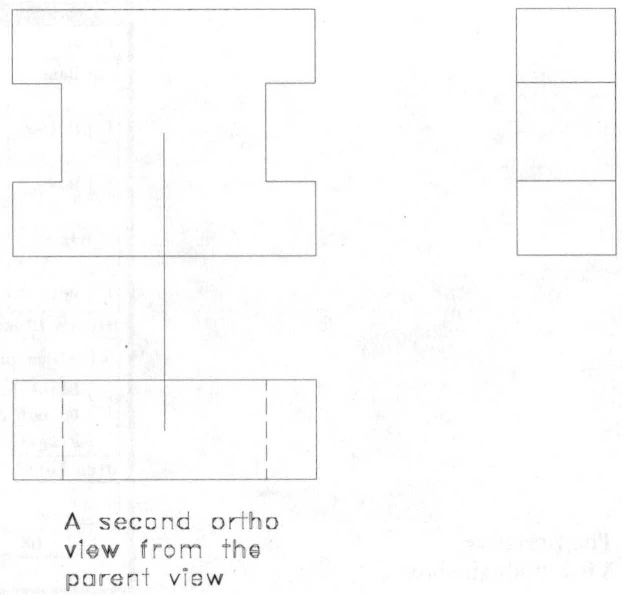

Fig. 2.18 Positioning the second orthographic view

The second view appears (Fig. 2.17)

7. Repeat item 6 to obtain a second orthographic view (Fig. 2.18).
   Figure 2.19 shows the **Designer Part** screen as a planar face is highlighted after being selected from a pictorial view of the part. Figure 2.20 shows the **Designer Drawing** screen with the three-view orthographic projection of the part.

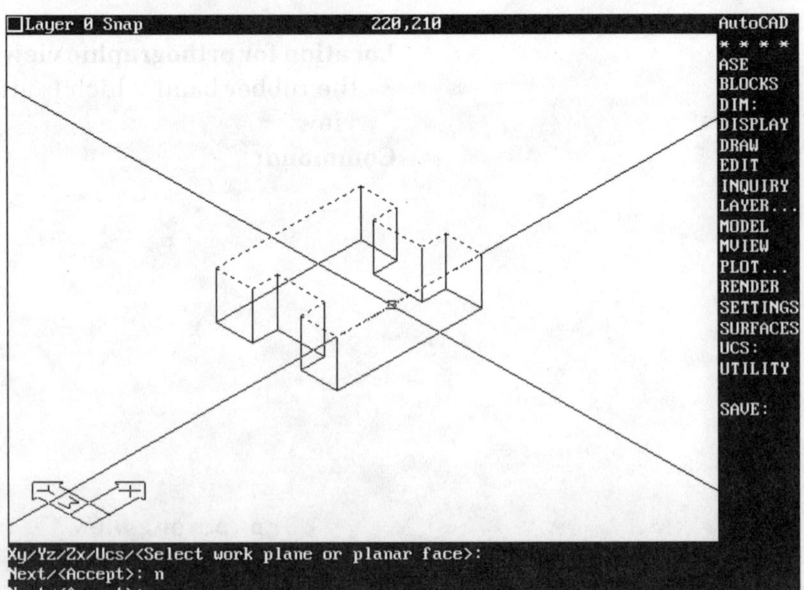

Fig. 2.19 Selecting a planar face from a pictorial view of the part extrusion

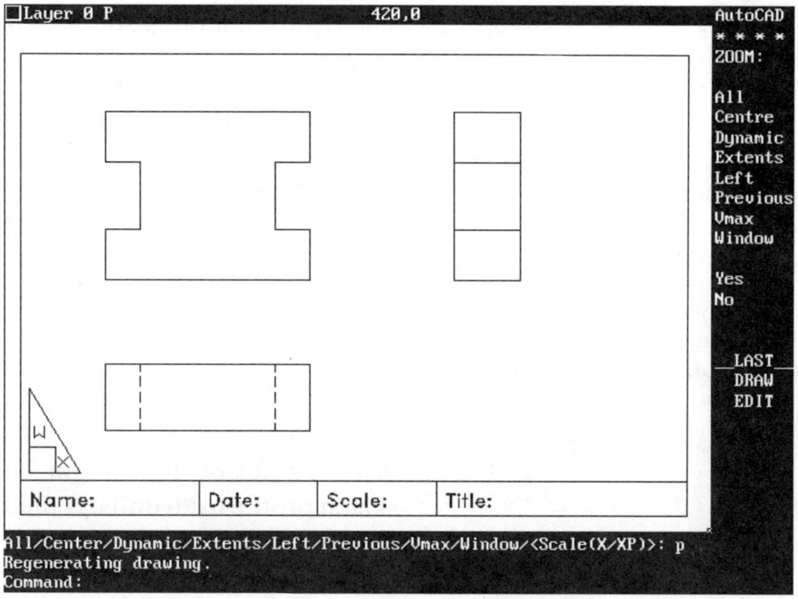

Fig. 2.20 The three-orthographic view of the extrusion in the **Designer Drawing** screen of **admine.dwg**

A second example – adding dimensions

1. Select **Add Dimension** from the **Designer** pull-down menu (Fig. 2.21) then draw the sketch outline as in Fig. 2.22.
2. At the Command Line:

Command: *enter* adpardim *right-click*
Select first item: *pick* the line 70 long
Select second item or place dimension: *pick* position for dimension
Undo/Hor/Ver/Align/Par/Dimension value <70>: *right-click*
Solved under constrained sketch requiring 5 dimensions/constraints.
Select first item: *pick* the line 20 long
Undo/Hor/Ver/Align/Par/Dimension value <20>: *right-click*
Solved under constrained sketch requiring 4 dimensions/constraints.
Select first item: *pick* the other line 20 long
Undo/Hor/Ver/Align/Par/Dimension value <20>: *right-click*
Solved under constrained sketch requiring 3 dimensions/constraints.
Select first item: *pick* one of the lines 10 long
Undo/Hor/Ver/Align/Par/Dimension value <10>: *right-click*
Solved under constrained sketch requiring 2 dimensions/constraints.
Select first item: *pick* the other line 10 long
Undo/Hor/Ver/Align/Par/Dimension value <10>: *right-click*
Solved under constrained sketch requiring 1 dimension/constraint.
Select first item: *pick* the arc
Undo/Hor/Ver/Align/Par/Dimension value <30>: *right-click*
Solved fully constrained sketch: *right-click*
Command:

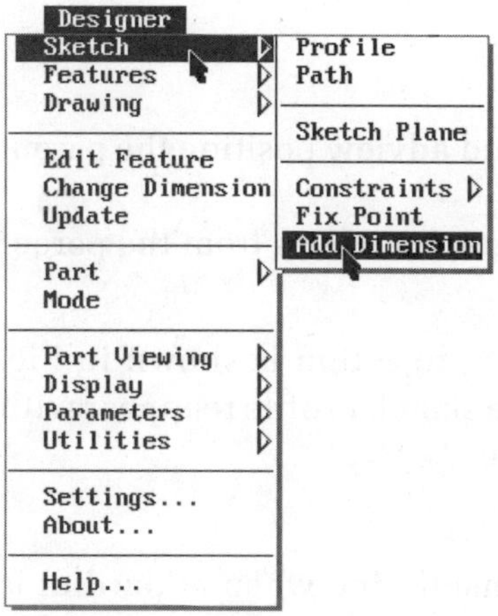

Fig. 2.21 Selecting **Add Dimension** from the **Designer** pull-down menu

The result of adding these dimensions is shown in Fig. 2.22.

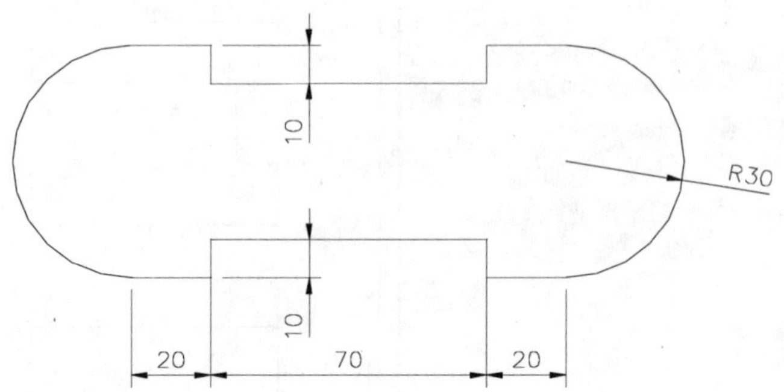

Fig. 2.22 Second example – adding dimensions to the sketch profile with the aid of **adpardim**

3. With the aid of the Designer command **adextrude**, extrude the sketch profile to 20 units. A pictorial view of the extrusion is given in Fig. 2.23.

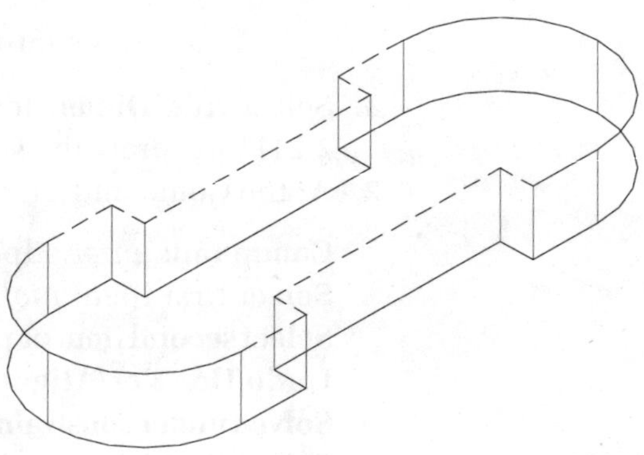

Fig. 2.23 The extruded profile with the top surface selected as the planar surface.

4. With the aid of the Designer command **adview** position the parent view in the **Drawing Mode** screen.
5. Again using **adview** add two orthographic views from the parent view.

The resulting three-view orthographic projection is shown in Fig. 2.24. Note that the dimensions from the sketch profile reappear with the orthographic projection.

Notes

1. The options appearing at the Command Line when **adpardim** is called have the following meanings:

   Undo – *entering* u undoes the last dimension to be added.
   Hor – *enter* h and the dimension to be entered will be horizontal.

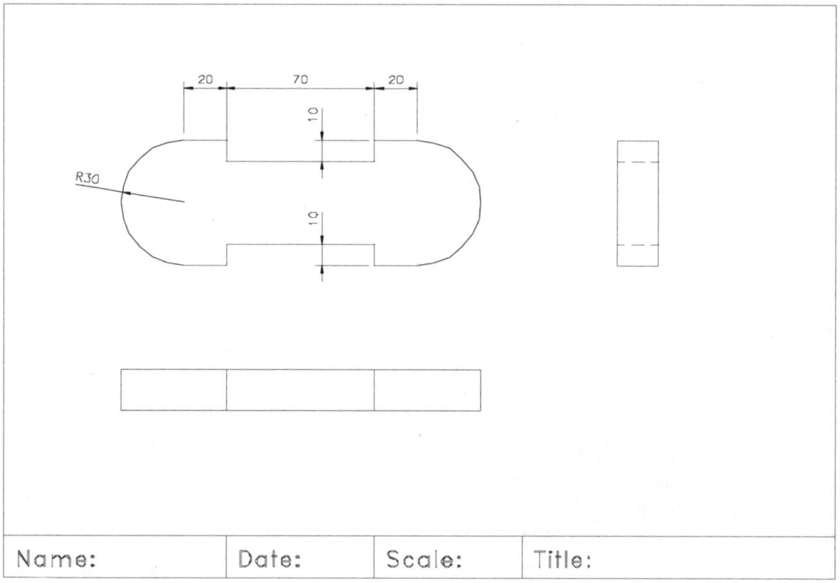

Fig. 2.24 Second example – the orthographic projection including the dimensions from the sketch profile

Ver – *enter* v and the dimension to be entered will be vertical.

Align – *enter* a and the dimension to be entered will be aligned with the object selected.

Par – *enter* p and select two points to obtain a dimension which is parallel to the *picked* points.

Hor – *enter* h and the dimension to be entered will be horizontal.

Dimension value <70>: – a *right-click* accepts the given default in bracket (in this example this is 70). Otherwise *enter* a required dimension number, followed by a *right-click*.

2. A sketch profile must be fully dimensioned/constrained before the full parametric values of a solid model generated from the profile can be gained. Note that a statement at the Command Line informs the operator when he/she has fully dimensioned (constrained) the sketch profile. More about constraints in a later chapter.
3. If the dimensioning of a sketch profile has not been fully solved, the following appears at the Command Line:

Remove a highlighted dimension or a constraint <Enter> to continue – and some dimensions on the profile will highlight.

If this statement appears, *right-click* and use the AutoCAD command **erase** to erase unwanted dimensions. Then go back to using **adpardim** in an attempt to fully dimension the profile.

4. Further dimensions can be added to an orthographic projection in the **Drawing Mode** screen if desired with the aid of the basic AutoCAD **dim** command. An example is given in Fig. 2.25.

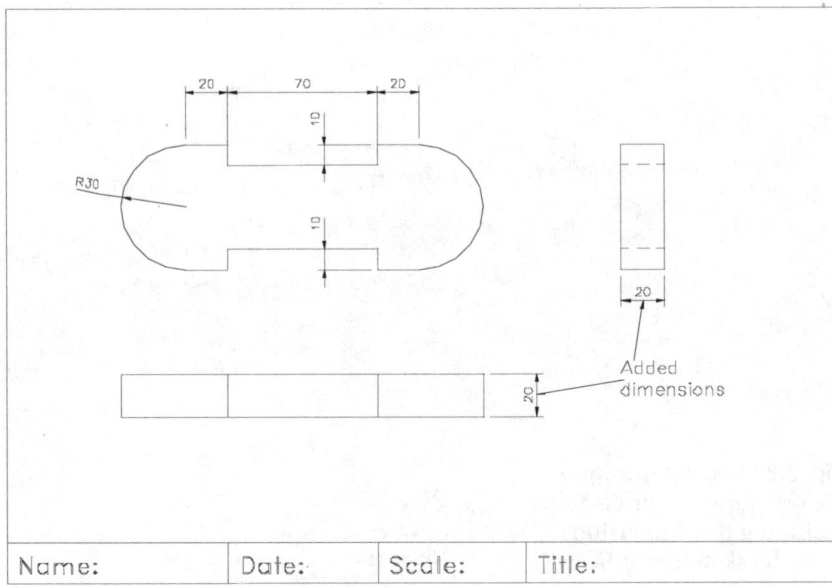

Fig. 2.25 Dimensions added to an orthographic projection with the aid of the AutoCAD **dim** command

Questions

1. Which two methods have been described to ensure that a Designer prototype drawing loads into the AutoCAD editor upon startup?
2. Why has the author decided to create his own prototype drawing file for Designer drawings?
3. Why should you not edit the contents of layers automatically formed when Designer commands are called?
4. In a Designer construction, what is a sketch profile?
5. There are two ways by which you can call the Designer extrusion command. What are they?
6. Why is it best to place a Designer solid into a pictorial viewing position before entering the **Drawing Mode** screen?
7. What is the difference between **Drawing Mode** and **Part Mode** in Designer?
8. What is meant by a 'Parent view'?
9. What is the minimum RAM requirement for a PC working with Designer?
10. Why is it necessary to fully dimension/constrain a sketch profile?

Exercises

Four simple exercises are given below, all of which can be drawn with the aid of Designer, using the methods described in this chapter. The reader can either:

1. Work the exercises in a standard AutoCAD drawing editor and add margins and title block – or:
2. Call a Designer prototype drawing and construct the exercise in that – or:
3. Make up his/her own Designer prototype drawing and work within that.

The procedure for each exercise is:

1. Construct a sketch outline.
2. Call **adprofile** and produce a sketch profile.
3. Call **adpardim** and add dimensions to the sketch profile.
4. Call **adextrude** and extrude the sketch profile.
5. Place the extrusion in a pictorial view with the aid of **vpoint**.
6. Call **adview** and place the resulting parent view.
7. Call **adview** again and add the orthographic views as necessary.
8. Add dimensions as needed with the AutoCAD **dim** command.
9. If thought fit, complete the title block by adding your name, the date, a scale and a suitable title.

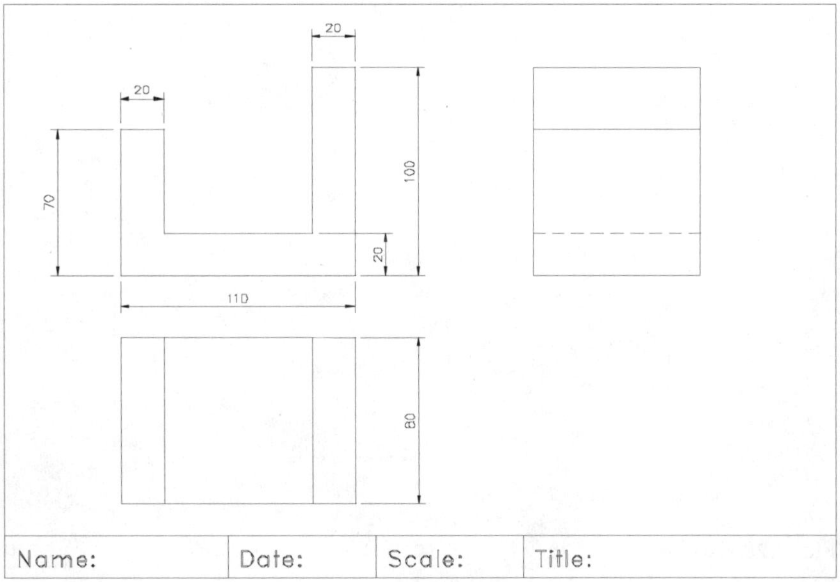

Fig. 2.26 Exercise 1

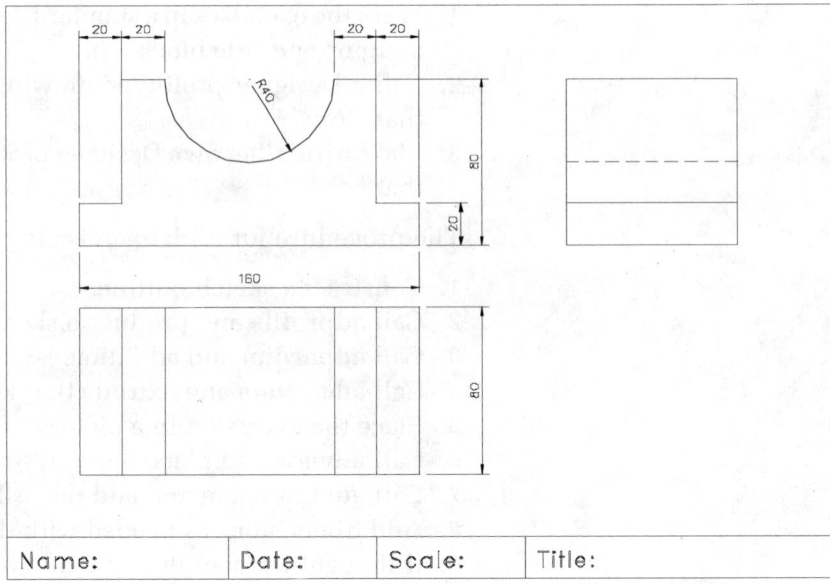

Fig. 2.27 Exercise 2

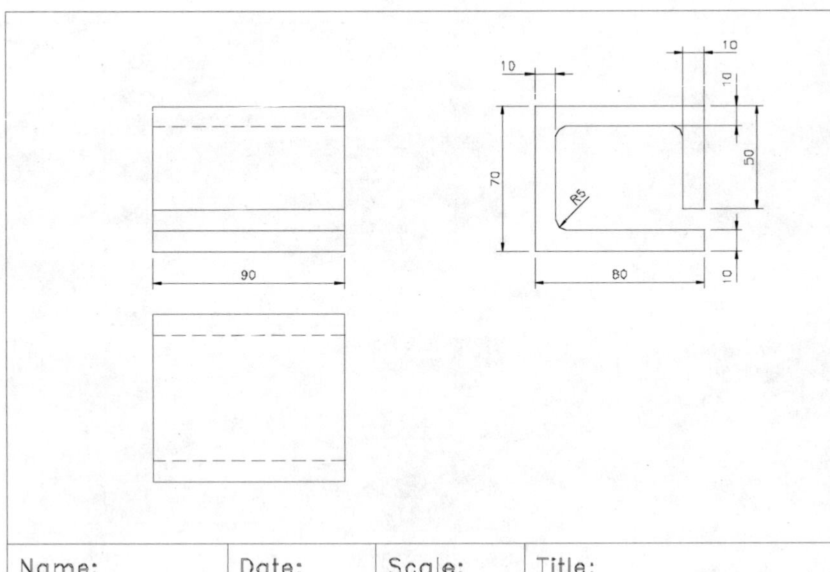

Fig. 2.28 Exercise 3

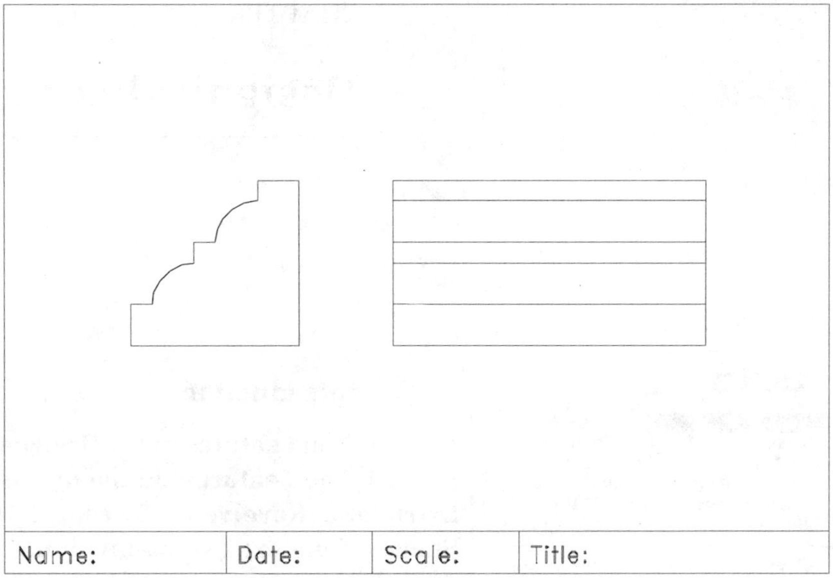

Fig. 2.29 Exercise 4

CHAPTER 3

Designer features

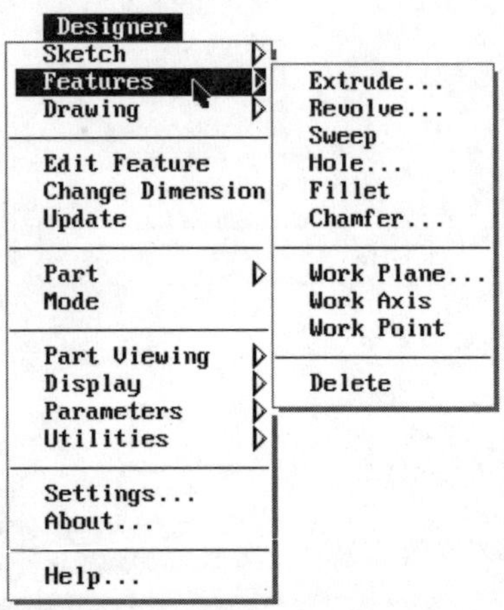

Fig. 3.1 The **Features** from the **Designer** pull-down menu

Introduction

Left-click on **Features** in the **Designer** pull-down menu as shown in Fig. 3.1 The **Features** sub-menu displays the **Features** commands **Extrude...**, **Revolve...**, **Sweep...**, **Hole...**, **Fillet** and **Chamfer...**. Some simple extrusions involving the **Extrude...** command were described in the previous chapter. Further work involving **Extrude...** will be given later in this book. In this chapter, we will be giving simple examples of the other **Features** commands. Some reference will also be made in this chapter to **Work Plane...** and **Work Axis**.

Examples

First example – using Revolve...

1. Construct the sketch profile (Fig. 3.2). Call **adpardim** and fully dimension the profile.
2. At the Command Line:

   Command: *enter* adrevolve *right-click*
   The **Designer Revolution** dialogue box appears (Fig. 3.4).
   In the dialogue box, *left-click* on the **Base** button, *left-click* on **By Angle** and *enter* 360 in the **Size Angle:** box. Then *left-click* on the **OK** button.
   Select axis of revolution: *pick* the axis
   Command:

   And the solid of revolution is formed.
3. At the Command Line:

   Command: *enter* vpoint *right-click*
   VPOINT Rotate/<View point> <0,0,1>: *enter* –1,–1,1 *right-click*
   Command:

   And the solid of revolution is seen in a pictorial view.

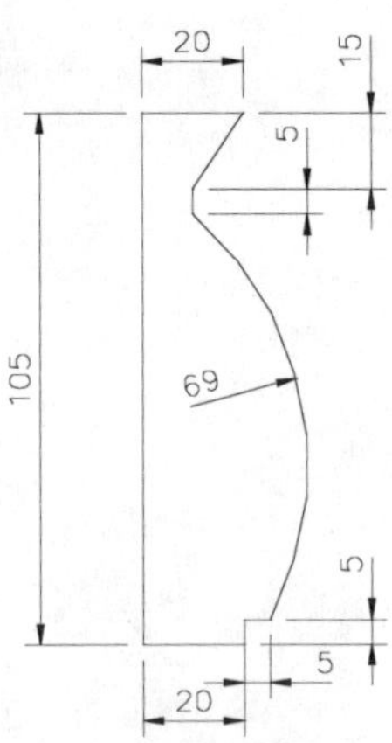

Fig. 3.2 The sketch profile for the first example

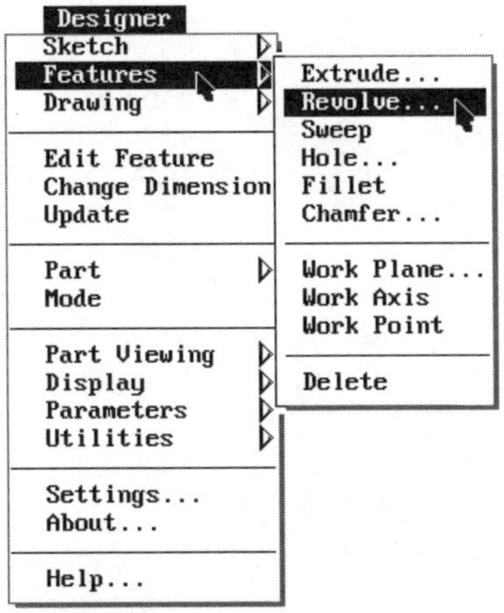

Fig. 3.3 Selecting **Revolve...** from the **Designer** pull-down menu

4. At the Command Line:

   Command: *enter* adworkaxis *right-click*
   Select cylindrical face: *pick* as in Fig. 3.6
   Command:

   And the work axis appears on the view.

5. At the Command Line:

   Command: *enter* adworkpln *right-click*
   The **Designer Work Plane** dialogue box appears. In the dialogue box, *left-click* in the check box next to **On UCS**, followed by another *left-click* on the **OK** button.
   Command:

   And the work plane appears on the view (Fig. 3.6).

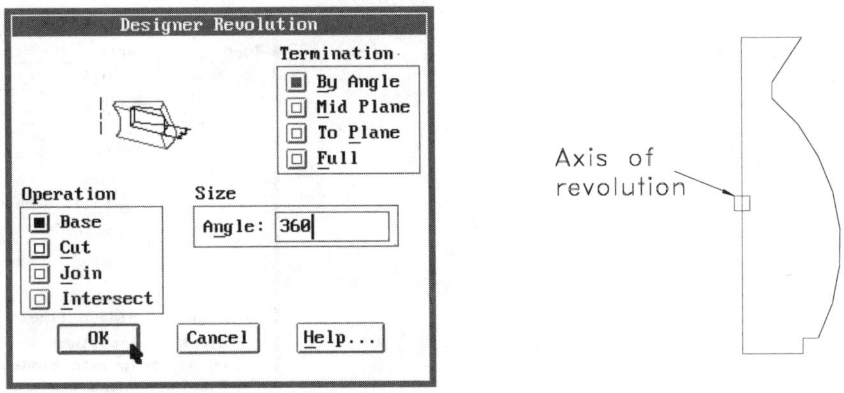

Fig. 3.4 The entries in the **Designer Revolution** dialogue box and selecting the axis of revolution on the sketch profile

6. At the Command Line:

   Command: *enter* adview *right-click*
   In the **Designer Drawing View** dialogue box which appears, accept the default settings (Fig. 3.7) and *left-click* on the **OK** button.
   Xy/Yz/Zx/UCS/<Select work plane or planar face>: *pick* the work plane
   Rotate/<Accept>: *right-click* (to accept)
   The **Designer Drawing** screen appears.
   View center: *pick* a suitable position *right-click*
   Command:

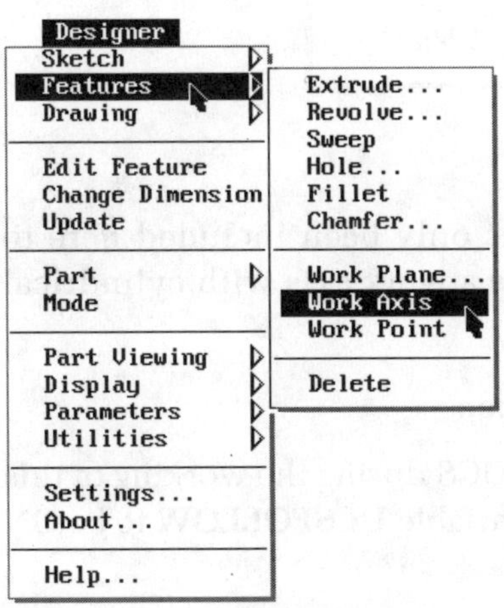

Fig. 3.5 Selecting **Work Axis** from the **Designer** pull-down menu

7. Call adview again and in the **Designer Drawing View** dialogue box, *left-click* on the **Ortho** button and add two further views in the **Designer Drawing** screen.
8. Erase unsuitable dimensions and re-dimension as necessary as indicated in Fig. 3.8.

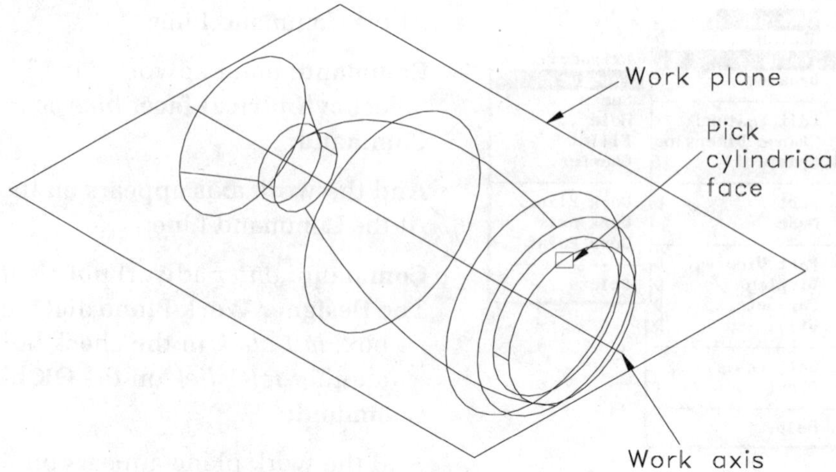

Fig. 3.6 A pictorial view of the first example showing the work axis and work plane

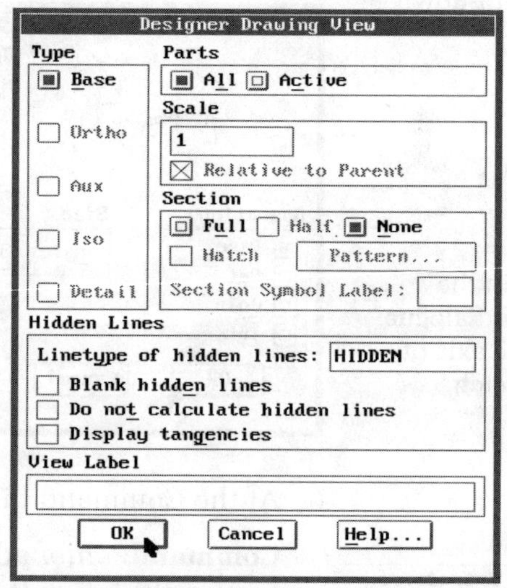

Fig. 3.7 The **Designer Drawing View** dialogue box showing the default settings

Note

The work axis shown in Fig. 3.6 has only been included here to demonstrate how easy it is to include a work axis with cylindrical parts.

Second example – using Sweep

1. It will be necessary to change the UCS during the working of this example. To enable this, set the variable **UCSFOLLOW** to be **ON** as follows:

   Command: *enter* ucsfollow *right-click*
   New value for UCSFOLLOW <0>: *enter* 1 *right-click*
   Command:

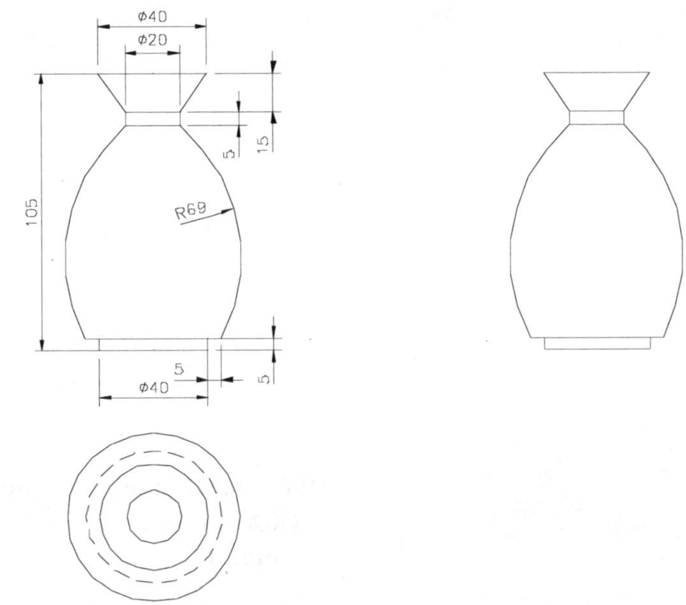

Fig. 3.8 First example – the resulting three-view orthographic projection

2. Draw the path line (Fig. 3.9).
3. At the Command Line:

   Command: *enter* adpath *right-click*
   Select objects for sketch.
   Select objects: *pick* the path line
   Solved under constrained sketch requiring 6 dimensions/ constraints.
   Specify start of path: *pick* the point where the path meets the sketch profile
   Command:

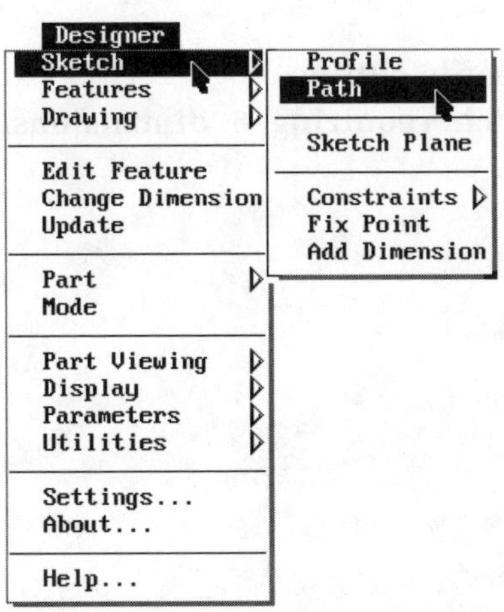

Fig. 3.9 Selecting **Path** from the **Designer** pull-down menu

4. Now set the UCS so that, when the sketch profile is drawn it will be on the current UCS. At the Command Line:

   Command: *enter* ucs *right-click*
   Origin/ZAxis/3point/Entity/View/X/Y/Z/Prev/Restore/Save/Del/ ?/<World>: *enter* 3 (3point) *right-click*
   Origin point: *pick* 1st point as in Fig. 3.9
   Point on positive part of the X-axis: *pick* 2nd point (Fig. 3.10)
   Point on positive-Y part of the UCS XY plane: *enter* .xy
   of *pick* 3rd point as in Fig. 3.10
   (need Z): *enter* 1 *right-click*
   Command:

5. At the Command Line:

   Command: *enter* z (Zoom) *right-click*

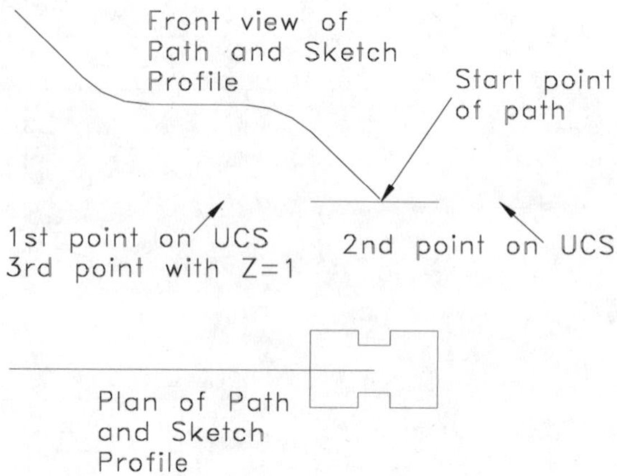

Fig. 3.10 Front and plan views of the path and the sketch profile for the second example

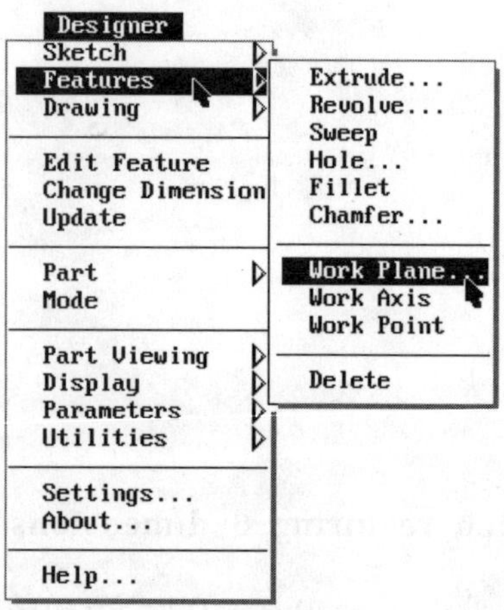

Fig. 3.11 Selecting **Work Plane** from the **Designer** pull-down menu

All/Center/Dynamic/Extents/Left/Previous/Vmax/Window/<Scale (X/XP)>: *enter* 1 *right-click*
Command:

6. Draw the sketch profile around the start point of the Path, so that the path start point is central to the profile.
7. To set the work plane on the same UCS as the sketch profile, at the Command Line:

Command: *enter* adskpln *right-click*
Xy/Yz/Zx/Ucs/<Select workplane or planar face>: *enter* u (for UCS) *right-click*
Command:

8. At the Command Line:

Command: *enter* adprofile *right-click*
Select objects for sketch.
Select objects: *pick* the sketch profile outline
Solved under constrained sketch requiring 6 dimensions/ constraints.
Command:

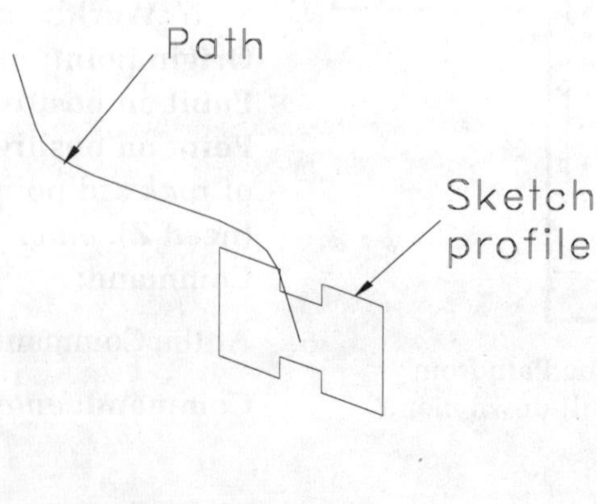

Fig. 3.12 Pictorial view of the path and sketch profile for the second example

9. To place the construction so far in a pictorial view, at the Command Line:

   Command: *enter* vpoint *right-click*
   VPOINT Rotate/<View point><0,0,1>: *enter* –1,–1,1 *right-click*
   Command:

10. **Zoom** to 1.
11. To form the sweep, at the Command Line:

    Command: *enter* adsweep *right-click*
    Select sweep path: *pick* (Fig. 3.12)
    Select sweep cross-section profile: *pick* sketch profile (Fig. 3.12)
    Parallel/<Normal>: *right-click* (to accept Normal)
    Command:

12. To produce the orthographic projection use **adview**. The results are shown in Fig. 3.13.

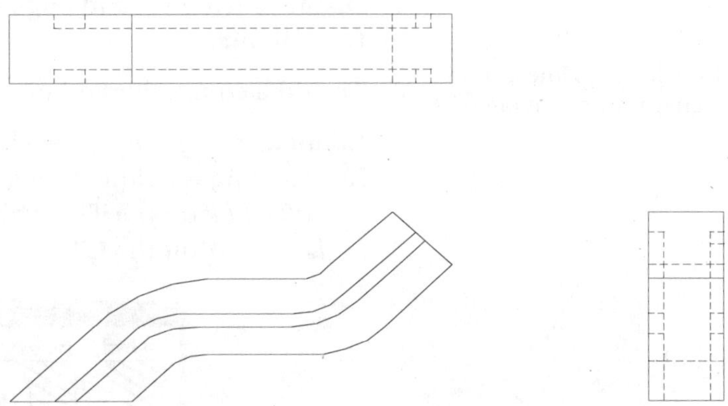

Fig. 3.13 The resulting three-view orthographic projection for the second example

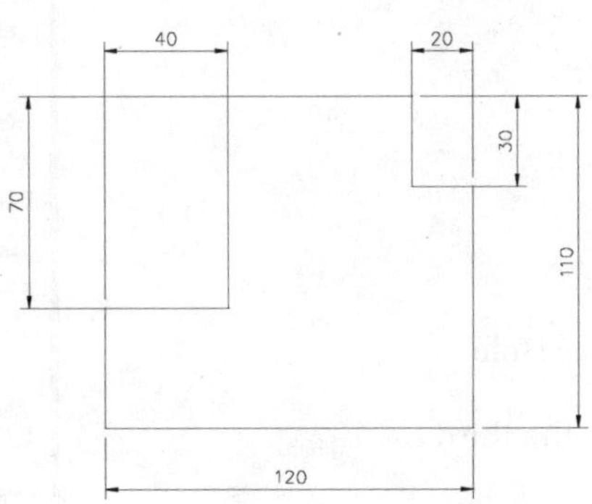

Fig. 3.14 The dimensioned Sketch Profile for the third example

Third example – using Holes

1. Draw the sketch profile outline, followed by **adprofile**.
2. Add dimensions with **adpardim**. See Fig. 3.14.
3. Extrude to 80 deep with **adextrude**.
4. **Vpoint** –1,–1,1 to obtain a pictorial view.
5. To add a through hole to the extrusion, at the Command Line:

Command: *enter* adhole *right-click*
In the **Designer Hole** dialogue box:
    Left-click on the **Through** button
    Left-click on the **Drilled** button
    Left-click on the **2 Edges** button
    Enter 20 in the **Dia:** box
    Left-click on **OK**
Select first edge: *pick*
Select second edge: *pick*
Select hole location: two lines appear parallel to the two picked edges. Move to a suitable position and *right-click*
Distance from first edge <45>: *enter* 40 *right-click*
Distance from second edge <60> *right-click* (because correct)
Command:

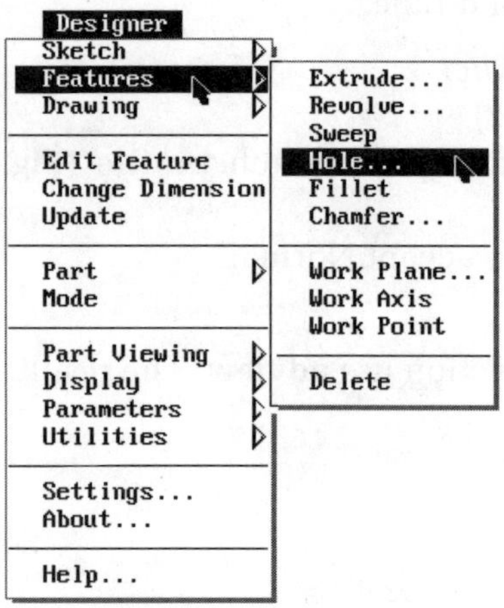

Fig. 3.15 Selecting **Hole...** from the **Designer** pull-down menu

6. To add a counterbored hole to the extrusion

Command: *right-click* (back to the **adhole** command sequence)
In the **Designer Hole** dialogue box
    Left-click on the **Through** button
    Left-click on the **C'Bore** button

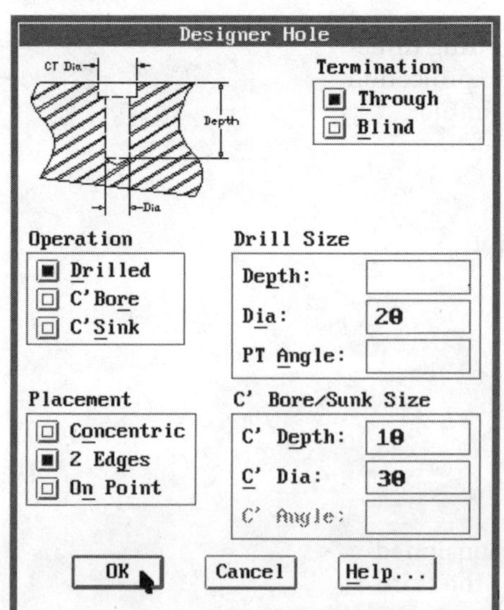

Fig. 3.16 The **Designer Hole** dialogue box for the counterbored hole in the third example

Left-click on the **2 Edges** button
Enter 20 in the **Dia:** box
Enter 10 in the **C'Depth:** box
Enter 30 in the **C'Dia:** box
Left-click on **OK**

Select first edge: *pick*
Select second edge: *pick*
Select hole location: two lines appear parallel to the two picked edges. Move to a suitable position and *right-click*
Distance from first edge <25>: *enter* 20 *right-click*
Distance from second edge <35> *enter* 40 *right-click*
Command:

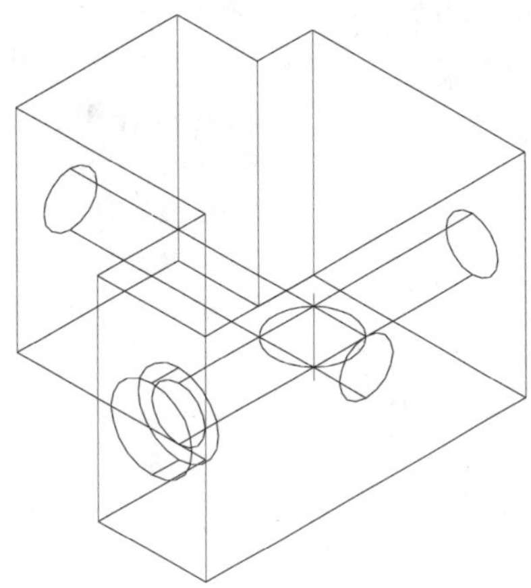

Fig. 3.17 The two holes in the extrusion as seen in a pictorial view

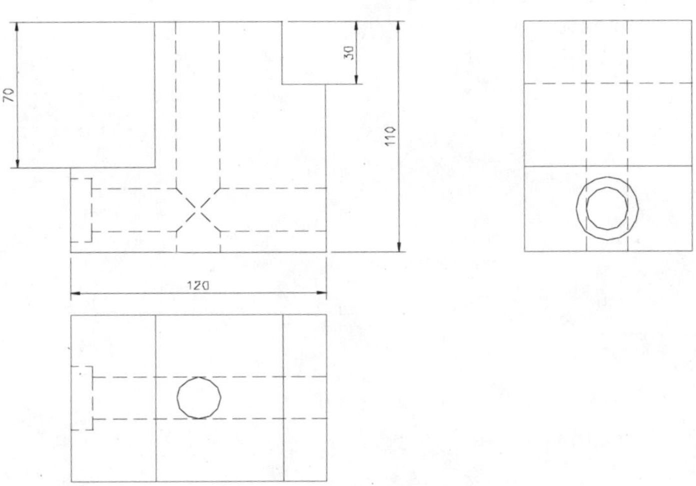

Fig. 3.18 The orthographic projection for the third example

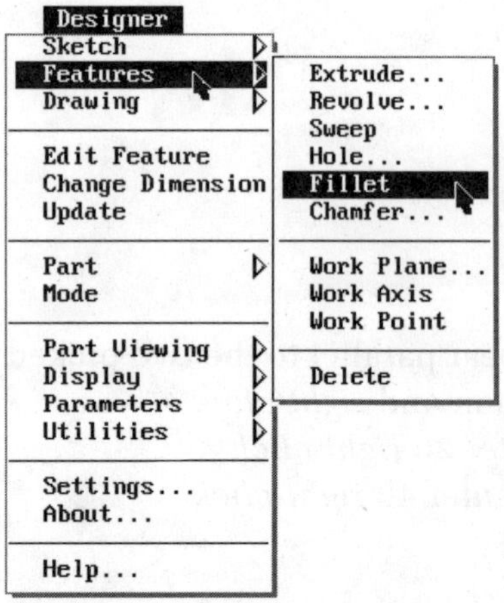

Fig. 3.19 Selecting **Fillet** from the **Designer** pull-down menu

The **Designer Hole** dialogue box details for the counterbored hole are shown in Fig. 3.16. The resulting holes in the extrusion are shown in Fig. 3.17.

7. Now with the aid of the Designer **adview** command insert three views in the **Drawing Mode** screen. The resulting orthographic projection is given in Fig. 3.18.

Fourth example – using Fillet

1. Construct the Sketch profile outline.
2. Call **adprofile** and select the outline.
3. Call **adpardim** and add dimensions to fully dimension the outline as shown in Fig. 3.20.
4. Call **adextrude** and extrude – **Base** and **Distance:** 30.
5. Call **vpoint** and place in pictorial view –1,–1,1 (Fig. 3.21).
6. At the Command Line:

Command: *enter* adfillet *right-click*
Select edge: *pick* (Fig. 3.21)
Select edge: *pick*
Select edge: *pick*
Select edge: *pick*

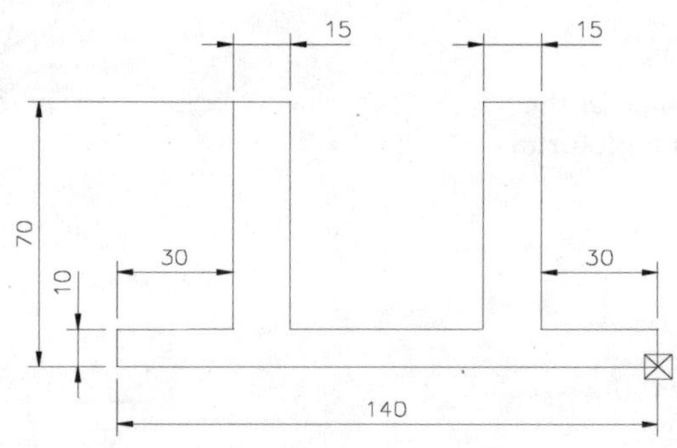

Fig. 3.20 The fully dimensioned Sketch Profile for the fourth example

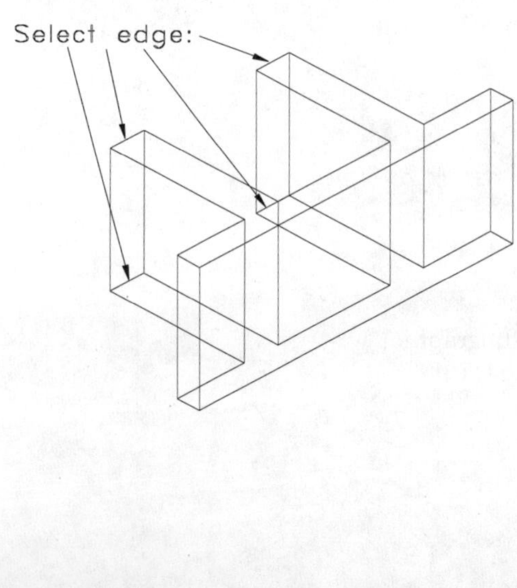

Fig. 3.21 Place the part in **vpoint**

Select edge: *right-click*
Fillet radius <0.5>: *enter* 30 *right-click*
Command:

7. Call **adfillet** again and add the fillets to the base corners (Fig. 3.22).

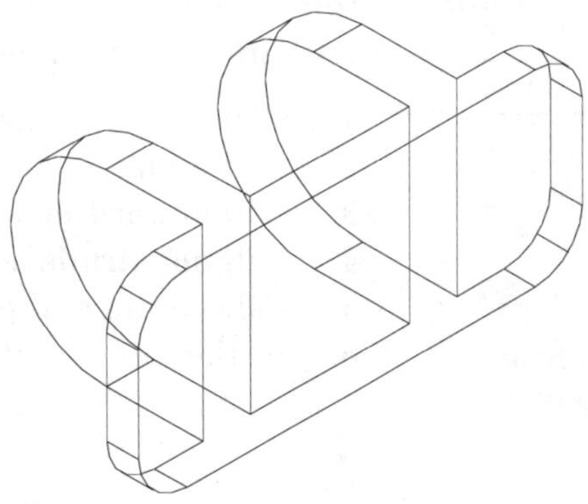

Fig. 3.22 The fourth example with fillets added

8. Call **adview** and position the three orthographic projection views as in Fig. 3.23.

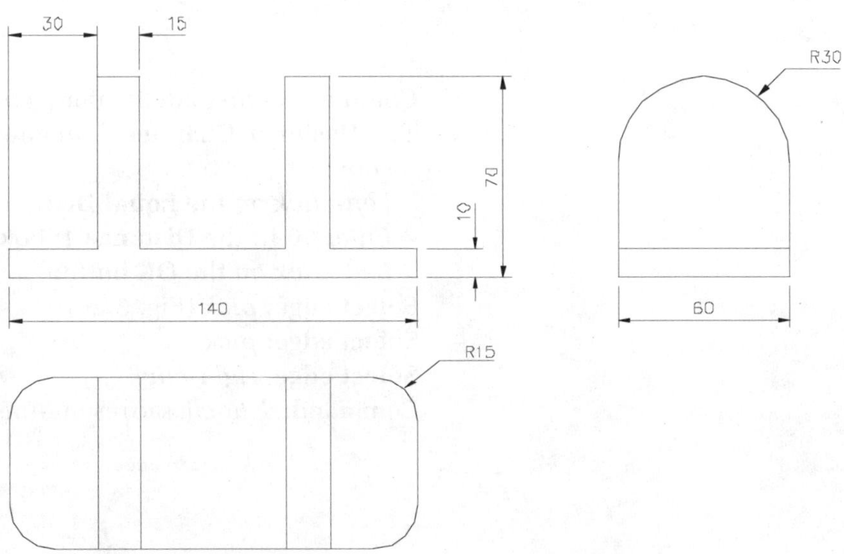

Fig. 3.23 Fourth example – the three-view orthographic projection in **Drawing Mode**

9. In this example some dimensions have been deleted and other added with the aid of the AutoCAD command **Dim**.

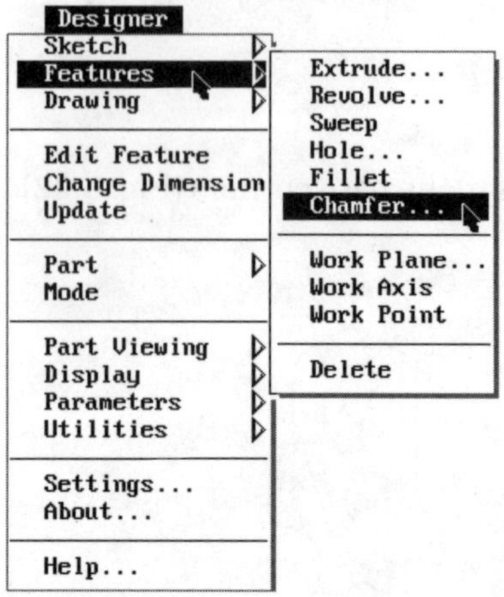

Fig. 3.24 Selecting **Chamfer...** from the **Designer** pull-down menu

Fifth example – using Chamfer

Note

As with the commands **Extrude...**, **Revolve...** and **Hole...**, the three fullstops after the name **Chamfer...** indicate that when the command is called, either from the **Designer** pull-down menu, or by *entering* the command name **adchamfer** at the Command Line, a dialogue box will appear on screen.

1. Construct the sketch outline.
2. Call **adprofile** and select the outline.
3. Call **adpardim** and dimension the sketch profile (Fig. 3.25).
4. Call **adextrude** and extrude 80 units.
5. Call **vpoint** and place in a pictorial view (Fig. 3.26).
6. At the Command Line:

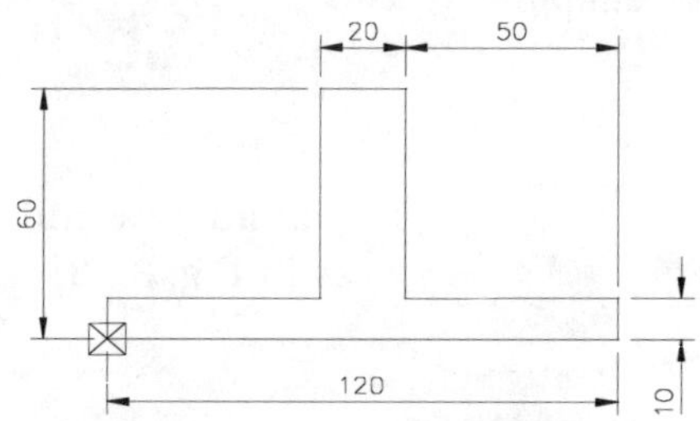

Fig. 3.25 The dimensioned Sketch profile for the fifth example

Command: *enter* adchamfer *right-click*

The **Designer Chamfer** dialogue box appears. In the dialogue box:

Left-click on the **Equal Distance** button

Enter 20 in the **Distance 1:** box

Left-click on the **OK** button

Select edge: *pick* (Fig. 3.26)

Select edge: *pick*

Select edge: *right-click*

Command: *right-click* to resume the **adchamfer** command sequence

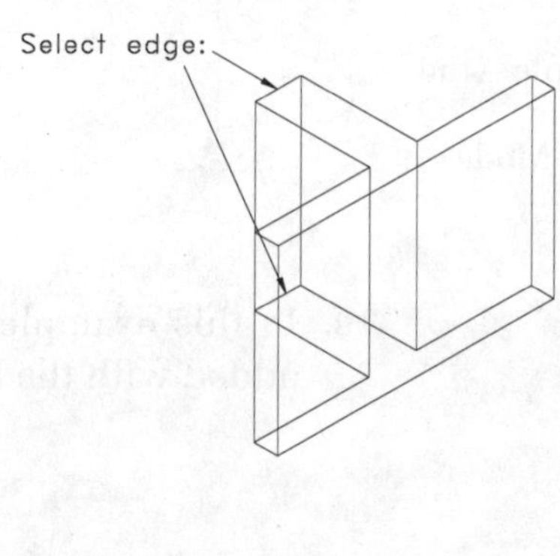

Fig. 3.26 The pictorial view of the extruded part

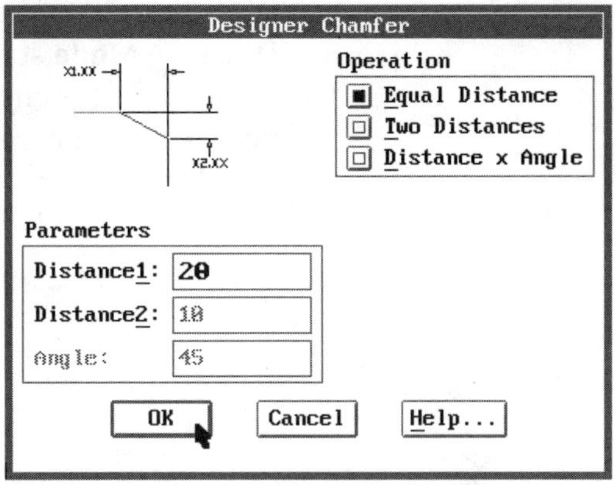

Fig. 3.27 The entries in the **Designer Chamfer** dialogue box for the fifth example

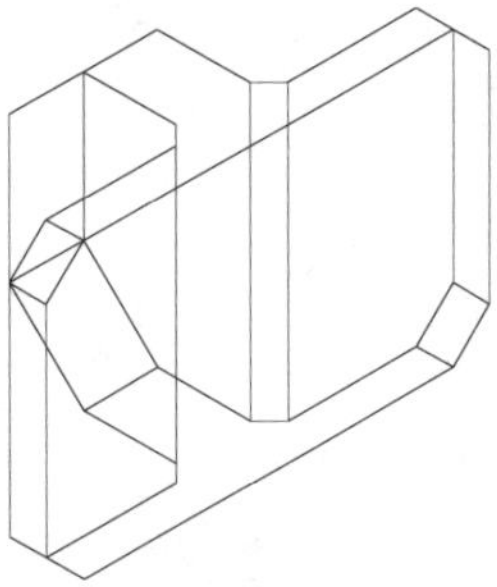

Fig. 3.28 The chamfers formed for the fifth example

And add the other chamfers to the base and to the internal edges. See Fig. 3.28.

7. At the Command Line:

Command: *enter* adhole *right-click*
In the **Designer Hole** dialogue box:
Left-click on the **Drilled** button
Left-click on the **Through** button
Left-click on the **2 Edges** button
Enter 15 in the **Dia:** box
Left-click on the **OK** button of the dialogue box
Select first edge: *pick*
Select second edge: *pick*
Distance from first edge <25>: *enter* 20 *right-click*
Distance from second edge <15>: *enter* 20 *right-click*
Command:

8. With the aid of **adhole** add a hole to the upright portion of the part. Diameter 25 at distances of 40 from the sides and 25 from the top edge.

9. With the aid of **adview** place three orthographic views in the **Drawing Mode** screen.
10. Erase old dimensions and add new dimensions as thought necessary. The resulting orthographic projection is given in Fig. 3.29.

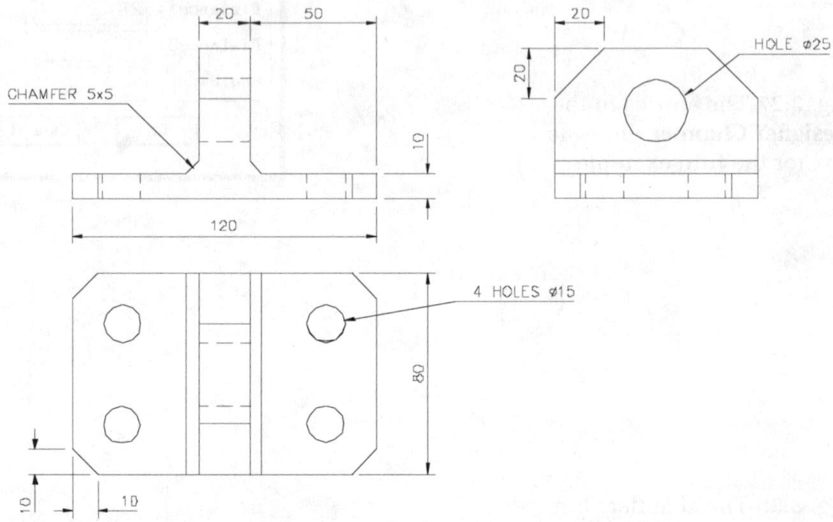

Fig. 3.29 The three-view orthographic projection for the fifth example

Sixth example – using the UCS

In all the examples given so far in both this and the previous chapters, the outlines for the sketch profiles have been drawn in the **WORLD** UCS. Readers who are familiar with the User Coordinate System of AutoCAD (UCS) may find it advantageous to construct sketch profiles on other UCS planes. This sixth example makes use of the UCS when constructing the sketch profile outline to obtain a different viewing position when calling **vpoint**.

1. At the Command Line:

   Command: *enter* ucsfollow *right-click*
   New value for UCSFOLLOW <0>: *enter* 1 *right-click*
   Command:

   Ucsfollow must be set **ON** (1) to allow the UCS to respond to changes in the positions of new UCS planes.
2. *Left-click* on **Settings...** in the menu bar, followed by another *left-click* on **UCS**, then another on **Presets...** (Fig. 3.30) and yet another on the **FRONT** icon in the **UCS Orientation** dialogue box. Finally *left-click* on the **OK** button of the dialogue box (Fig. 3.31). The UCS is now reset.

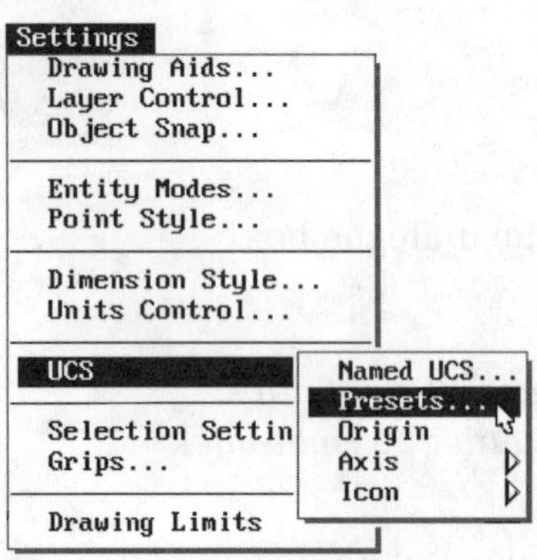

Fig. 3.30 Selecting **UCS Presets...** from the **Settings** pull-down menu

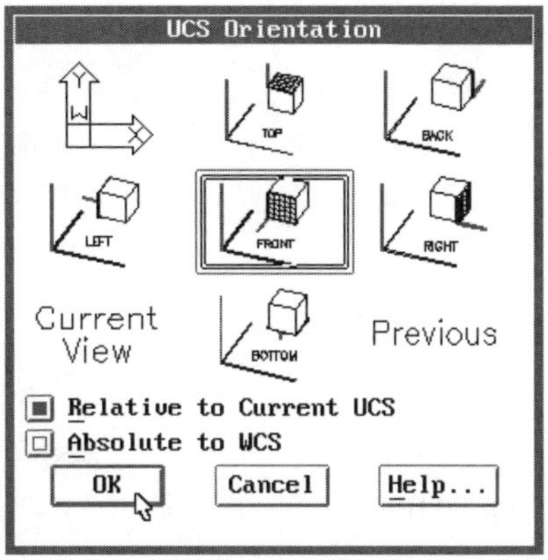

Fig. 3.31 The **UCS Orientation** dialogue box

3. Construct the sketch profile outline on this UCS.
4. Unless the current UCS (FRONT) is set as the Designer sketch plane, **adprofile** will not recognise the sketch outline drawn on the FRONT UCS. To set the sketch plane:

Command: *enter* adskpln *right-click*
Xy/Yz/Zx/Ucs/<Select work plane or planar face>: *enter* u (Ucs) *right-click*
Rotate/<Accept>: *right-click*
Command:

Failure to set the sketch plane to the current UCS will result in the following message when **adprofile** is called:

Geometry not planar or not in current sketch plane.
Invalid items selected for profile.
Command:

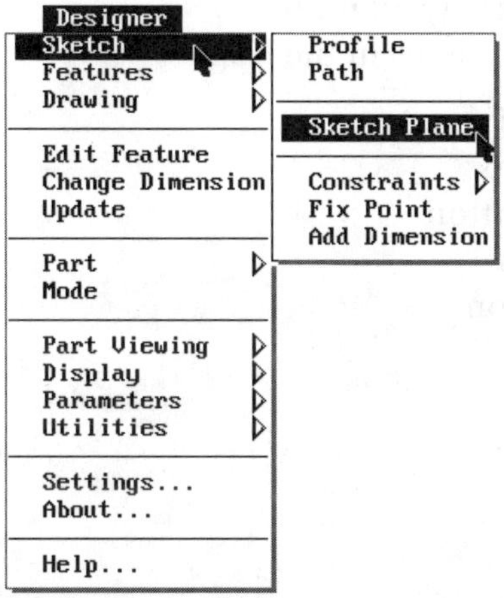

Fig. 3.32 Selecting **Sketch Plane** from the **Designer** pull-down menu

5. Call **adprofile**, select the outline to form the sketch profile.
6. Call **adpardim** and dimension the sketch profile.
7. Call **adextrude** and extrude 60 units.

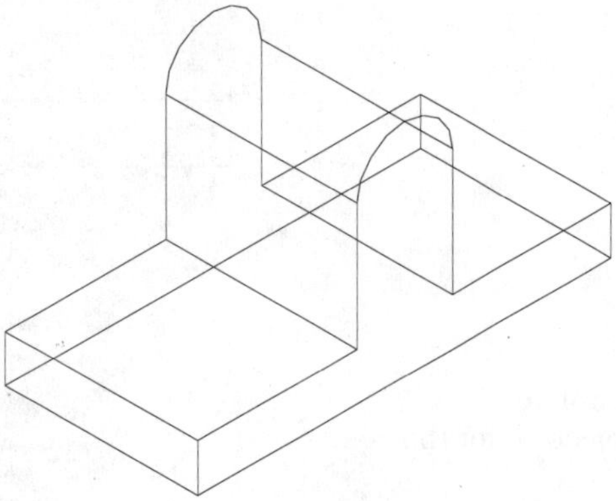

Fig. 3.33 The extruded profile of the sixth example in a pictorial view

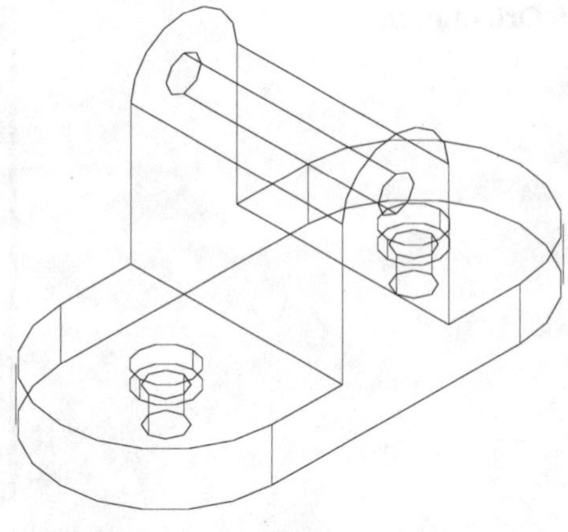

Fig. 3.34 Sixth example showing fillets and holes in a pictorial view

8. Call **vpoint** and place in a pictorial view (Fig. 3.33).
9. Call **adfillet** and fillet the base corners 30 units.
10. Call **adhole** and add counterbored holes in the base:

Command: *enter* adhole *right-click*
In the **Designer Hole** dialogue box:
Left-click on the **Concentric** button
Left-click on the **C'Bore** button
Left-click on the **Through** button
Enter 10 in the **Dia:** box
Enter 5 in the **C'Bore Depth:** box
Enter 15 in the **C'Bore Dia:** box
Left-click on **OK**

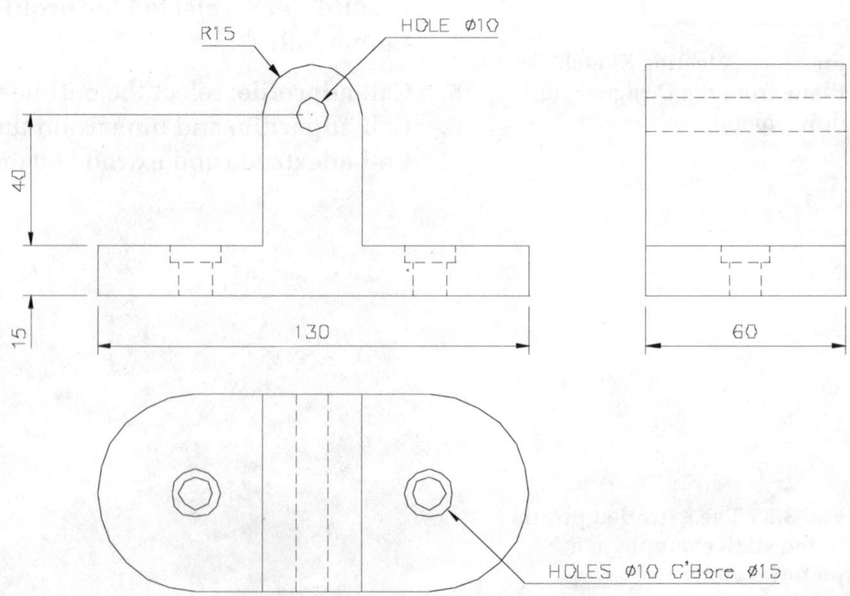

Fig. 3.35 The completed orthographic projection for the sixth example

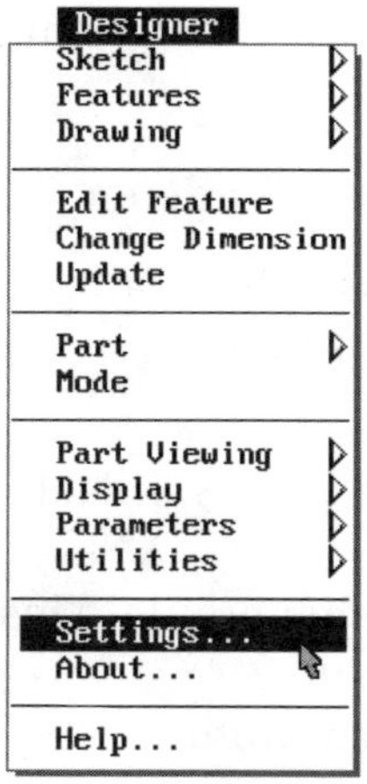

Fig. 3.36 Selecting **Settings...** from the **Designer** pull-down menu

Select work plane or planar edge: *pick*
Select concentric edge: *pick* the curve of one of the filleted ends of the base
Command: *right-click* to bring back the options for the second base hole

Figure 3.36 shows the fillets and holes formed in the extrusion while in a pictorial view.

11. Call **adhole** again to add the 10 diameter hole through the upright.
12. Call **adview** and place three views in the **Drawing Mode** screen (Fig. 3.35)

Note

As shown in Figs 3.33 and 3.34, the upright position of the pictorial view may be found to be more suitable than the views obtained when the sketch profile is drawn on the **WORLD** UCS (WCS).

Notes

1. All the orthographic projections shown so far in the book have been in First angle projection.
2. To ensure that drawings are in the desired angle of projection:
   (a) *Left-click* on **Designer** in the menu bar, followed by another *left-click* on **Settings...** in the pull-down menu (Fig. 3.36).
   (b) In the **Designer Settings** dialogue box (Fig. 3.37) *left-click* on the **Drawing Settings...** button.
   (c) In the **Drawing Variables** dialogue box which appears *left-click* on the **First Angle** button.
3. AutoCAD Designer is for the designing of parametric engineering parts. Hence the name **Part** in Part Mode. So far we have not been

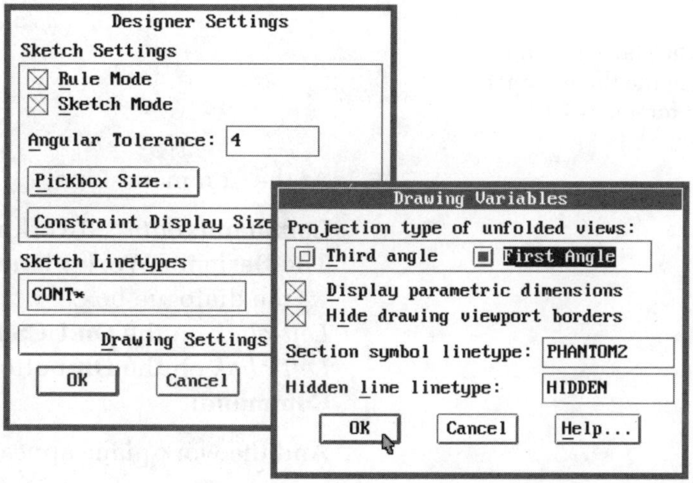

Fig. 3.37 Setting for **First Angle** projection in the **Drawing Variables** dialogue box

concerned with parametrics. These will be dealt with later in this book.

Seventh example – more about *adextrude* and *adview*

This example makes use of the setting of parameters in the dialogue boxes connected with **adextrude** and **adview**, as well as showing some methods of setting sketch planes.

1. Set **Ucsfollow** to 1 to ensure that any changes in the UCS will take place.
2. On the World UCS, draw the outline for the sketch profile. This will be the same as the left-hand view of Fig. 3.38.
3. Call **adprofile** and make the outline into a sketch profile.
4. Call **adextrude** and extrude the profile 50 units.
5. Still in the **WORLD** UCS, call the UCS command:

   Command: *enter* ucs *right-click*
   Origin/ZAxis/3point/Entity/View/X/Y/Z/Prev/Restore/Save/Del/?/<World>: *enter* 3 (3point) *right-click*
   Origin point: *pick* 1st point as in Fig. 3.38
   Point on positive part of the X-axis: *pick* 2nd point (Fig. 3.38)
   Point on positive-Y part of the UCS XY plane: *enter* .xy
   of *pick* 3rd point as in Fig. 3.38
   (need Z): *enter* 1 *right-click*
   Command:

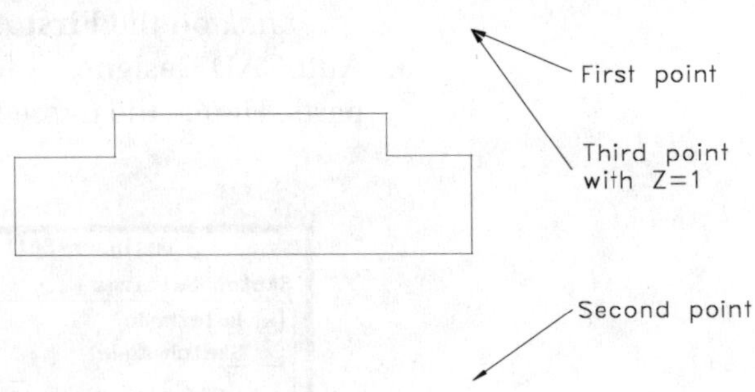

Fig. 3.38 The extrusion showing the three points picked for a new UCS

6. At the Command Line:

   Command: *enter* adworkpln *right-click*
   The **Designer Work Plane** dialogue box appears (Fig. 3.39). In the dialogue box:
   Left-click on the **On UCS** button
   Left-click on the **OK** button
   Command:

   And the work plane appears on the UCS (Fig. 3.40).

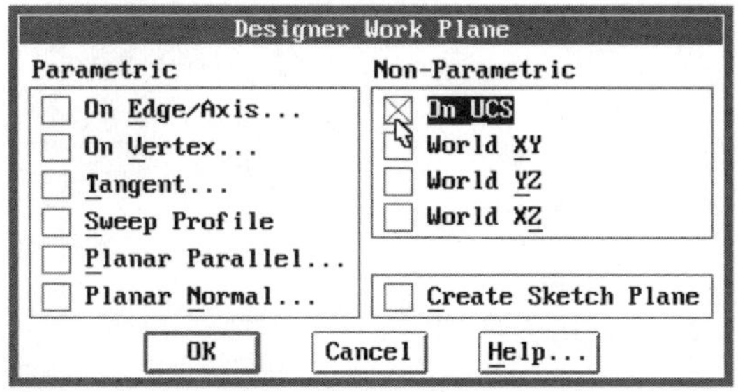

Fig. 3.39 The **Designer Work Plane** dialogue box

7. On the new work plane construct the outline for the hole in the part as shown in Fig. 3.40.

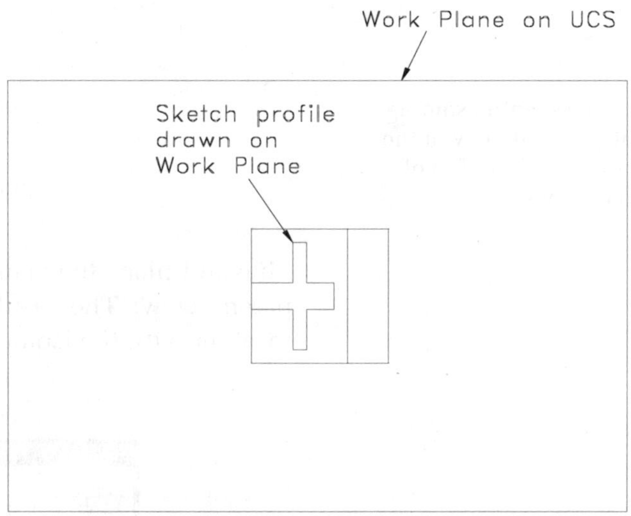

Fig. 3.40 Seventh example. The new work plane on the 3 point UCS

8. Call **vpoint** and place the part in a pictorial view (Fig. 3.41)
9. Call **adextrude** and in the **Designer Extrusion** dialogue box:

   Left-click on the **Through** button
   Left-click on the **Cut** button
   Enter 200 in the **Distance:** box (much larger than required to ensure the cut goes all the way through)
   Left-click on the **OK** button

   Direction Flip/Accept: *right-click* (to accept the direction of the arrow)
   Command:

10. Call **adview** and with its aid place two views of the part with its cut into the **Drawing Mode** screen.
11. Call **adview** again and *left-click* on the **Iso** button in the dialogue box as shown in Fig. 3.43. Follow the instructions at the Command

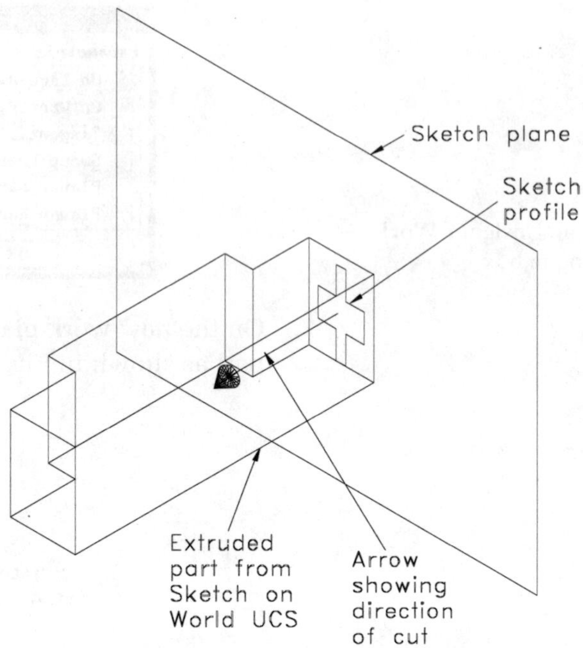

Fig. 3.41 The seventh example – a **vpoint** pictorial view of the part and the sketch profile of the cut to be made

Line and place the isometric view in position in relation to the parent view. The resulting two-view orthographic projection, together with the isometric view is shown in Fig. 3.44.

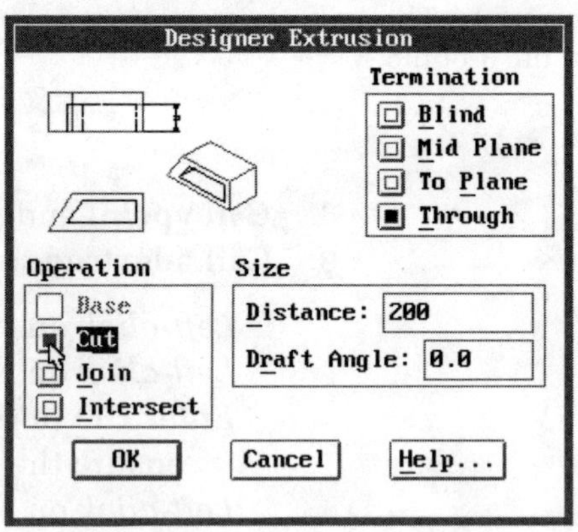

Fig. 3.42 The **Designer Extrusion** dialogue box showing a cut through

Notes

1. Unless a new work or sketch plane is constructed for a sketch profile on a UCS other than the WCS, a sketch cannot be accepted by Designer as a sketch profile from which one can Extrude, Revolve or Sweep.

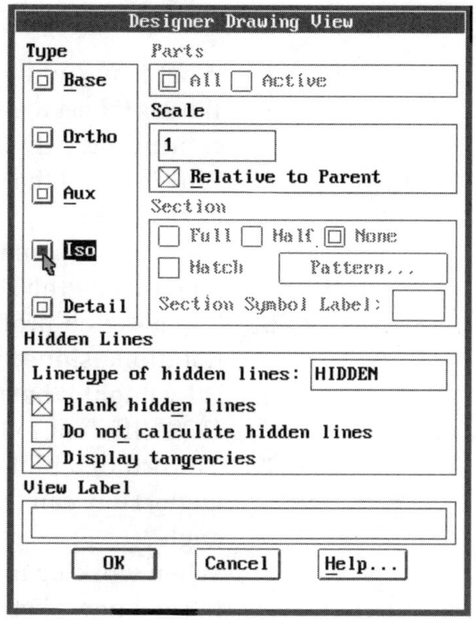

Fig. 3.43 The **Designer Drawing View** dialogue box showing **Iso** selected

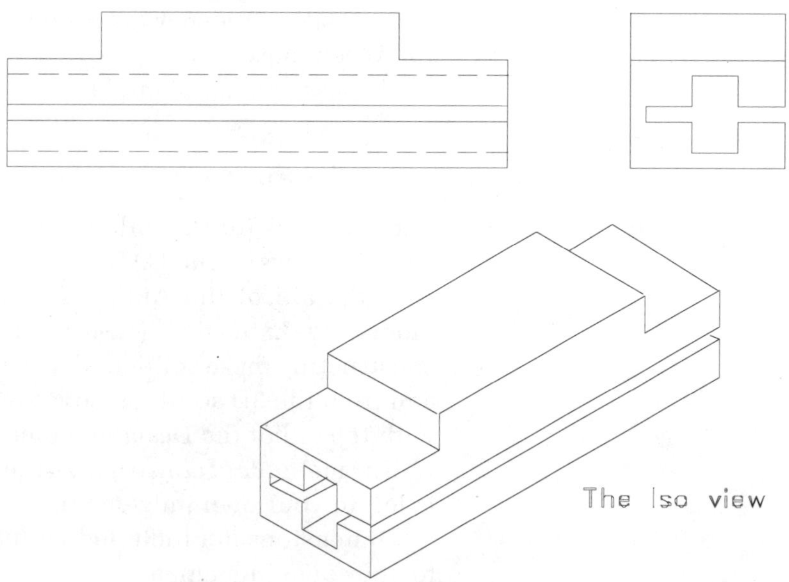

Fig. 3.44 The two-view orthographic projection and isometric drawing for the seventh example

2. When making a **Cut** while using **adextrude**, it is advisable to check that the **Distance:** set for the cut is sufficiently long.
3. The **Flip** arrow appearing when a cut is called shows the direction in which the cut is being made. Answering **Distance Flip** with f causes the arrow to be reversed and the cut to be made in the opposite direction.

Questions

1. What is meant by the term *feature* in connection with **Designer**?
2. Why is it best to place a part into a **vpoint** viewing position before continuing with Designer commands?
3. Why is it best that the variable **Ucsfollow** be set **ON** when working in Designer?
4. How can an isometric view be included with an orthographic view when using the Designer command **adview**?
5. Can a sketch profile be extruded with **adextrude** if the profile is not dimensioned?
6. Why might it be better to construct a sketch profile for a part on a UCS different to the WCS?
7. The orthographic projections shown so far in this book are in first angle. How can this be changed so that the projections are in third angle?
8. When working in a UCS different to the WCS, why is it necessary to set a new sketch plane?
9. What is the purpose of the **Flip** arrow which appears when **Cut** is set in the **Designer Extrusion** dialogue box?
10. When constructing a Designer **Revolve**, can the surface of revolution be less than a full circle?

Exercises

The drawings for the following exercises are shown in the form of pictorial views of AutoCAD solid models, which have been constructed with the aid of the AutoCAD extension software, the Advanced Modelling Extension (AME). The reader is advised to attempt constructing these solid models with the aid of Designer commands and from the 3D solids so constructed develop orthographic views with the aid of the Designer command **adview**.

The methods of constructing the models with Designer commands is left to your own judgement.

Dimensions not included with the exercise drawing are also left to your own judgement.

1. Figure 3.45. A 3D solid model drawing of a slide is given. Construct a Designer 3D solid from the information given with Fig. 3.45 and, from your 3D solid, construct a three-view third-angle orthographic projection.

   Include an isometric view with your orthographic views.
2. Figure 3.46. A 3D solid model drawing of a fork is shown, together with the pin assembly use to join two forks end to end to each other.

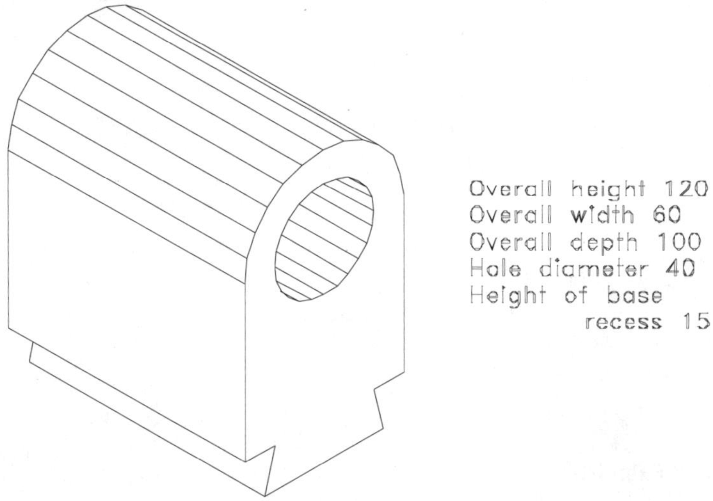

Fig. 3.45 Exercise 1

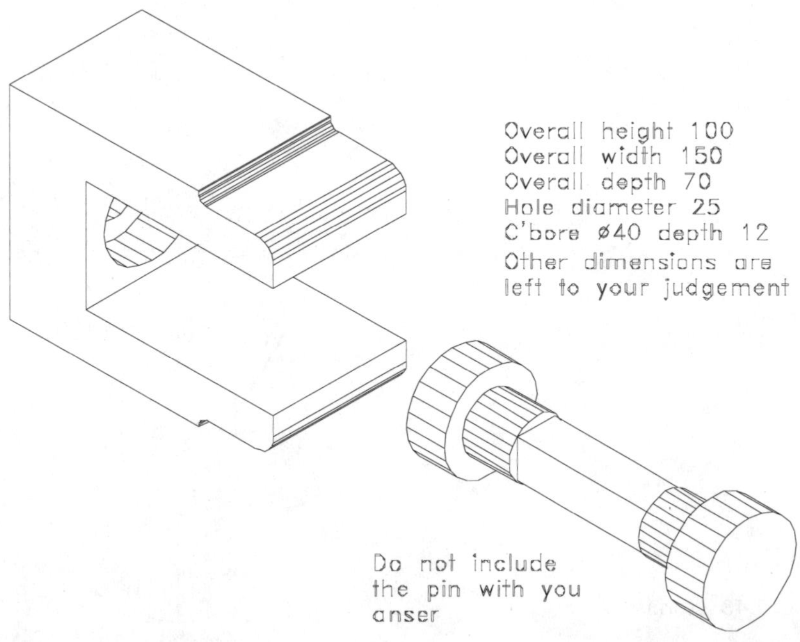

Fig. 3.46 Exercise 2

Do not attempt to draw the pin. Construct a Designer 3D solid model of the fork. From your solid model construct a first-angle three-view orthographic projection. Include an isometric view with your orthographic views.

3. Figure 3.47. A 3D solid model drawing of an angle bracket is given. Construct a Designer 3D solid model drawing to the given dimensions. From your 3D solid obtain a three-view third-angle orthographic projection. Add an isometric view to your orthographic projection.

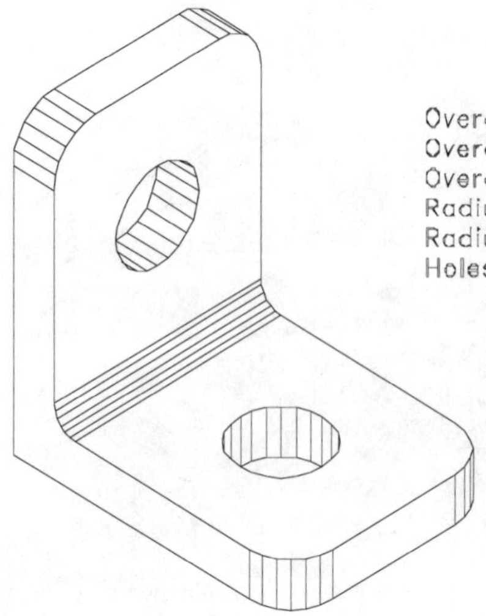

Fig. 3.47 Exercise 3

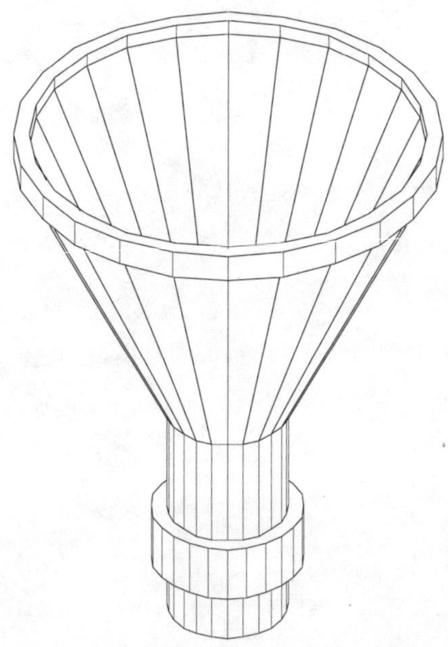

Fig. 3.48 Exercise 4

4. Figure 3.48. From the given dimensions construct a Designer 3D solid model, from which construct a two-view third-angle orthographic projection. Include an isometric view with your drawing.
5. Figure 3.49. A 3D solid model of a bracket is given. Construct a Designer 3D solid model of the bracket from the given dimensions. You will need to use the **Cut** option from the **Designer Extrusion** dialogue box to complete your solid model drawing. From your solid model develop a first-angle orthographic projection in three views and include an isometric view.

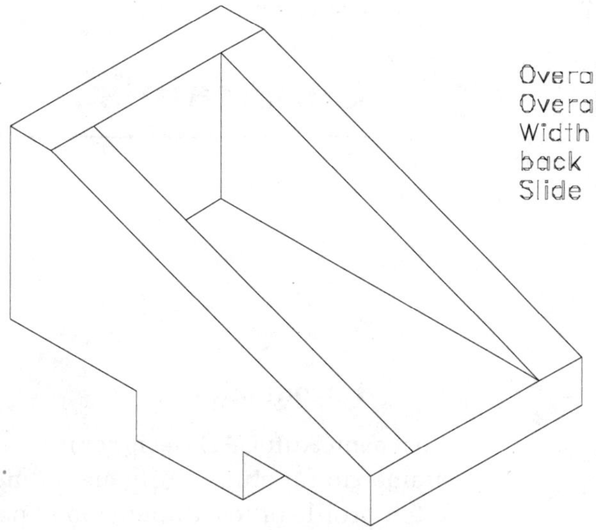

Fig. 3.49 Exercise 5

CHAPTER 4

Constraints and parametrics

Introduction

The reason AutoCAD Designer is a valuable designing tool lies in its parametric functions. Any amendment to a dimension to either a sketch profile or to a dimensioned part will result in the changes as they affect the single dimension, parametrically changing the whole sketch or part. Two features of the software – *constraints* and the command **adeditfeat** (edit feature) control the parametric function.

Sketch profiles

When the Designer command **adprofile** is called and the sketch selected, Designer automatically applies constraints to the outline. Not only are constraints applied, which can be viewed with the aid of the command **adshowcon**, but sketch outlines are modified to a set of rules among which are the following:

1. Lines which are nearly horizontal are forced to horizontal.
2. Lines which are nearly vertical are forced to vertical.
3. Lines which are nearly parallel are forced parallel.
4. Lines and arcs or circles nearly tangential are forced tangential.
5. Lines and other objects near to one another become attached.

The limits to these restraints applied by **adprofile** are governed by the size of the Designer *pickbox*, This is set within the **Designer**

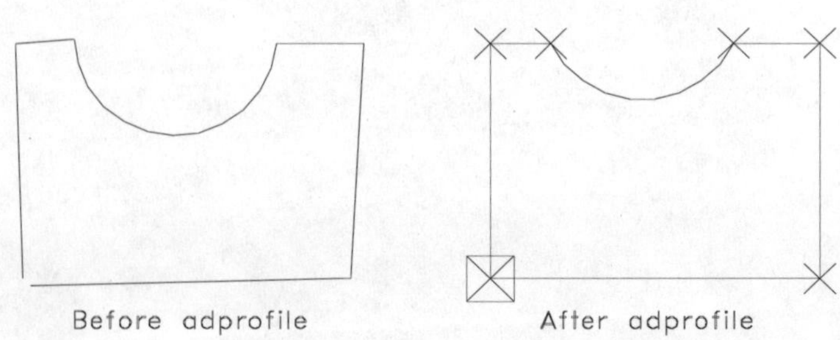

Fig. 4.1 An untidy sketch which has been forced to observe **adprofile** rules

Settings dialogue box as shown in Fig. 4.2. As an example, lines not vertical outside the limits of the pickbox size remain at the angle at which they were drawn. Lines not vertical within the limits of the pickbox sizes are forced to vertical when **adprofile** is called.

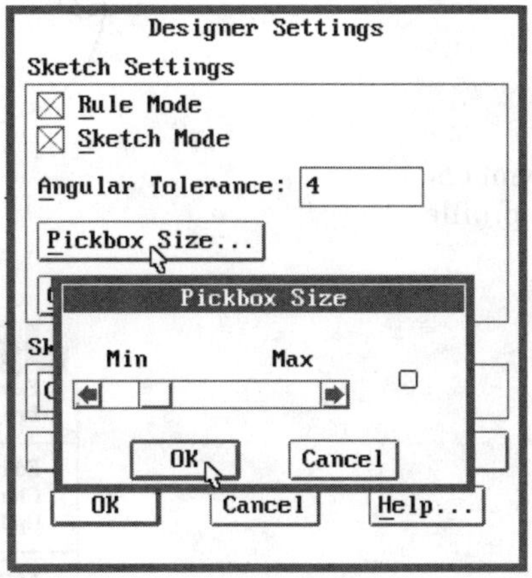

Fig. 4.2 Setting the Designer pickbox size in the **Designer Settings** dialogue box

Constraints

Call the command **adshowcon** and at the Command Line:

Command: *enter* adshowcon *left-click*
All/Select/Next/<eXit>: *enter* a (All) *right-click*

And symbols showing the constraints in a fully constrained sketch appear on the sketch profile. Examples are given in Fig. 4.3 (for a path) and Fig. 4.4 (for a sketch profile). Note that the symbols only show while the command **adshowcon** is active. They disappear with a second *right-click* to the above command prompts sequence.

In the **adshowcon** command sequence, the prompts have the following meanings:

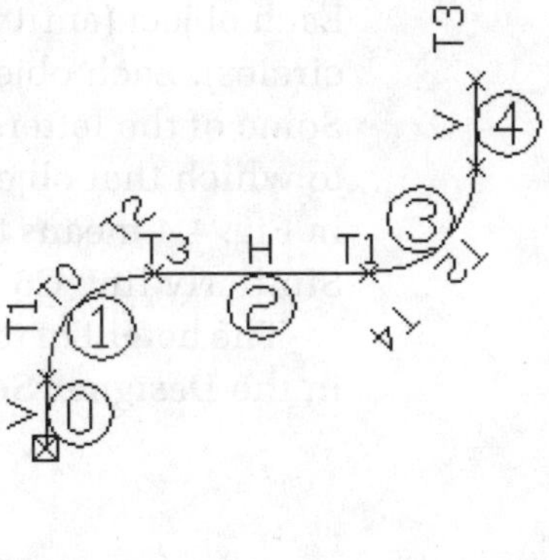

Fig. 4.3 Constraint symbols showing on a path

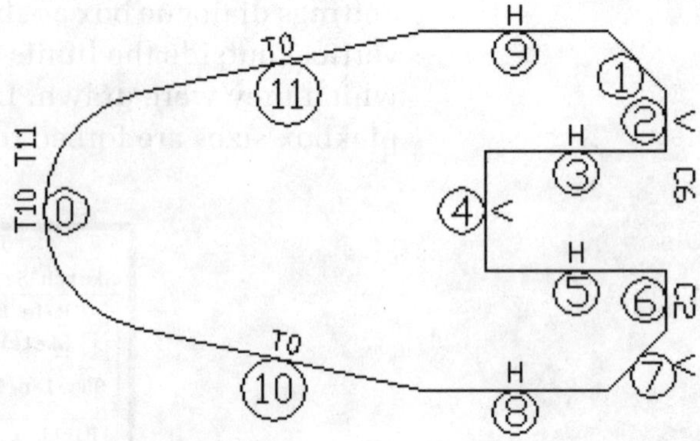

Fig. 4.4 Constraint symbols showing on a sketch profile

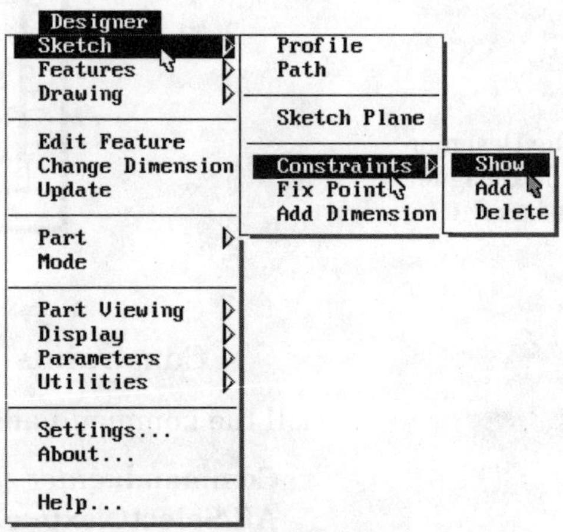

Fig. 4.5 Selecting **Show Constraints** from the **Designer** pull-down menu

All – all the constraint symbols are shown on the path or sketch.
Select – *pick* any object within a sketch and the constraints related to that object show.
Next – the constraints symbols appear one after the other as each *n*, followed by a *right-click* is *entered*.

The meanings of the constraint symbols

Each object (entity) in a sketch profile is numbered (the numbers in circles). Each object also carries a letter. The figures are in circles. Some of the letters are followed by a number referring to the object to which that object is related. Thus the object with the symbol C2 in Fig. 4.4 means that the line C2 is collinear (in line) with entity 2. Similarly line C6 is in line with entity 6.

The height of the constraints symbols is controlled by the size set in the **Designer Settings** dialogue box (Fig. 4.6).

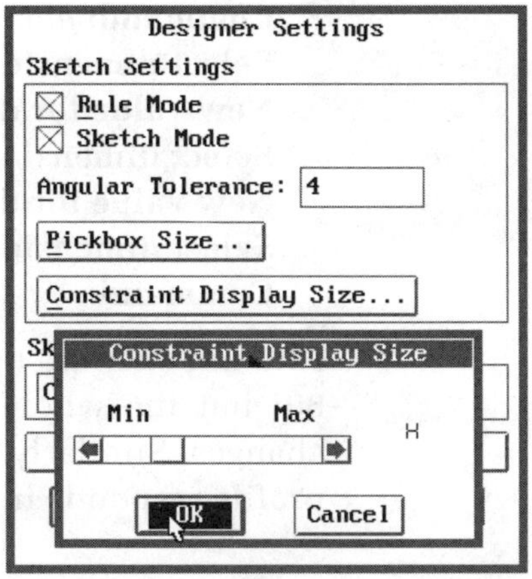

Fig. 4.6 Setting the **Constraints Display Size** in the **Designer Settings** dialogue box

Meanings of constraint letters

H – horizontal – i.e. in line with the X axis.
V – vertical – i.e. in line with the Y axis.
PE – lines which are perpendicular to each other.
PA – lines parallel to each other.
T – entities tangential to each other.
C – entities collinear with each other.
J – end points of two entities are joined.
XV – the centres of circles have the same X coordinate.
YV – the centres of circles have the same Y coordinate.
R – arcs and/or circles have the same radius.

Examples

First example – editing dimensioned sketch profiles

Taking the sketch profile of Fig. 4.7 (Dimensioned in Fig. 4.9) as an example, Fig. 4.9 shows what happens to the fully dimensioned/constrained sketch profile when dimensions are edited with the aid of the Designer command **admoddim**. The Command Line sequence for this command are:

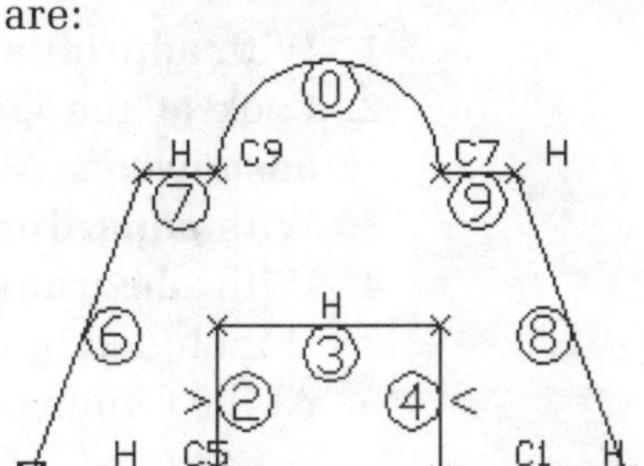

Fig. 4.7 The constraints showing on the sketch profile of the first example (Fig. 4.9)

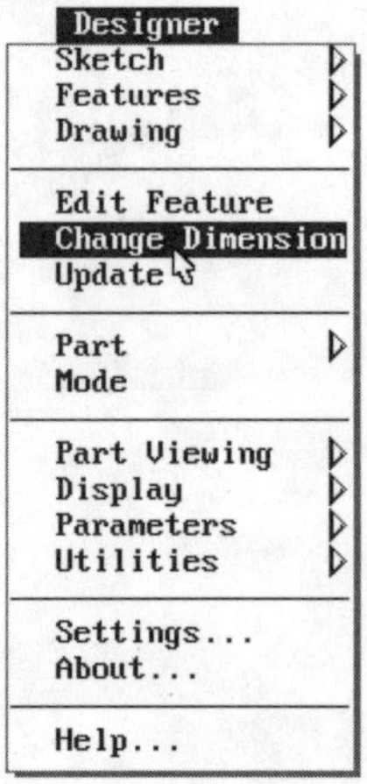

Fig. 4.8. Selecting **Change Dimensions** from the Designer pull-down menu

Command: *enter* admoddim *right-click*
Select dimension to change: *pick* one of the 69° dimensions
New value for dimension <69>: *enter* 60 *right-click*
Select dimension to change: *pick* the other 69° dimensions
New value for dimension <69>: *enter* 60 *right-click*
Select dimension to change: *right-click*
Command:

And not only are the two angular dimensions changed from 69° to 60° but the whole sketch changes to accommodate the angular changes. Similarly when other dimensions are changed the sketch profile responds in a parametric form.

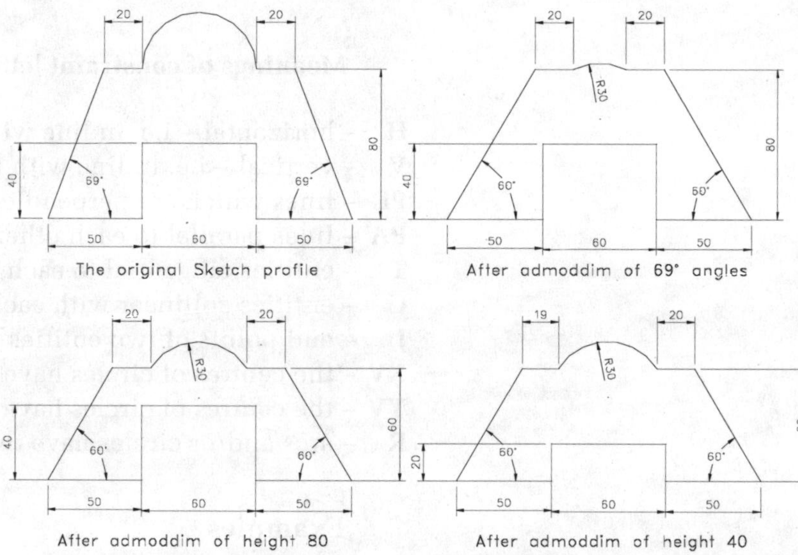

Fig. 4.9 Editing dimensions of the sketch profile of the first example with the aid of **admoddim**

Second example – changing dimensions in an extrusion

To demonstrate the parametric functions resulting from changing a dimension in a feature, first construct the sketch outline (Fig. 4.10), sizes for which are given in Fig. 4.12. Then:

1. With **adprofile** form the sketch profile for the extrusion.
2. Look at the constraints as shown in Fig. 4.10 with the aid of **adshowcon** (All).
3. With **adpardim** fully dimension the sketch outline.
4. With **adextrude** extrude the sketch through 80 units. The extrusion is included in the drawings of Fig. 4.12.
5. At the Command Line:

   Command: *enter* adeditfeat *right-click*

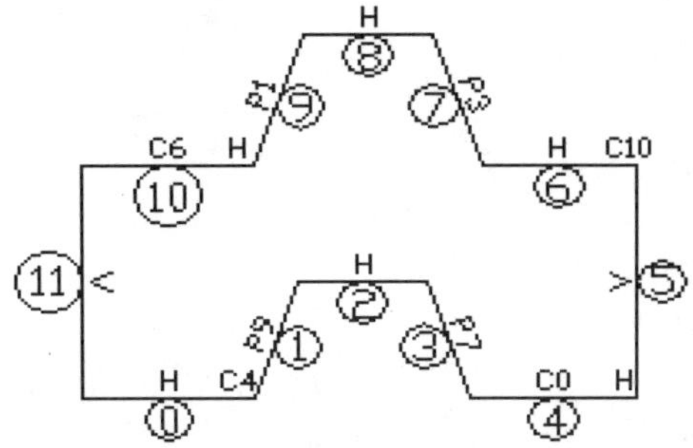

Fig. 4.10 The sketch profile for demonstrating parametric dimensions in the second example

Sketch/<Select Feature>: *pick* the extrusion
The dimensions of the sketch profile and the extrusion height appear on the feature
Select dimension to change: *pick* the 80 dimension of the extrusion
New value for dimension <80>: *enter* 40 *right-click*
Select dimension to change: *right-click*
Command:

6. At the Command Line:

Command: *enter* adupdate *right-click*
Updating feature 2 of 2 (type: Extrude):
Command:

And, as shown in Fig. 4.12, the extrusion becomes 40 units in height. Also included with Fig. 4.12 are examples of **adeditfeat** dimensional changes to other dimensions of the extruded feature.

7. Call **adview** and include orthographic views of the changed feature. Two of these are given in Figs 4.13 and 4.14.

Note

At the Command Line prompt of the **adeditfeat** sequence:

Sketch/<Select Feature>:
if an s (for sketch) in *entered* as a response to the line as follows:
Command: *enter* adeditfeat *right-click*
Sketch/<Select Feature>: *enter* s *right-click*

The feature changes to the original dimensioned sketch profile.

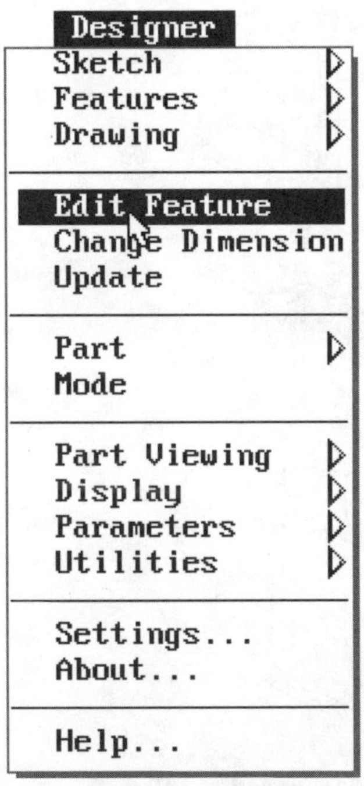

Fig. 4.11 Selecting **Edit Feature** from the **Designer** pull-down menu

Third example – editing the dimensions of a revolved solid

This example shows the changing of dimensions and the resulting parametric changes involving a Designer extrusion. The sequence of working was:

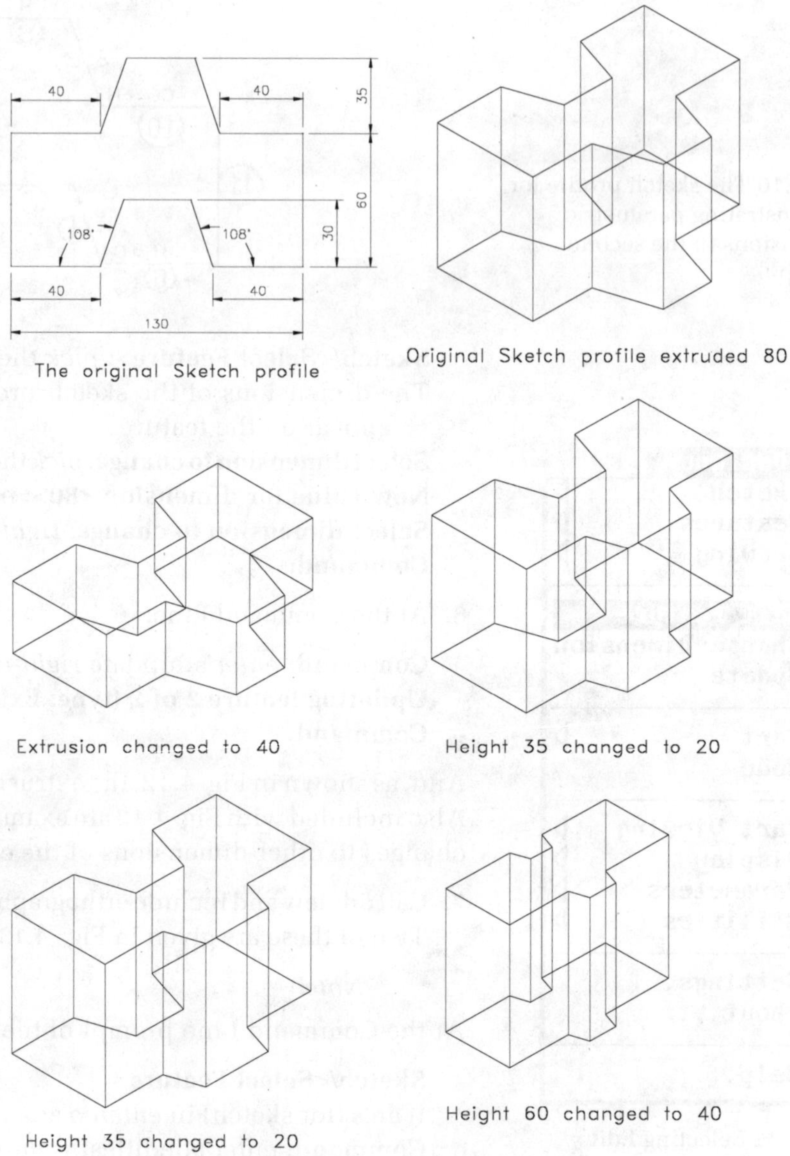

Fig. 4.12 Examples of parametrics associated with the changing of dimensions in a feature

1. Draw the outline.
2. Call **adprofile** and change the outline to a sketch profile.
3. Call **adshowcon** to inspect the constraint symbols (Fig. 4.16).
4. Call **adpardim** and dimension the sketch profile (Fig. 4.17).
5. Call **vpoint** and place the feature in a pictorial view.
6. Call **adeditfeat** and change dimensions as indicated in Fig. 4.18.

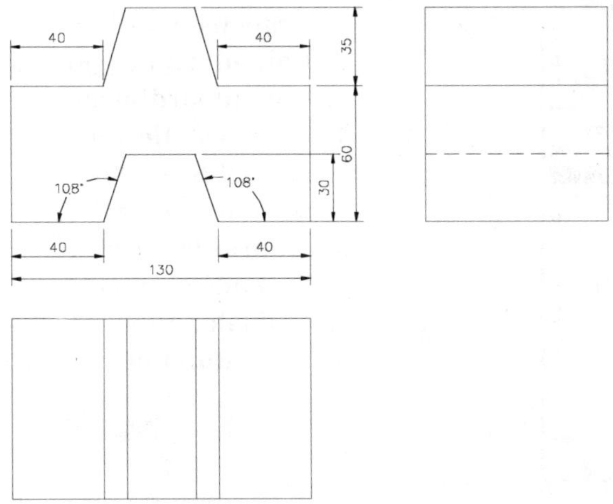

Fig. 4.13 The **adview** orthographic projection of the second example

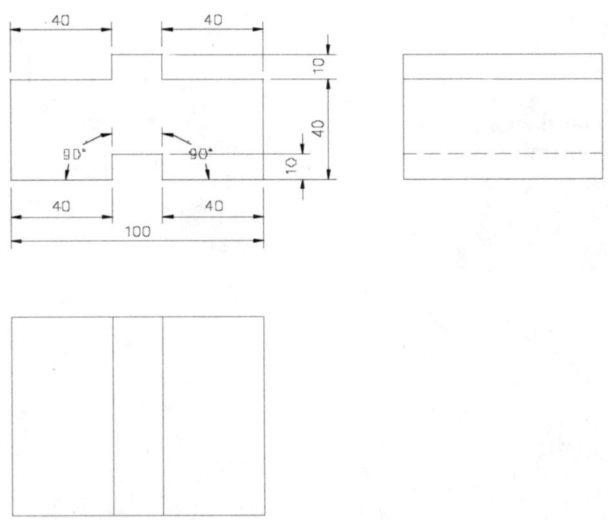

Fig. 4.14 The **adview** orthographic projection of the feature in which the 108° angles have both been changed to 90° in the second example

Note

Another method of obtaining a pictorial view is to call the Designer command **adpartview** and place the feature in an Isometric view from the options available with **adpartview**.

Fourth example – editing a sweep

This example follows the same procedures as for the previous examples, except that the path was constructed on the WCS and the sketch profile on a UCS constructed with the 3point option. The sequence is:

1. Draw path outline.
2. Call **adprofile** and change outline into a sketch profile.
3. Call **adpardim** and dimension the sketch profile.
4. Call **Ucsfollow** and set it ON (1)
5. Call **UCS** and **3point** and construct the new UCS on which to draw the outline for the sketch profile.
6. **Adprofile** the sketch.
7. Call **adsweep** and construct the sweep.
8. Call **adeditfeat** and change the dimensions as though fit (Fig. 4.20).
9. Call **adupdate** to update changes in dimensions.

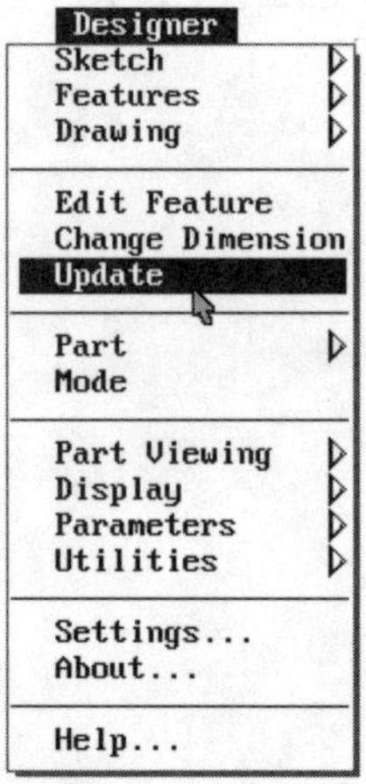

Fig. 4.15 Selecting **Update** from the **Designer** pull-down menu

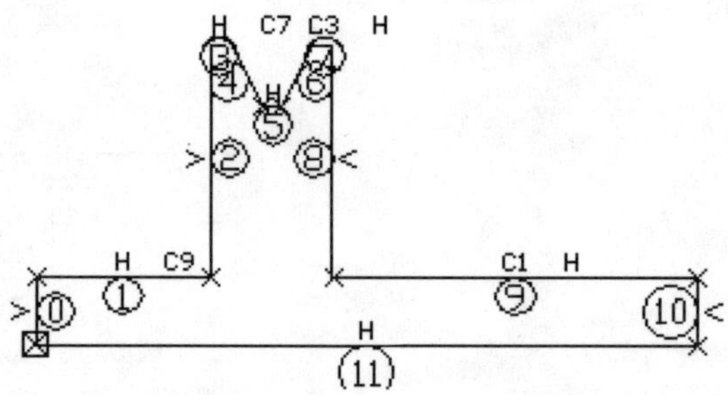

Fig. 4.16 The sketch profile showing constraint symbols in the third example

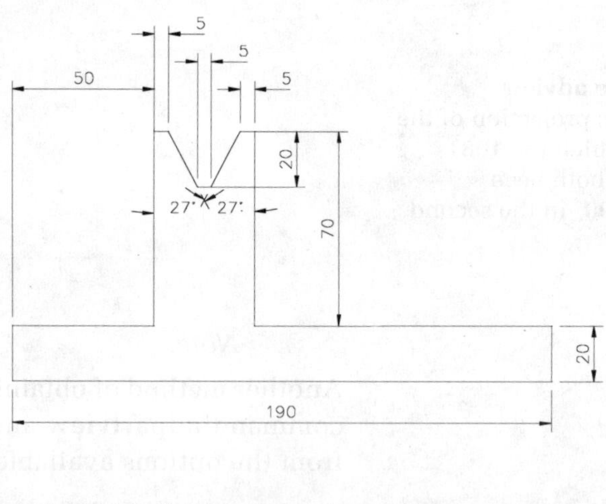

Fig. 4.17 The dimensioned sketch profile for the third example

Fifth example – changing dimensions in other features

The same procedures as have been described so far in this chapter can equally as well be applied to changing the dimensions of Designer holes, and extrude cuts. Figures 4.21 and 4.22 show original features and the result of using **adeditfeat** on the holes and the extruding cut in the two features.

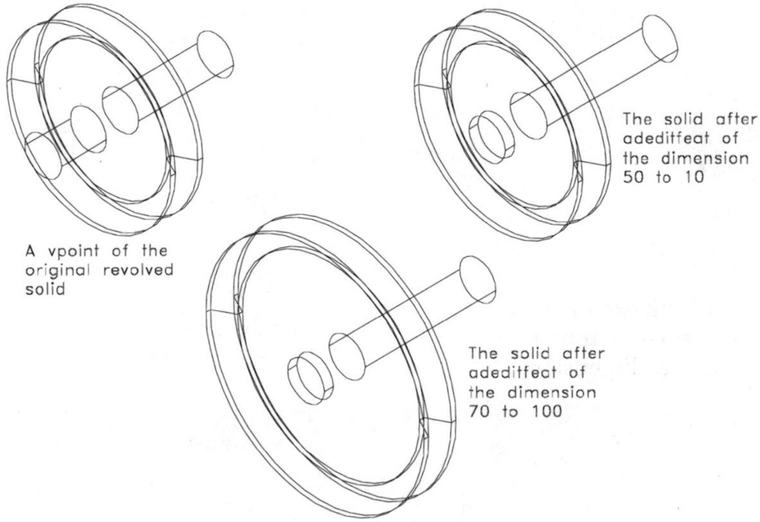

Fig. 4.18 The original solid of extrusion of the third example, together with two examples of the solid after **adeditfeat** and changes to dimensions

Designer Part viewing command

In earlier chapters it was suggested that, with **Ucsfollow** set on (to 1), and using the **FRONT** UCS from **UCS Presets...** that a better viewing position could be obtained for placing the feature being acted upon in a pictorial position. Another method of obtaining a good viewing

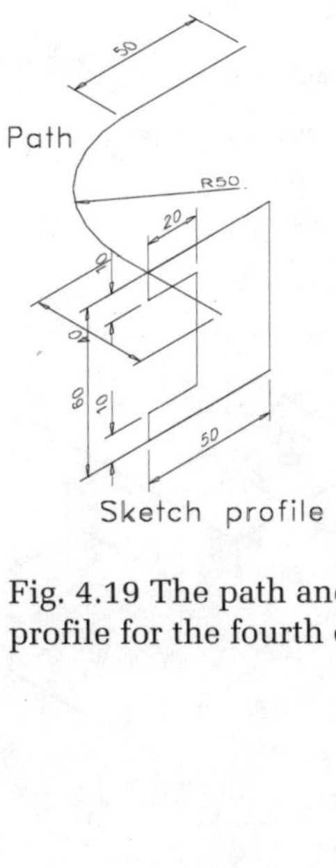

Fig. 4.19 The path and sketch profile for the fourth example

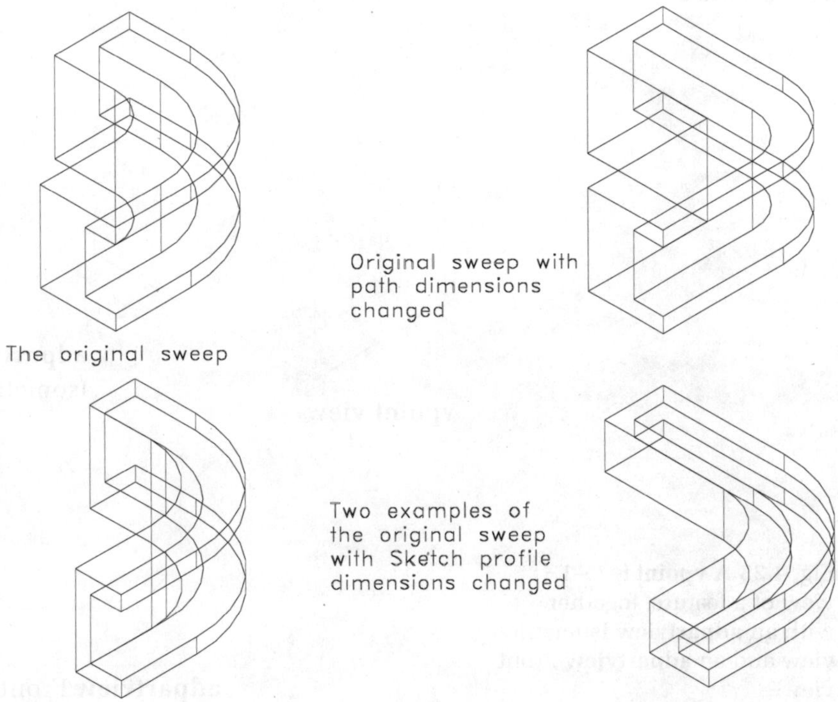

Fig. 4.20 Fourth example – the original sweep and the results of changing path dimensions and sketch profile dimensions

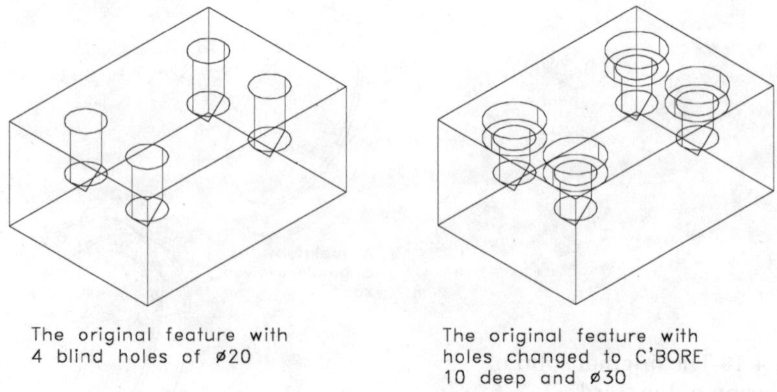

Fig. 4.21 Fifth example. The effects of **adeditfeat** on holes and changing dimensions

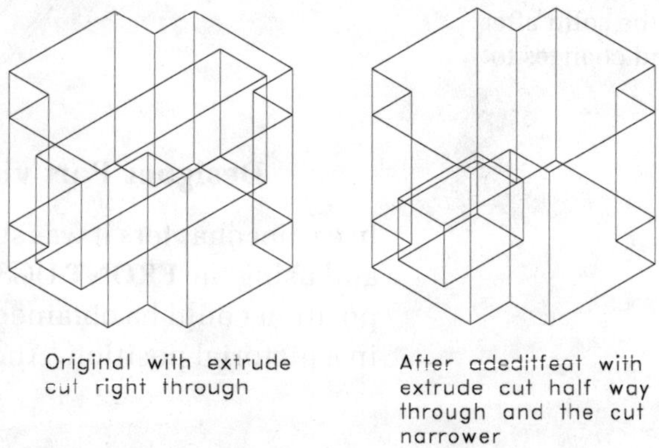

Fig. 4.22 Fifth example. The effects of using **adeditfeat** on an extrude cut

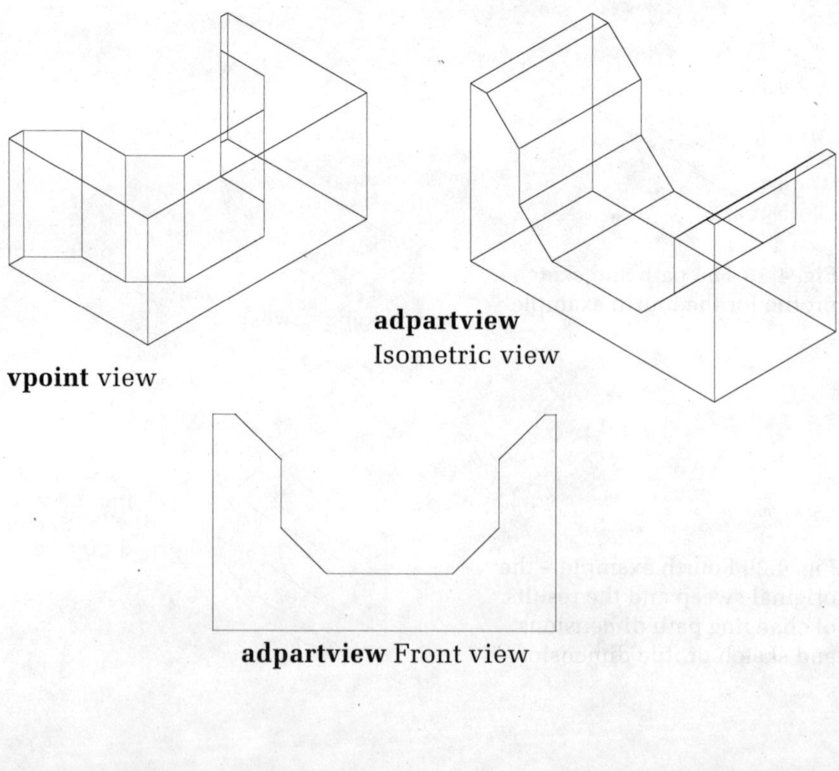

Fig. 4.23 A **vpoint** (–1,–1,1) view of a feature, together with an **adpartview** Isometric view and an **adpartview** Front view

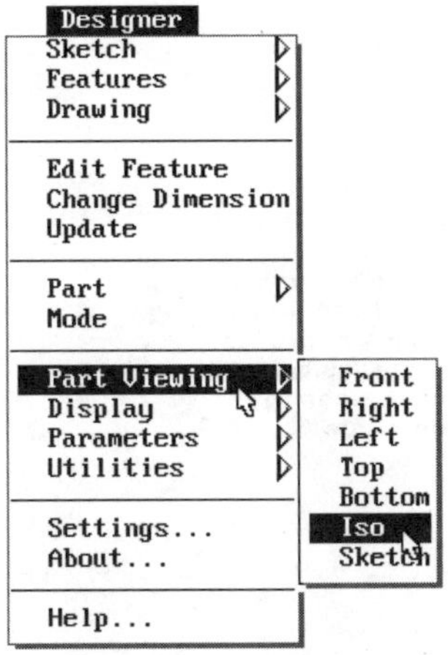

Fig. 4.24 Selecting **Part Viewing** options from the **Designer** pull-down menu

position is to call the Designer command **adpartview**. When called, the Command Line shows:

Command: *enter* adpartview *right-click*
View option Front/Right/Left/Top/Bottom/Isometric/<Sketch>:

Depending upon the operator's response, the feature on screen automatically assumes the position required. Figure 4.23 shows the **vpoint** view at –1,–1,1, together with the **adpartview** isometric (i) option view and the **adpartview** front (f) option view. Figure 4.24 shows the command called by selection from the **Designer** pull-down menu.

Further examples

Number 1

Figure 4.25 is a Designer solid model made up from a number of sketch profiles drawn on the WCS, with the holes **cut extruded** into a **base extrusion**. The two tags were then drawn on a 3point UCS and on a new **adskpln** and added by **join extrusions** to the remainder of the solid.

Figure 4.26 includes notes indicating the methods of construction and Fig. 4.27 is the **adview** orthographic projection of the solid.

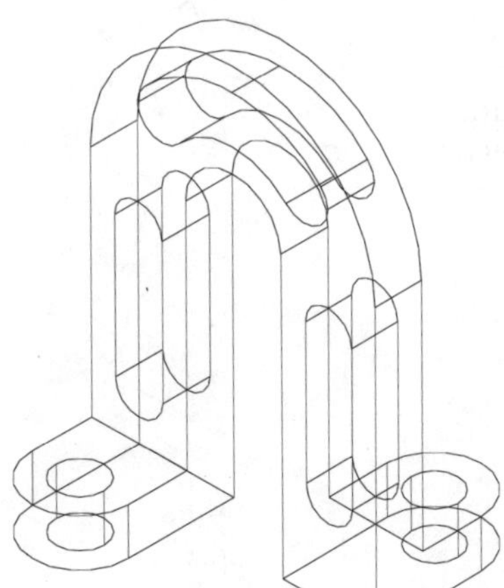

Fig. 4.25 Further examples – number 1

Number 2

This example (Fig. 4.28) was extruded from two sketch profiles which were **join extruded** to each other (Fig. 4.29). The hole in the right-hand end of the solid was added with the command **adhole**.

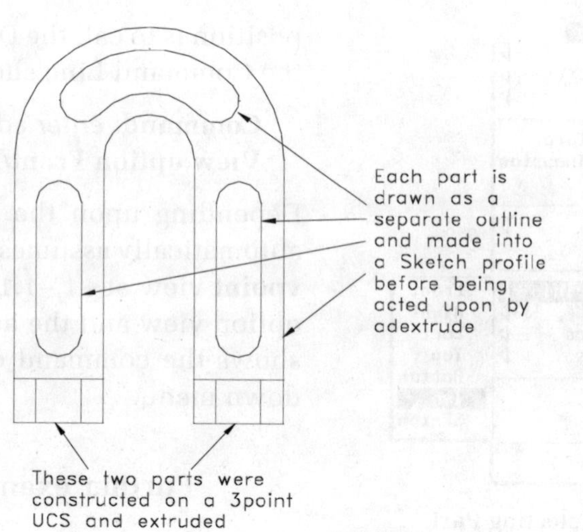

Fig. 4.26 The methods of construction of Fig. 4.25

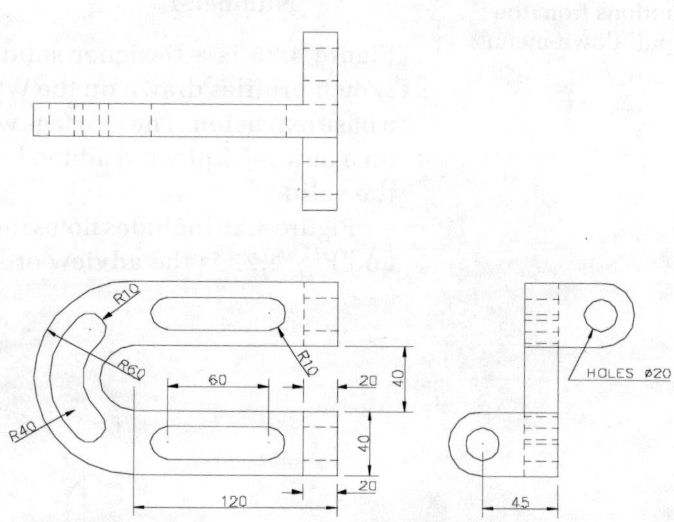

Fig. 4.27 The **adview** third-angle orthographic projection of Fig. 4.25. Dimensions were added to the views

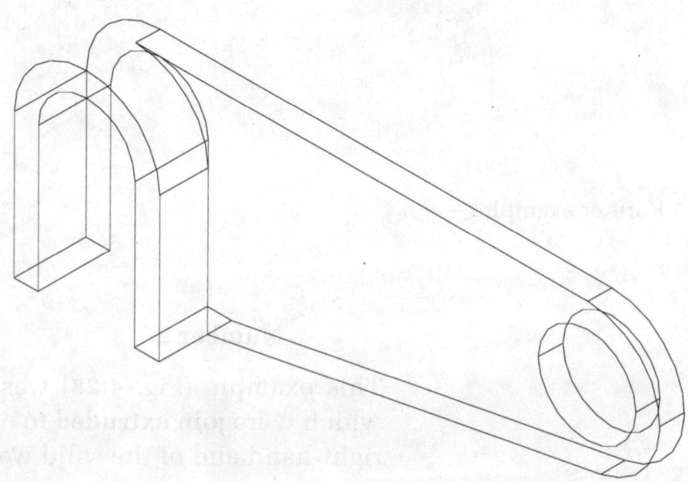

Fig. 4.28 Further examples – number 2

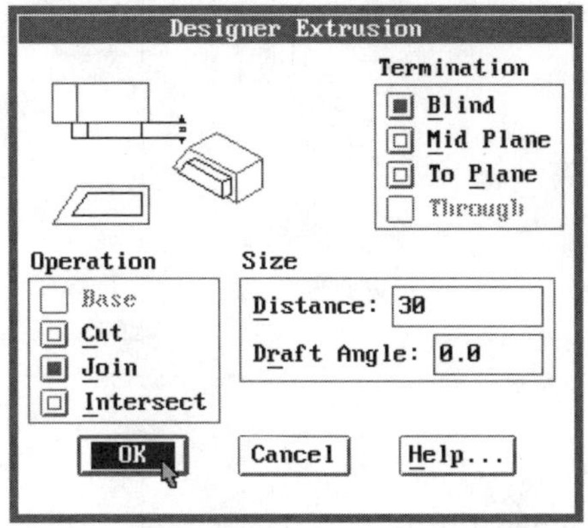

Fig. 4.29 The settings in the **Designer Extrusion** dialogue box to obtain a **Join** extrusion

Number 3

Figure 4.30 is an isometric view of the Designer 3D solid model shown in a three-view third-angle orthographic projection in Fig. 4.31.

The outline for the base of the solid was constructed as a sketch profile.
Holes were added with the aid of **adhole**.
The vertical part was added with the aid of Designer **join extrude**.
The horizontal cylinder was added as an extrusion on a new sketch plane on a 3point UCS.
The hole through the central cylinder was added as a **cut extrude**.

The three-view third-angle orthographic projection was constructed with the aid of the Designer command **adview**.

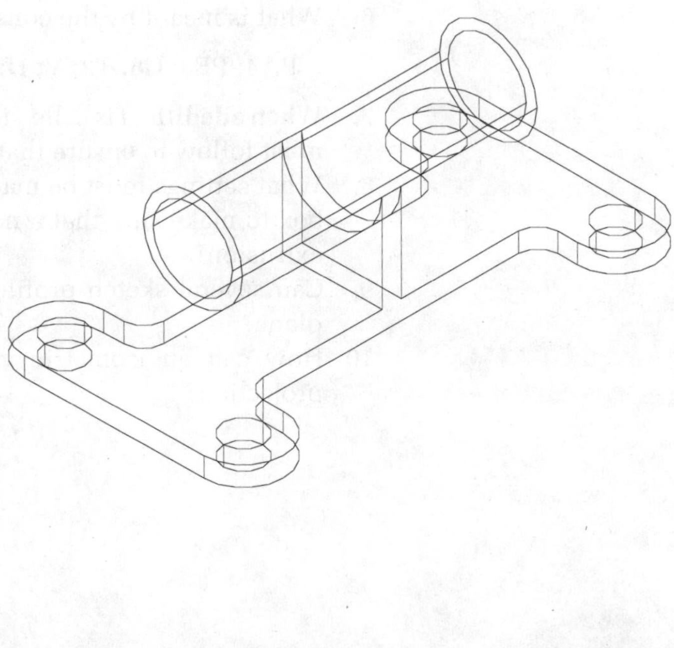

Fig. 4.30 Further examples – number 3

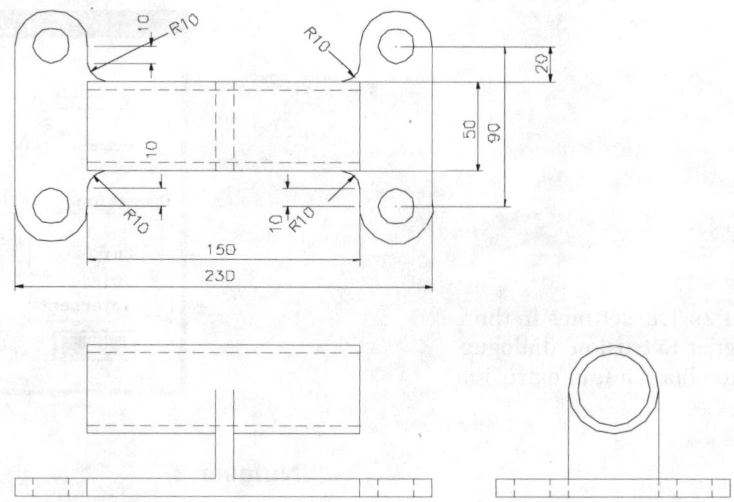

Fig. 4.31 The three-view third-angle orthographic projection obtained from the part shown in Fig. 4.30

Questions

1. When placing a Designer feature into a pictorial view it is probably better to use the Designer command **adpartview** than to use the AutoCAD command **vpoint**. Why is this so?
2. The Designer command **adprofile** 'cleans up' untidy outlines intended to be used as sketch profiles. How is this carried out?
3. Why is it necessary to fully dimension a sketch profile before changing it into a Designer feature with commands such as **adrevolve**?
4. What is the difference between a Designer path and a Designer sketch profile?
5. What happens when **adshowcon** is called and the option **Next** is chosen?
6. What is meant by the constraints symbols:

   PA4; PE3; C8; T2; V; H; XV2; YV5?

7. When **adeditfeat** is called to change dimensions, which command must follow to ensure that the change takes effect?
8. What settings must be made in the **Designer Extrusion** dialogue box to make sure that a new extrusion cuts through an existing extrusion?
9. Can several sketch profiles be constructed on the same sketch plane?
10. How can an isometric view be obtained in an orthographic projection?

Exercises

1. A Designer three-view third-angle orthographic projection of a post stand is given in Fig. 4.32.

   Construct the feature to the given dimensions and, with the aid of the Designer command **adeditfeat**, change some of its dimensions and hence test the Designer parametric functions on the part.

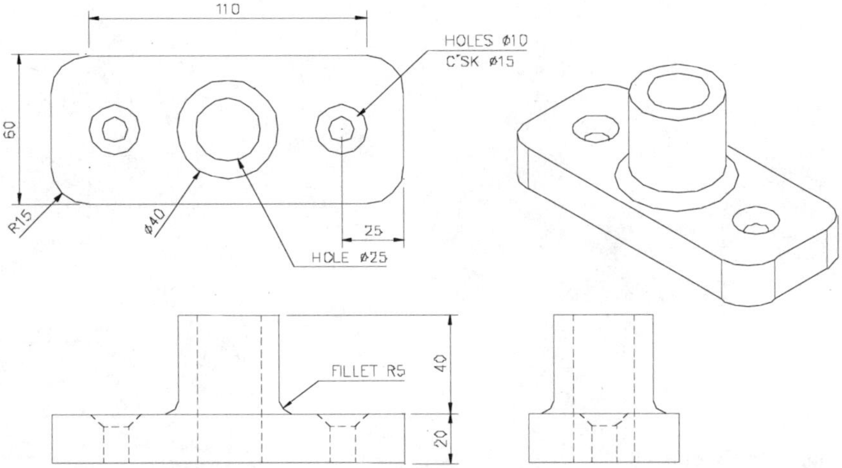

Fig. 4.32 Exercise 1

2. Figure 4.33 is a Designer three-view orthographic projection, together with an isometric view of an engineering component. With the aid of Designer construct a feature for the part and from it construct the given orthographic projection.

   Using **adeditfeat**, change some of the dimensions of the part and show the resulting changes in another orthographic projection with the aid of **adview**.

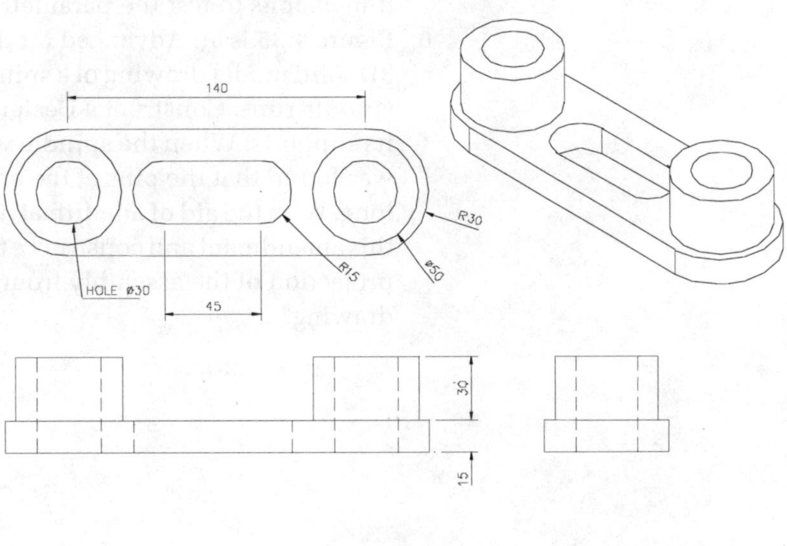

Fig. 4.33 Exercsie 2

3. Figure 4.34 is a Designer third-angle projection of a part. Construct the given drawing, including the isometric view with the aid of Designer. Change some dimensions with **adeditfeat** and from the updated feature produce a new orthographic projection in first angle.

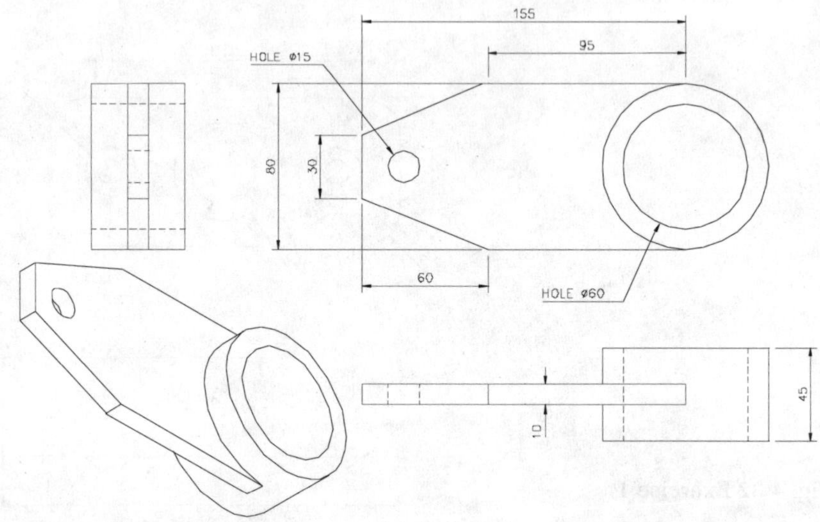

Fig. 4.34 Exercise 3

Further exercises

4. Construct Designer orthographic projections of Fig. 4.30 on page 63 to the dimensions given in Fig. 4.31. Experiment with the Designer command **adeditfeat** to change the parametric shapes of the feature.
5. Construct the drawing (Fig. 4.28) on page 62 and amend some of its dimensions to test the parametric functions of the software.
6. Figure 4.35 is an Advanced Modelling Extension (AME) exploded 3D solid model drawing of a spindle and two supports in which the spindle runs. Construct a Designer solid model of the spindle and its supports. When the spindle was first designed for its purpose it was found that the pins at the ends of the spindle were 10 mm too long. With the aid of **adeditfeat**, update the design to accommodate this amendment and construct a three-view first-angle orthographic projection of the assembly from your Designer 3D updated model drawing.

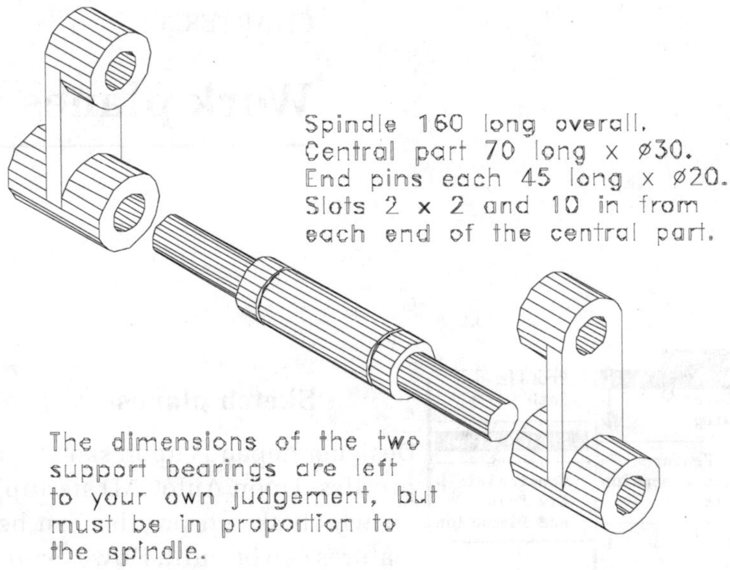

Fig. 4.35 Exercise 6

CHAPTER 5

Work planes and sketch planes

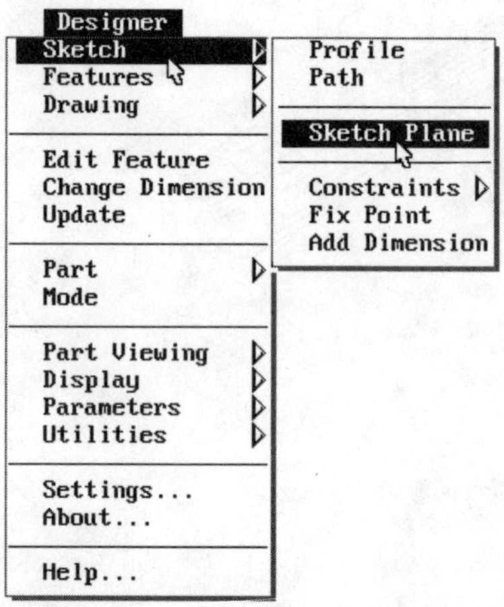

Fig 5.1 Selecting the command **Sketch Plane** from the **Designer** pull-down menu

Sketch planes

Designer depends upon sketch planes on which to construct sketch profiles. Upon AutoCAD startup, the WCS acts as the sketch plane on which sketch profiles can be constructed and from which 3D features can be built. However, once a different XY plane other than the WCS is required for other sketch profiles, a new sketch plane must be formed. A sketch plane is, in fact, a two-dimensional (2D) plane of infinite size, with X and Y axes. Only one sketch profile can be in action at any one time.

Sketch planes are not visible on the Designer screen. Because a sketch profile can only be constructed on a sketch plane, each feature in a 3D Designer model must be derived from a sketch profile constructed on a sketch plane.

The command **adskpln** is used to position the sketch plane as required, as will be seen in examples in this chapter.

1. The UCS icon on a sketch plane

In order to see the effect of aligning the UCS as a sketch plane, first set the variable **ucsicon** to show at an origin. When the UCS icon is displayed at the sketch plane origin, the X and Y symbols on the UCS icon show the operator the directions of the two axes of the sketch plane.

Figure 5.2 shows the Designer 3D model used to show one of the methods of changing the sketch plane position. New sketch planes were formed as follows:

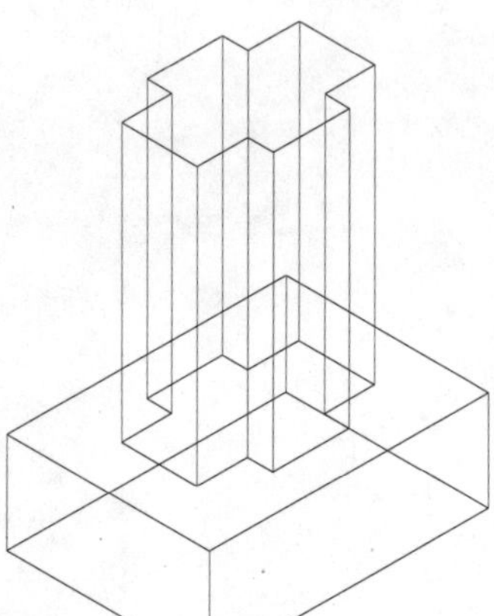

Fig. 5.2 The Designer model for Example 1

1. Set the variable **ucsicon** to show the icon at the origin. At the Command Line:

   Command: *enter* ucsicon *right-click*
   ON/OFF/All/Noorigin/ORigin/ <ON>: *enter* or *right-click*
   Command:

Fig. 5.3 *Pick* work plane or planar face

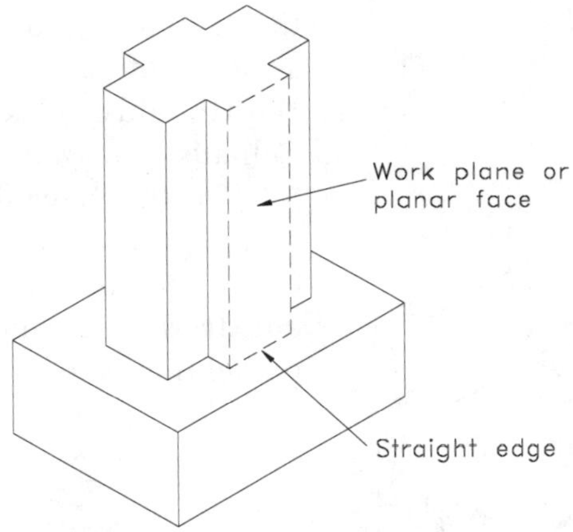

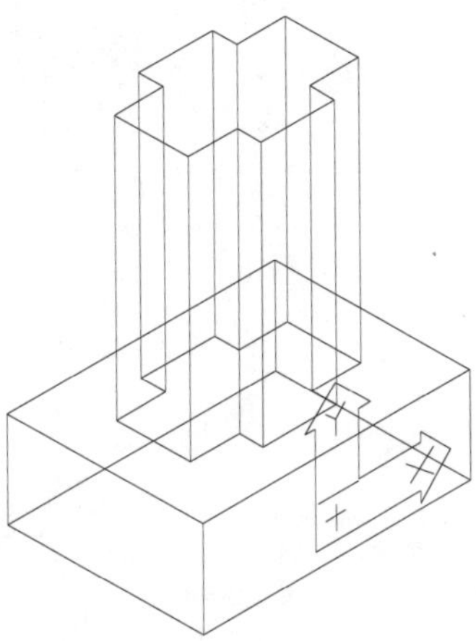

Fig. 5.4 The UCS icon appearing at the sketch plane origin

2. At the Command Line:

   Command: *enter* adskpln *right-click*
   Xy/Yz/Zx/Ucs/<Select work plane or planar face>: *pick* (Fig. 5.3)
   Next/Accept: *right-click* if it is the planar face required
   X/Y/Z/<Select work axis or straight edge>: *pick* (Fig. 5.3)
   Rotate/Accept: *right-click* if the UCS icon is in required position, X and Y axes as desired. If not *enter* r (Rotate) and the icon rotates through 90°. See Fig. 5.4
   Command:

3. At the Command Line:

   Command: *enter* adpartview *right-click*
   View option Front/Right/Top/Bottom/Isometric/<Sketch>: *right-click*
   Command:

The view changes to the sketch plane. On the sketch plane construct

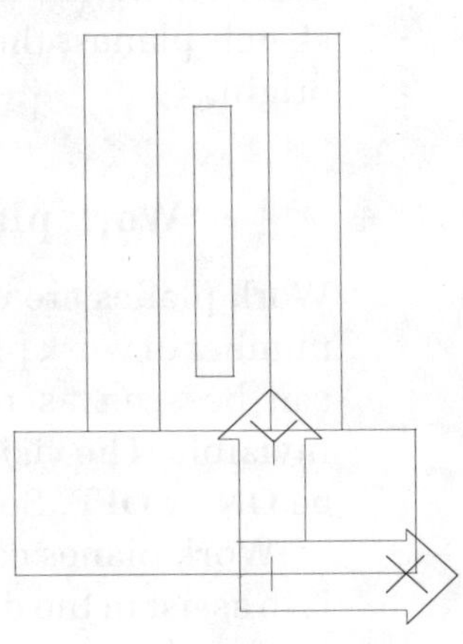

Fig. 5.5 An outline drawn on the new sketch plane

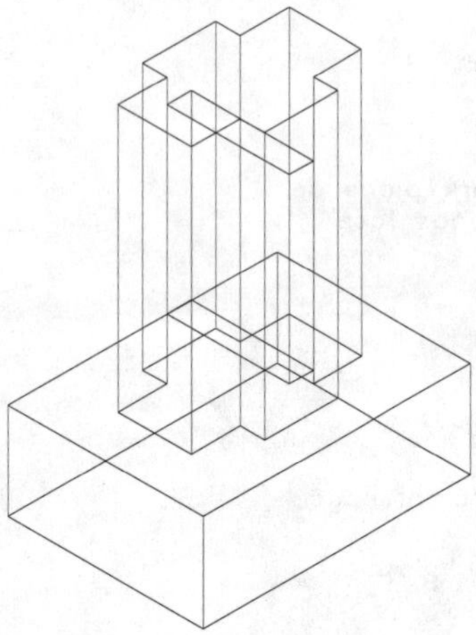

Fig. 5.6 The **Cut extrusion**

the outline Fig. 5.5. Call **adprofile** and convert the outline to a sketch profile.

4. With the aid of **adextrude (Cut)** extrude the sketch profile (Fig. 5.6).
5. Call **adskpln** again and reset the sketch plane as indicated in Fig. 5.7. On this new sketch plane construct an outline for another sketch profile (Fig. 5.8).
6. Call **adprofile** and change the outline to a sketch profile. Call **adextrude (Cut)** and extrude the cut through the height of the 3D model (Fig. 5.9).

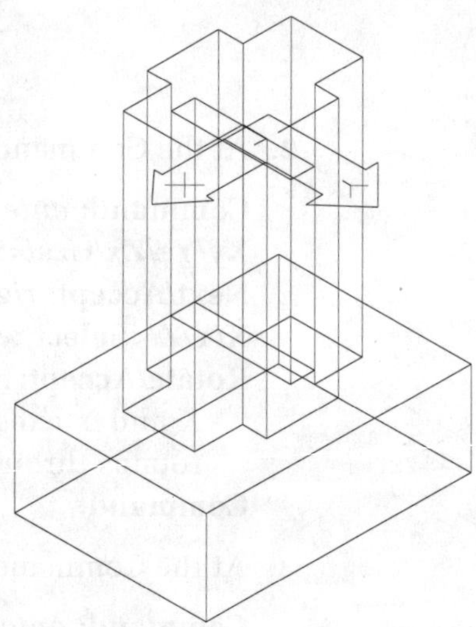

Fig. 5.7 Re-setting the sketch plane

Note

The UCS icon has been placed at the sketch profile origin in this example only to demonstrate to the reader that the sketch plane is in position. When an operator becomes more skilled at establishing sketch planes, the variable **ucsicon** need not be set to show at the origin.

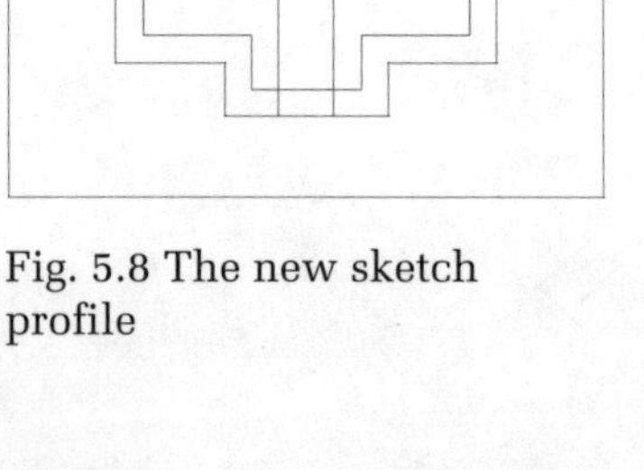

Fig. 5.8 The new sketch profile

Work planes

Work planes are used for different purposes to sketch planes. Any number of work planes can exist in a drawing at the same time. They can be seen as rectangular outlines if desired, or can be made invisible. The visibility is set by the Designer command **adplndsp** to be **ON** or **OFF**. See also Fig. 5.10.

Work planes can be used for a variety of purposes, one of which is to assist in the defining of a sketch plane. As has already been seen

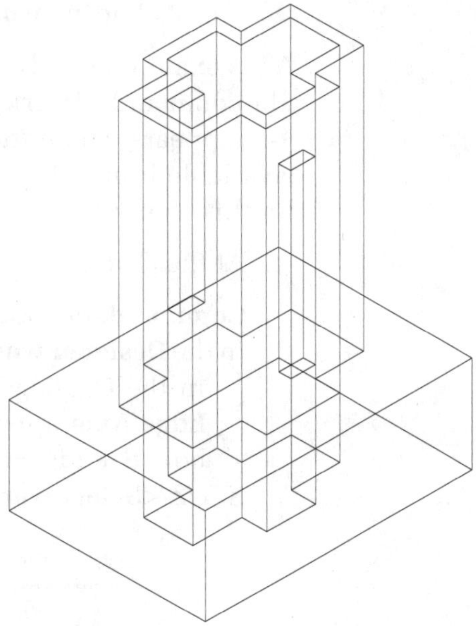

Fig. 5.9 The completed 3D model

in the options for the command **adskpln**, a work plane can be selected as one of the features for positioning of a sketch plane.

It must be noted that sketch profiles cannot be constructed on work planes. Work planes can however be used to set a sketch plane on their surface. It is not necessary to construct a work plane in order to define a sketch plane. As was shown earlier, the options for the command **adskpln** required either a planar face (part of a 3D feature already in existence) or a work plane.

Work planes, unlike sketch planes can be displayed with the drawing and can be erased or edited with other AutoCAD editing commands if desired.

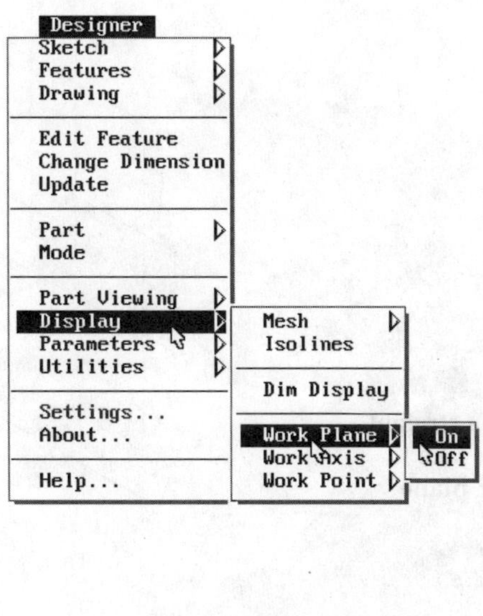

Fig. 5.10 Setting the work plane to be visible or not from the **Designer** pull-down menu

2. Setting work planes

This example involves the same 3D model as for example 1. When the command **adworkpln** is called, the **Designer work plane** dialogue box appears. There are a number of possible settings for a work plane available from this dialogue box. Two different settings are shown in this example.

1. At the Command Line:

Command: *enter* adworkpln *right-click*
In the **Designer work plane** dialogue box which appears *left-click* in the **On Edge/Axis** check box. A second dialogue box **On Edge/Axis** appears. *Left-click* in the **Planar Parallel** check box. See Fig. 5.11.
X/Y/Z/<Select work axis or straight edge>: *pick* (Fig. 5.12)

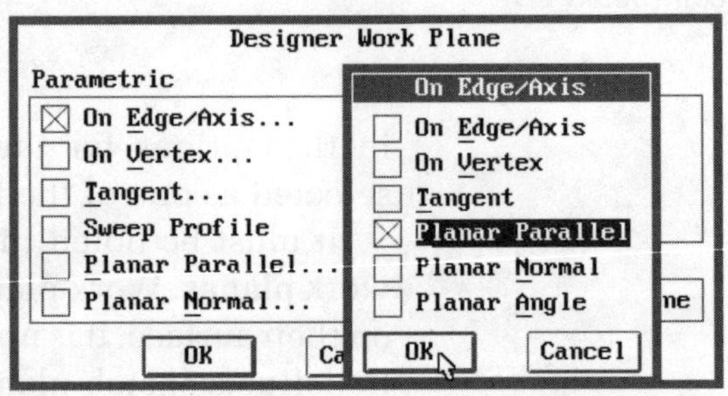

Fig. 5.11 Settings in the **Designer work plane** dialogue box

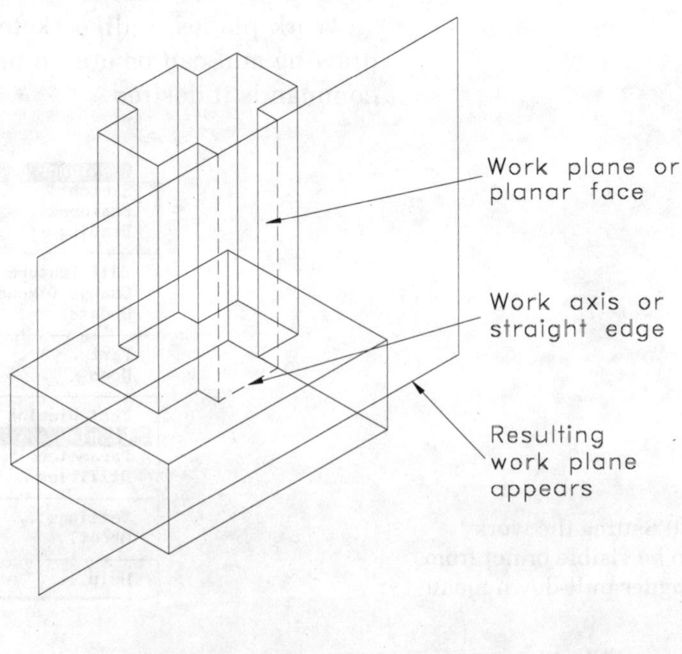

Fig. 5.12 *Picking* a straight edge and a planar face to determine a work plane

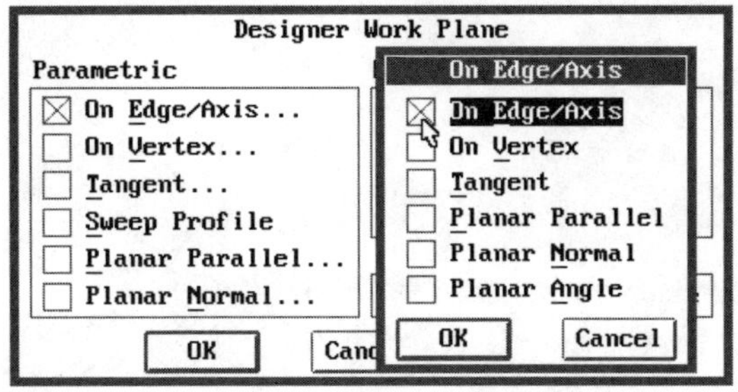

Fig. 5.13 Selecting **On Edge/Axis** in both dialogue boxes of the **Designer work plane** dialogue box

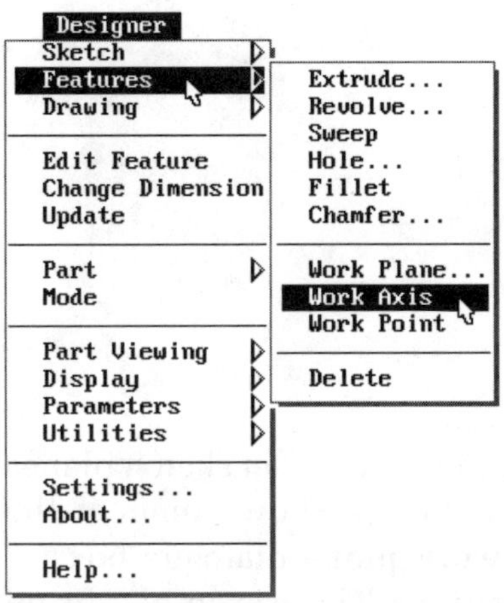

Fig. 5.14 Selecting **Work Axis** from the **Designer** pull-down menu

Xy/Yz/Zx/Ucs/<Select work plane or planar face>: *pick*
Next/<Accept>: *right-click*
Command:

2. Call **adworkpln** again and, in the **Designer work plane** dialogue box choose settings as shown in Fig. 5.13. When the options appear at the Command Line, *pick* straight edges as shown in Fig. 5.15.

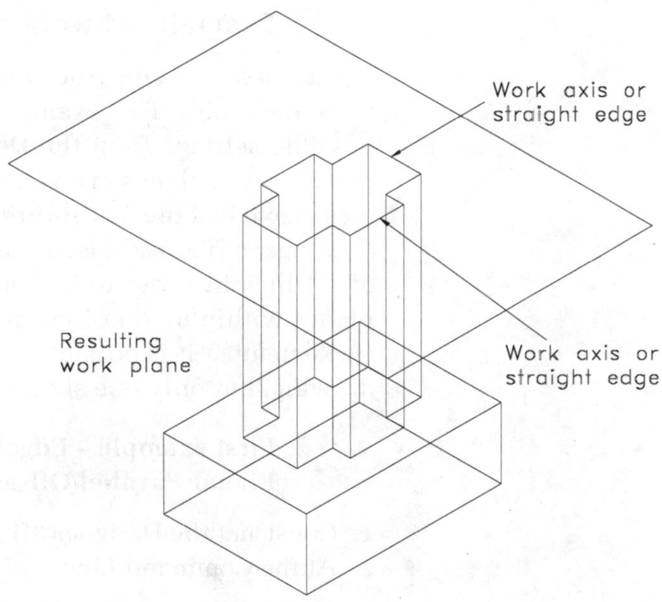

Fig. 5.15 The work plane formed by selecting straight edges as shown

Work axes

Work axes can be added to those parts of a Designer model which have cylindrical faces. They appear on the drawing as centre lines passing through the centre of the cylinder to which they refer. Examples of work axes placed on a Designer model are shown in Fig. 5.16. To add a work axis to a model:

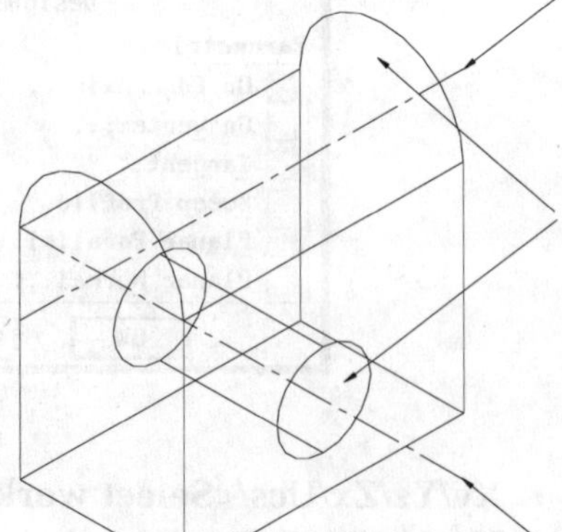

Fig. 5.16 Designer Work axes

Command: *enter* adworkaxis *right-click*
Select cylindrical face: *pick*
Command:

Examples of work planes

It is necessary to construct work planes in order to set sketch planes with their aid. The examples which follow show some of the possible settings from the **Designer work plane** dialogue box for placing work planes in a variety of positions. These examples by no means exhaust the possibilities for placing work planes in Designer drawings and the reader is advised to experiment with other combinations of settings in order to become familiar with the placing of work planes within his/her Designer drawings.

Remember it is possible to have any number of work planes in a drawing, but only one sketch profile is operative at any one time.

First example – Edge/Axis and Edge/Axis followed by Planar Parallel/Offset

1. Construct the Designer 3D model shown in Fig. 5.18.
2. At the Command Line:

Command: *enter* adworkaxis *right-click*
Select cylindrical face: *pick*
Command:

And repeat for the second Work Axis (Fig. 5.18).

3. At the Command Line:

Command : *enter* adworkpln *right-click*
In the **Designer work plane** dialogue box *left-click* in check boxes

as shown in Fig. 5.17, followed by *left-clicks* on the **OK** buttons.

X/Y/Z/<Select work axis or straight edge>: *pick* (Fig. 5.18)
X/Y/Z/<Select work axis or straight edge>: *pick* (Fig. 5.18)
Command:

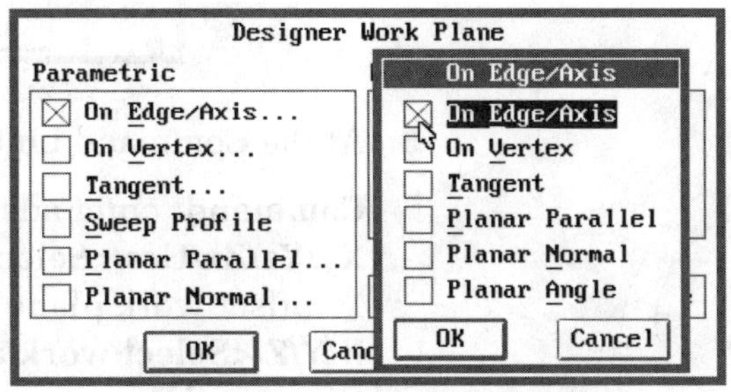

Fig. 5.17 Settings in the **Designer work plane** dialogue box for the first example

4. At the Command Line:

Command: *enter* adworkpln *right-click*
In the **Designer work plane** dialogue box *left-click* in check boxes as shown in Fig. 5.19, followed by *left-clicks* on the **OK** buttons.
Offset <1>: enter 30 *right-click*
Command: (Fig. 5.18)

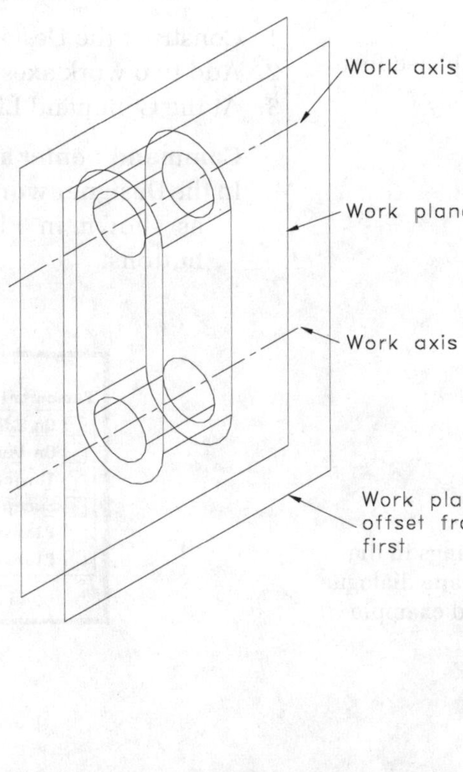

Fig. 5.18 The two work planes for the first example

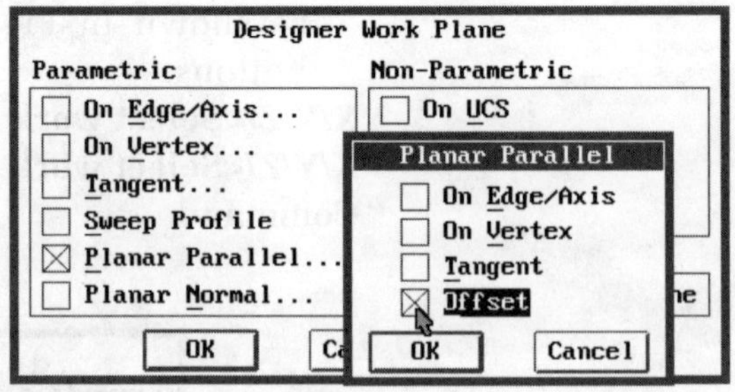

Fig. 5.19 Settings in the **Designer work plane** dialogue box for the second work plane of the first example

5. At the Command Line:

Command: *enter* adskpln *right-click*
Xy/Yz/Zx/Ucs/<Select work plane or planar face>: *pick* the offset work plane
X/Y/Z/<Select work axis or straight edge>: *pick* a Work Axis
Command:

6. At the Command Line:

Command: *enter* adviewpart *right-click*

and *right-click* to the options to place the model in the **Sketch** view.

7. Construct the outline for the sketch profile of the hole running through the model.
8. Call **adextrude** and **cut extrude** the profile. The result is shown in Fig. 5.20.

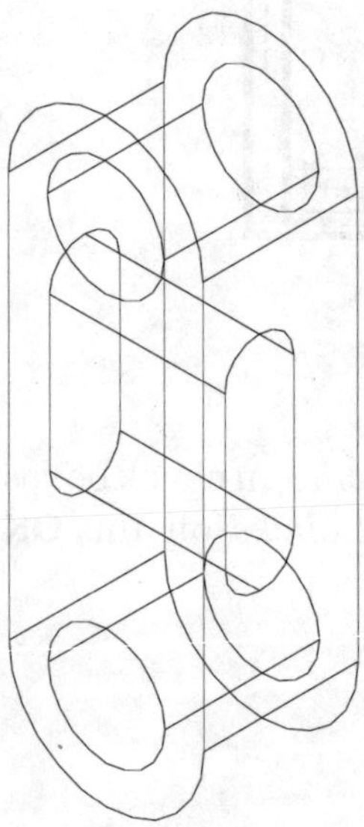

Fig. 5.20 The completed first example

Second example – Tangent and Planar/Parallel

1. Construct the Designer model as shown in Fig. 5.22.
2. Add two work axes to the model (Fig. 5.22).
3. At the Command Line:

Command : *enter* adworkpln *right-click*
In the **Designer work plane** dialogue box *left-click* in check boxes as shown in Fig. 5.21, followed by *left-clicks* on the **OK** buttons.

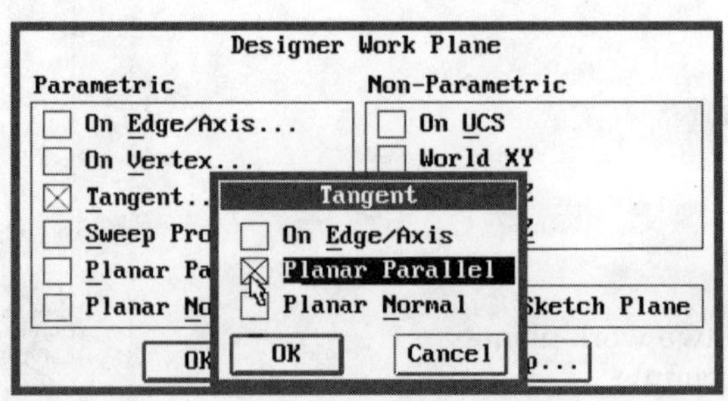

Fig. 5.21 The settings in the **Designer work plane** dialogue box for the second example

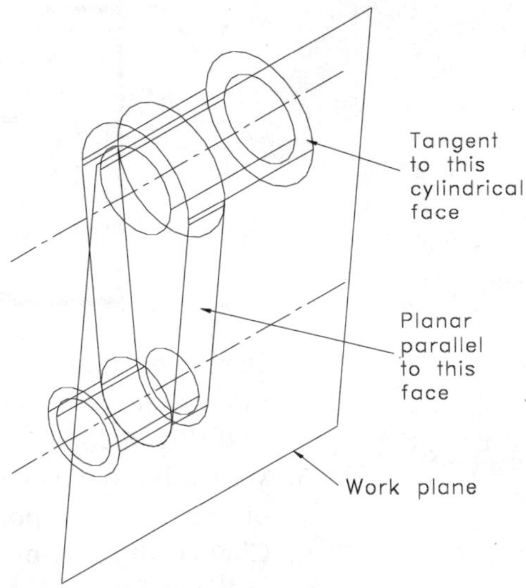

Fig. 5.22 The work axes and work plane for the second example

Select cylindrical face: *pick* (Fig. 5.22)
Xy/Yz/Zx/Ucs/<Select work plane or planar face>: *pick* (Fig. 5.22)
Flip/<Accept>: *right-click*
Command:

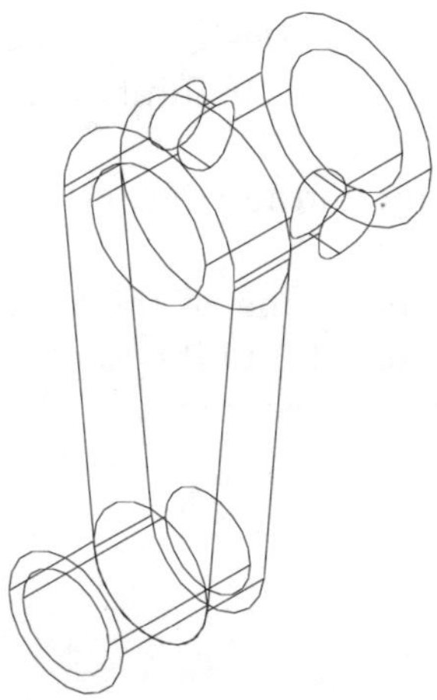

Fig. 5.23 The completed second example

4. Call **adskpln** and set the sketch plane to the work plane and one of the work axes.
5. Call **adpartview** and place the model in the default **Sketch** view.
6. Construct the outline (a circle) for the slanting hole and with **adprofile** turn it into a sketch profile.
7. Call **adextrude** and **cut extrude** the slanting hole in the model (Fig. 5.23)

Third example – Edge/Axis and Planar Parallel

1. Construct the Designer 3D model as shown in Fig. 5.25.
2. Add a work axis as shown in Fig. 5.25.
3. At the Command Line:

Command : *enter* adworkpln *right-click*
In the **Designer work plane** dialogue box *left-click* in check boxes as shown in Fig. 5.24, followed by *left-clicks* on the **OK** buttons.
X/Y/Z/Select work axis or straight edge: *pick* (Fig. 5.25)
Xy/Yz/Zx/Ucs/<Select work plane or planar face>: *pick* (Fig. 5.25)
Flip/<Accept>: *right-click*
Command:

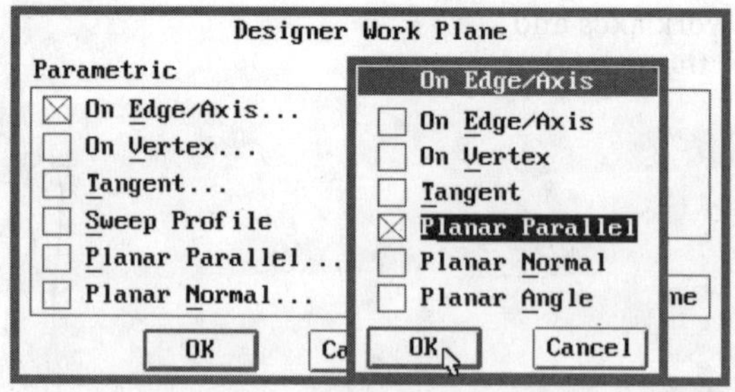

Fig. 5.24 The settings in the **Designer work plane** dialogue box for the third example

4. Using the **Planar Parallel/Offset** settings of the **Designer work plane** dialogue box add another work plane 2.5 units in front of the first (Fig. 5.25.
5. With **adviewpart** set the part in its **Sketch** view and add the outline of one of the supporting webs.
6. Change the **adviewpart** to isometric and make one of the web outlines into a sketch profile and **join extrude** it 5 units. Repeat with the second web outline. An **adview** in three views of the completed part is shown in Fig. 5.26.

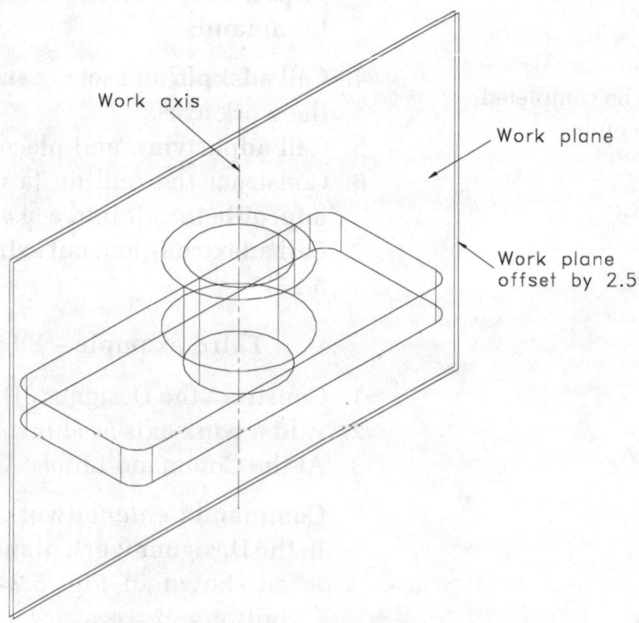

Fig. 5.25 Third example showing the work axis and work planes

Fourth example – another Edge/Axis and Edge/Axis

This example again makes use of the **Edge/Axis** and **Edge/Axis** settings in the **Designer Work Axis** dialogue box and selecting

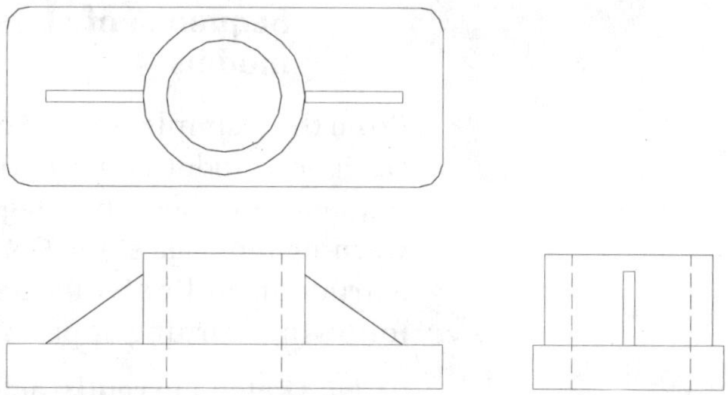

Fig. 5.26 Third example – orthographc views of the completed part

straight edges as indicated in Fig. 5.27. The work plane was then used as one of the parts for setting the sketch plane, and by constructing a sketch profile on this sketch plane the rectangular hole shown in Fig. 5.28 was **cut extruded** through the model.

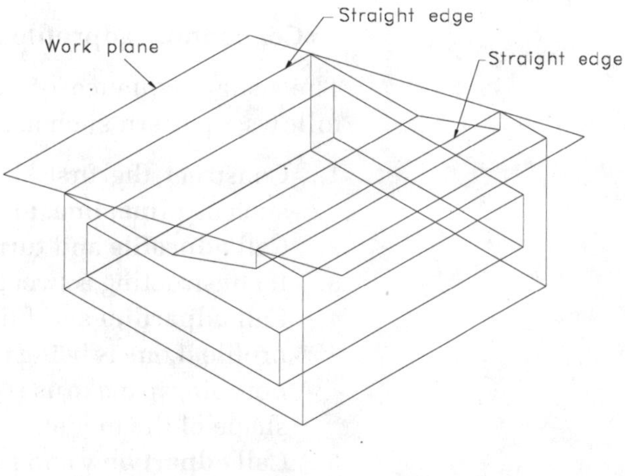

Fig. 4.27 The work plane for the fourth example

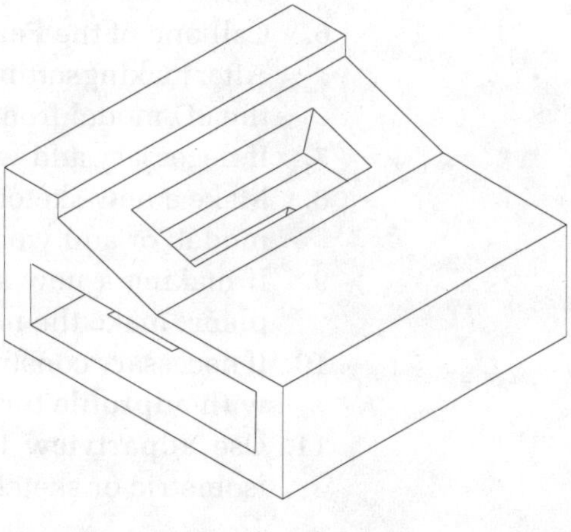

Fig. 5.28 The completed fourth example

Sequence of steps when constructing most Designer models

From the examples given so far in this book, it will be seen that most Designer model constructions involve a more or less prescribed sequence of stages. If a stage is missed, Designer will usually give a warning message at the Command Line. For example, if one tries to extrude an outline which has not been made into a sketch profile, the following warning appears at the Command Line:

No sketch currently active. Use ADPROFILE to make one.

It does not matter whether the operator *enters* Designer command names at the Command Line, or selects the command name from the pull-down menu. The only difference is that, when a command name is selected from the pull-down menus, the name appears at the Command Line preceded by a dash, to be followed by the same options sequences as if the name was *entered* from the keyboard, as shown in this example:

Command: _adprofile

The usual sequence of stages in constructing a Designer model follows a pattern such as:

1. Construct the first sketch outline using AutoCAD commands, such as **pline**, **line**, **arc**, **circle,** etc.
2. Call **adprofile** and turn the outline into a sketch profile.
3. If constructing a sweep, construct the Path profile.
4. Call **adpardim** and fully dimension the sketch profile (and Path profile if one is being used). This stage is not necessary if you are not going to make use of the dimensions for editing the parametric shape of the model.
5. Call **adpartview** and place the model in an isometric (preferably) view.
6. Call one of the **Features** – such as **adextrude**, **revolve**, **adsweep**. After making settings in the appropriate dialogue box(es), construct the 3D model from these settings.
7. If necessary add work axes to the model.
8. Make a new sketch plane for other features to be included in the model; or add work planes to the model.
9. If making a new sketch plane involves the selection of a work plane, make the new sketch plane at this stage.
10. If necessary construct a new outline on the new sketch plane and with **adprofile** turn it into a sketch profile.
11. Use **adpartview** between stages to place the model in either isometric or sketch view.

12. **Adextrude cut** or **adextrude join** as necessary, taking care that the **Flip** arrow is pointing in the right direction.
13. Add work planes and new sketch planes as necessary to complete the model.
14. Call **adview** and place orthographic views as required.
15. If necessary re-dimension the drawing, or add dimensions as necessary.

Note

All the above stages may not be needed. It depends upon the complexity of the model being constructed. Some further stages may have to be included, such as the addition of holes with **adhole**, or off fillets with **adfillet**, or chamfers with **adchamfer**. But basically the procedures for constructing any Designer 3D model will follow a series of steps such as those outlined above.

Questions

1. What happens if you try to **adextrude** an outline which has not be changed into a sketch profile?
2. Why is it necessary to add work planes to a Designer model while it is under construction?
3. How many sketch planes can be active at any one time?
4. How many work planes can be placed in a drawing at any one time?
5. How many work axes can be placed in a drawing at any one time?
6. Why use the **Isometric** option of the **adviewpart**?
7. Can you see a work plane in a drawing?
8. Can you see a sketch plane in a drawing?
9. It has been suggested early in this chapter that the UCS icon be set at the **ORigin**. Why was this suggestion made?
10. Calling the **adpartview** command and accepting the default **<Sketch>** option is used fairly frequently when engaged in constructing a complex drawing. Why is this so?

Exercises

The reader is advised to follow the instructions for the examples given in this chapter and, working to any reasonable sizes, attempt constructing them. It is also advisable to add dimensions to the sketch profiles with **adpardim**, so that you can test the parametric value of Designer when such dimensions are changed with **adeditfeat**.

1. Figure 5.29 is a dimensioned plan of the plate shown in an Advanced Modelling Extension 3D model in Fig. 5.30. Construct a Designer model to the given dimensions, assuming that the plate is 10 mm thick. Construct an **adview** orthographic projection of your model and dimension it.

   Attempt using the sketch profile dimensions to change the parametric shape of the plate.

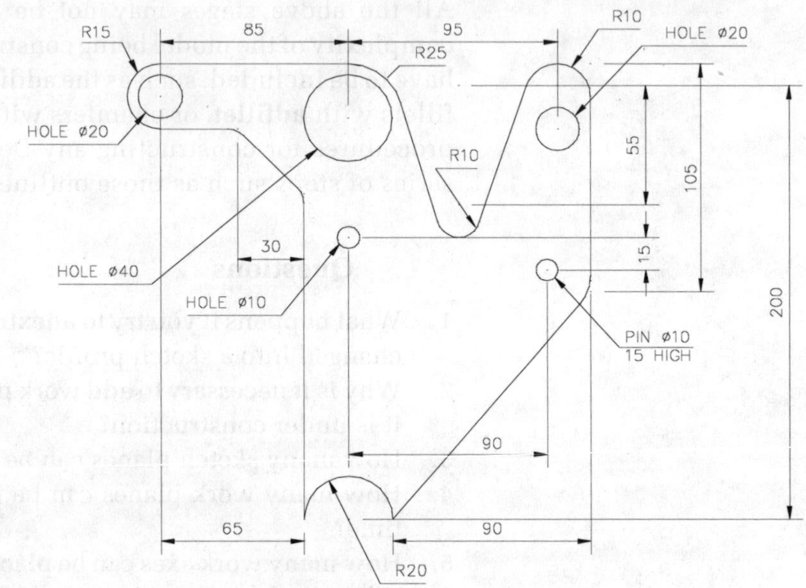

Fig. 5.29 Exercise 1 – dimensions

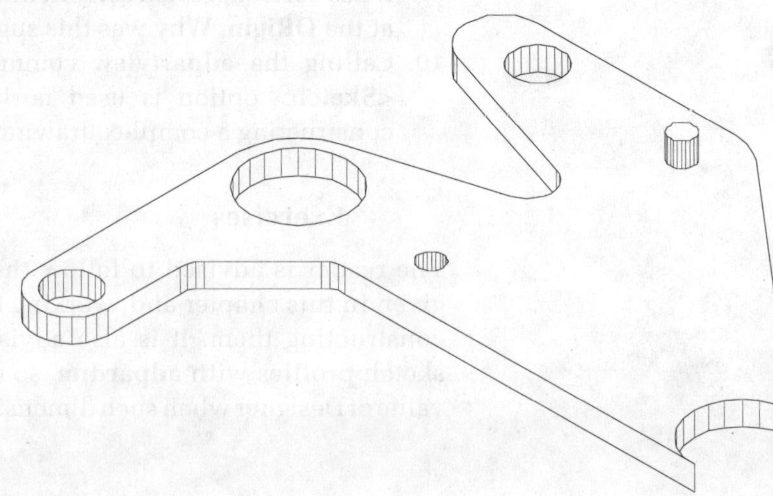

Fig. 5.30 3D solid model drawing for Exercise 1

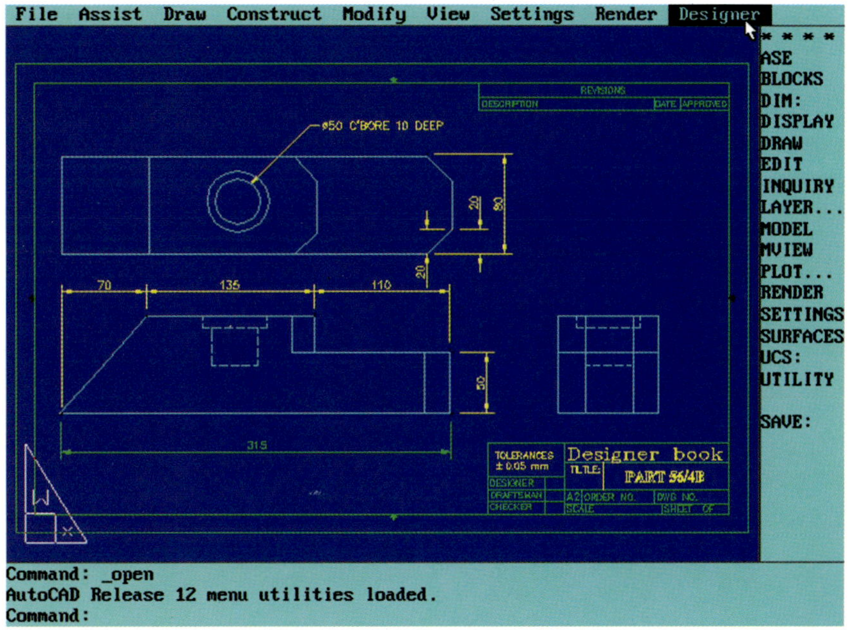

Plate I A three-view third-angle orthographic projection in the Designer **Drawing Mode** editor operating within AutoCAD Release 12 (DOS)

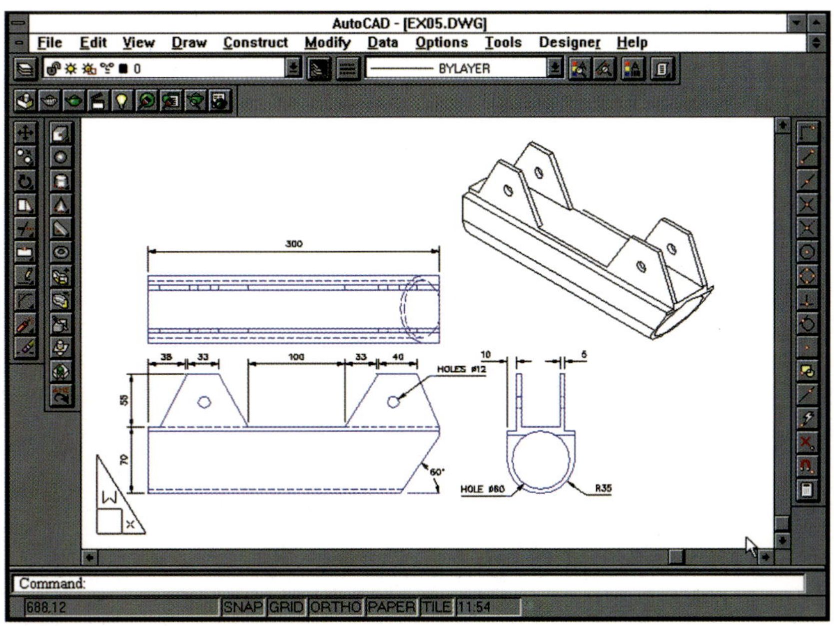

Plate II A three-view third-angle orthographic projection, with an isometric view, in the Designer **Drawing Mode** editor operating within AutoCAD Release 13 (Windows)

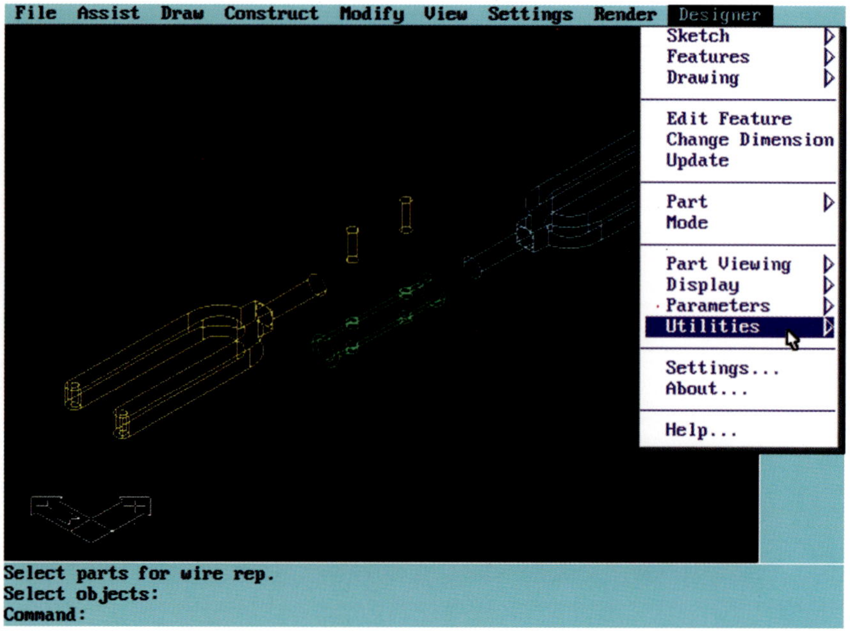

Plate III A four-part 3D Designer model in the **Part Mode** editor of AutoCAD Release 12 (DOS)

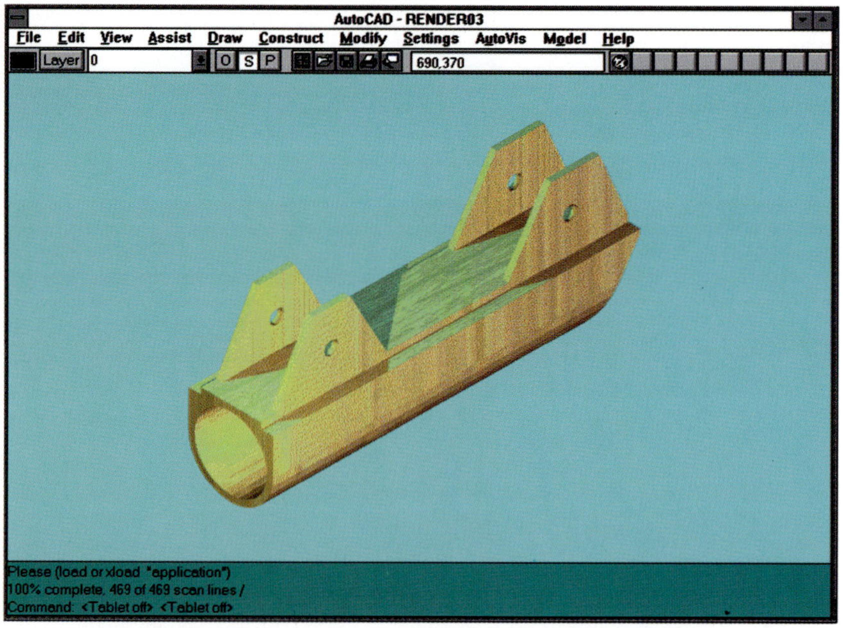

Plate IV An AutoVision rendering of a 3D Designer model in AutoCAD for Windows. Note, however, that Designer will not work within AutoCAD for Windows

Plate V Parametric views of three 3D Designer models in the **Part Mode** editor of AutoCAD Release 12 (DOS). Two of the models were loaded using the **Part In** command

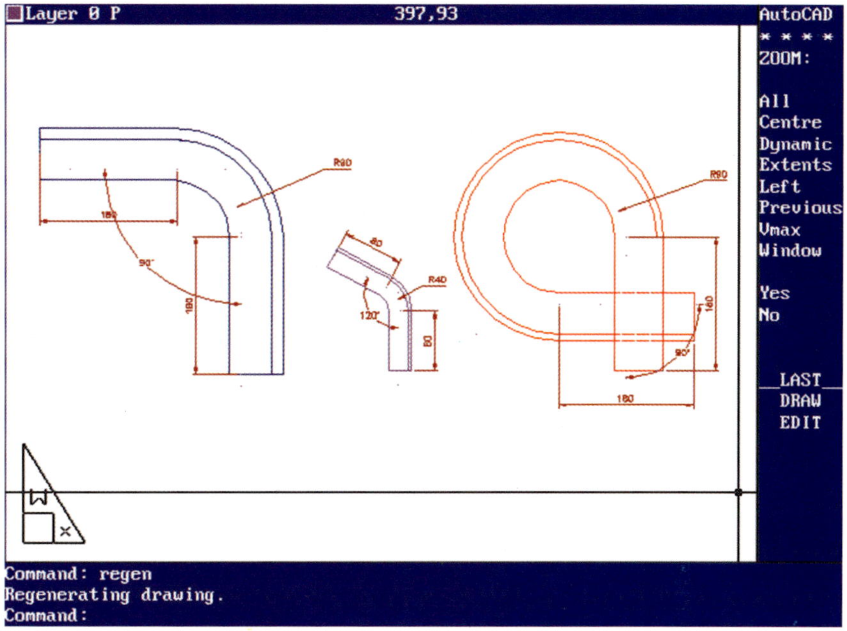

Plate VI The three parametric models shown in Plate V in **Drawing Mode** after calling **adview**

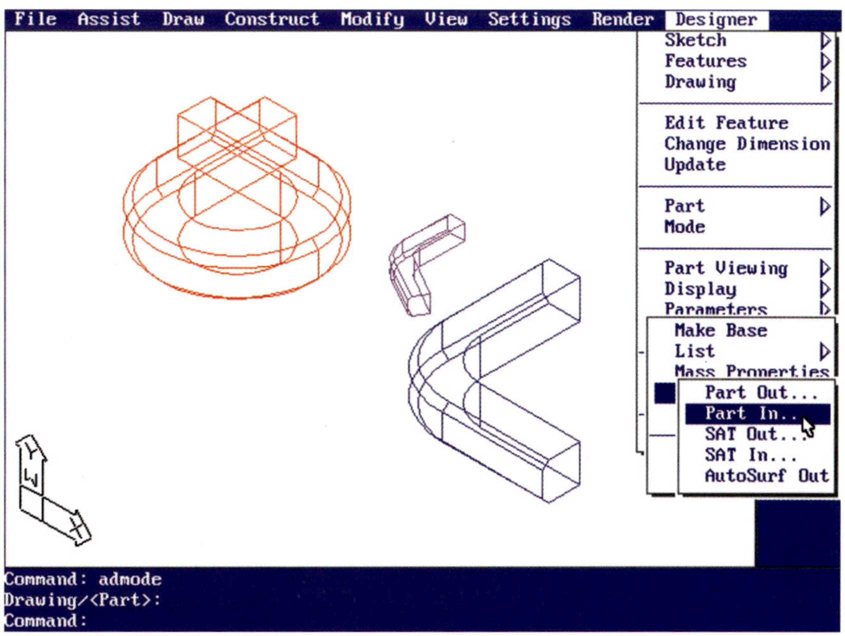

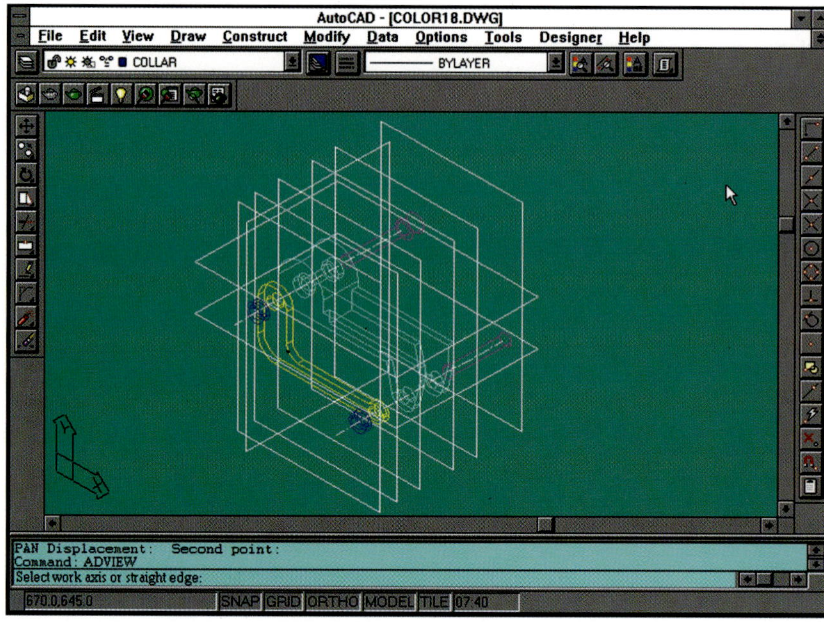

Plate VII Constructing a 3D Designer model in **Part Mode** using AutoCAD Release 13 (Windows)

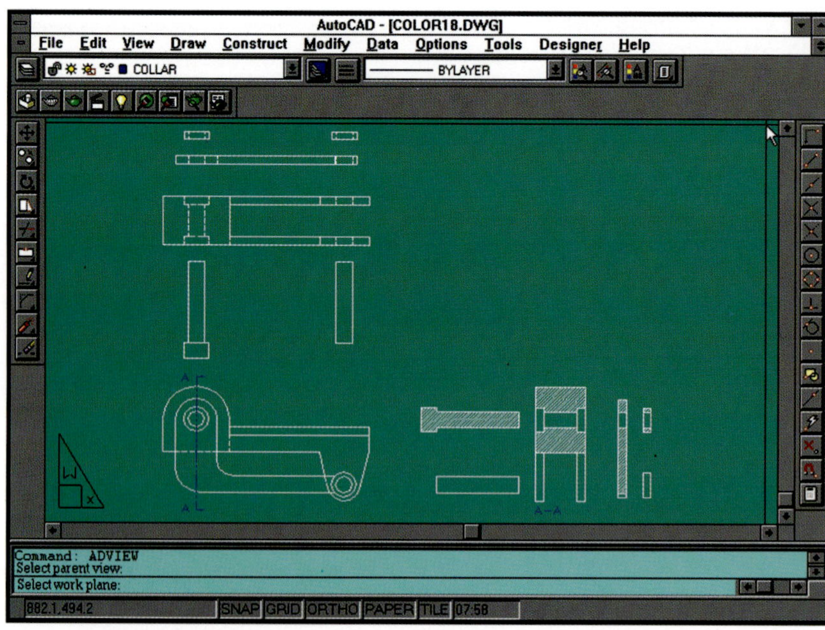

Plate VIII A third-angle orthographic projection, including a sectional view in **Drawing Mode** of the model shown in Plate VII

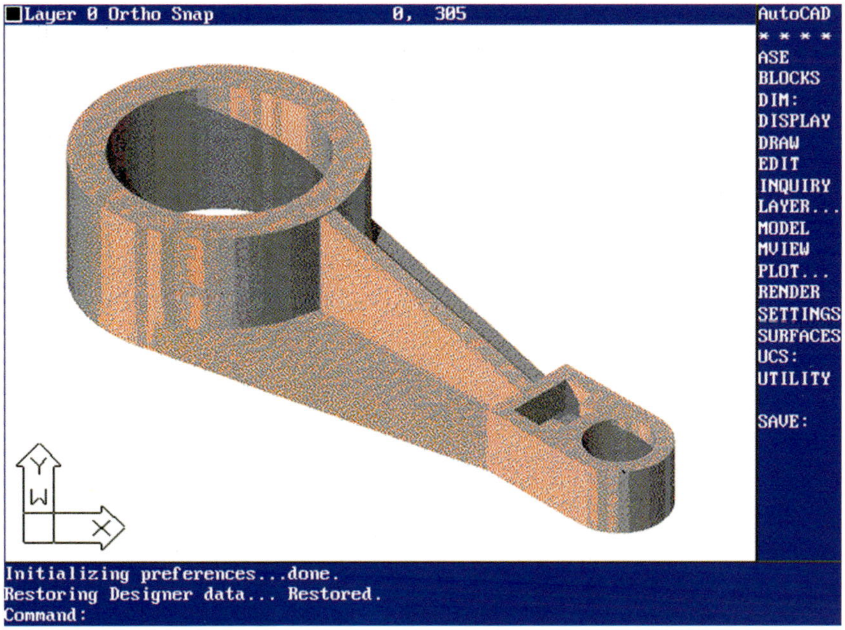

Plate IX A rendering of a 3D Designer model in AutoCAD Release 12 (DOS)

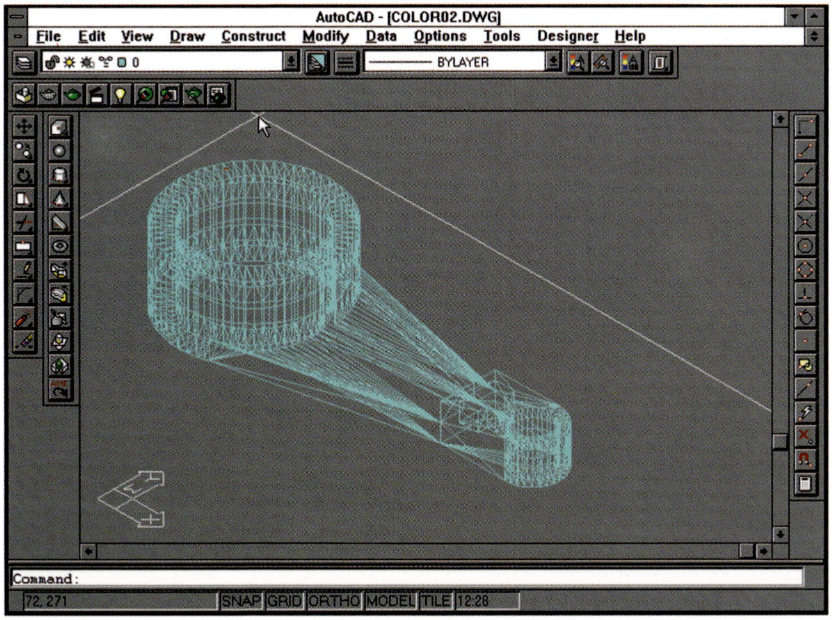

Plate X An **admesh** view of the 3D model shown in Plate IX in AutoCAD Release 13 (Windows)

Plate XI The 3D Designer model in Plate IX rendered using AutoVision within AutoCAD with a different screen colour

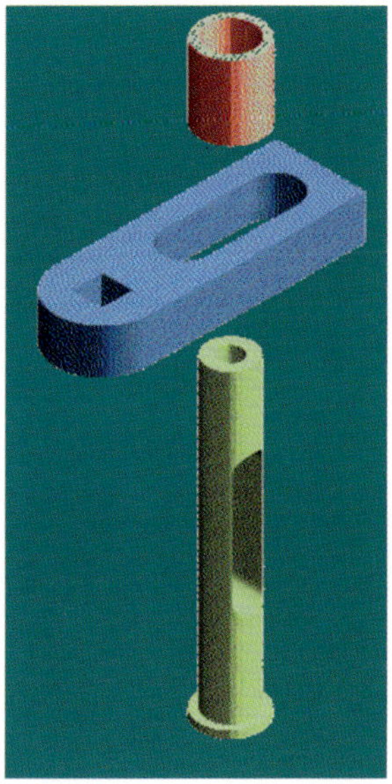

Plate XII An AutoVision rendering of a three-part 3D Designer model. Each part has been rendered as a different material

Plate XIII A 3D Designer model rendered using AutoCAD Render

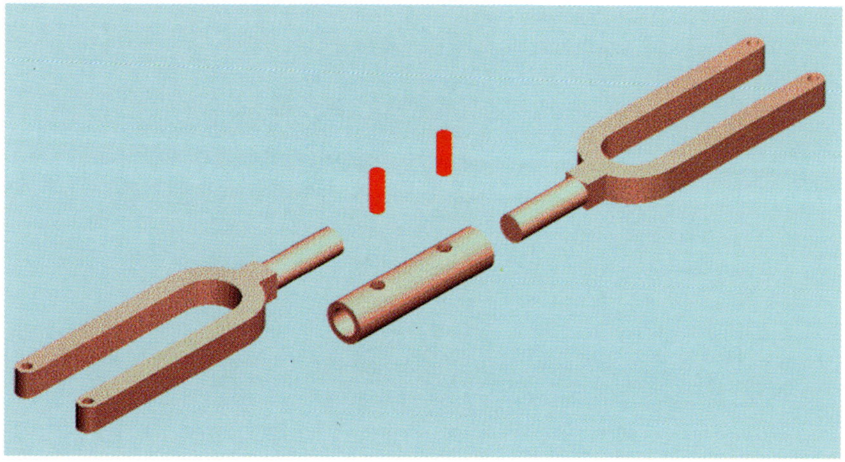

Plate XIV The four-part 3D Designer model shown in Plate III rendered in two materials using AutoVision

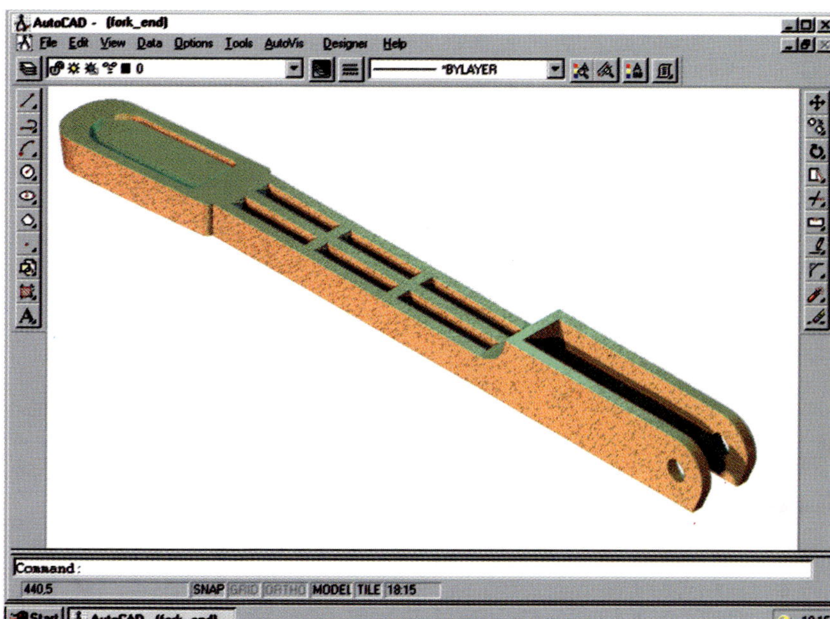

Plate XV An AutoVision rendering of a 3D Designer model created in Designer Release 2 working within AutoCAD Release 13 for Windows 95, involving the use of coloured spotlights

Plate XVI An AutoVision rendering of a 3D Designer model of an electronic probe

Plate XVII An AutoVision rendering of a garden table model, constructed in Designer Release 2 and displayed in AutoCAD Release 13 for Windows 95. The material used is white ash

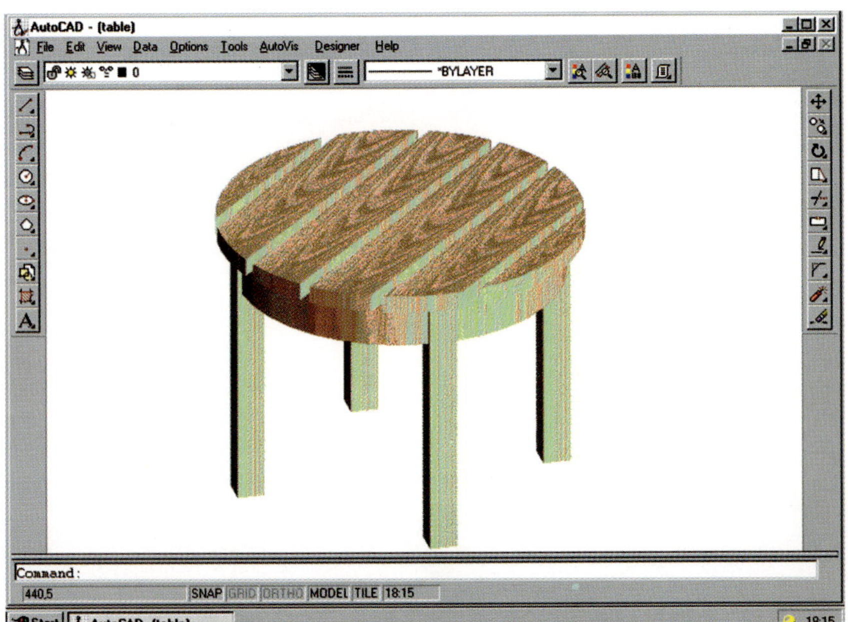

2. Figure 5.31 is a dimensioned plan view of a footstep clip from an invalid's wheelchair. Figure 5.32 is an AME 3D solid model drawing of the clip.

   Construct a Designer 3D solid model drawing of the clip, including dimensions.

   It was found that the distance between the two holes of the clip was too great for the clip to fit onto the foot fittings of the chair and that the distance should have been 70 mm. Using **adeditfeat** amend the dimension and check that the parametricity of your drawing is good.

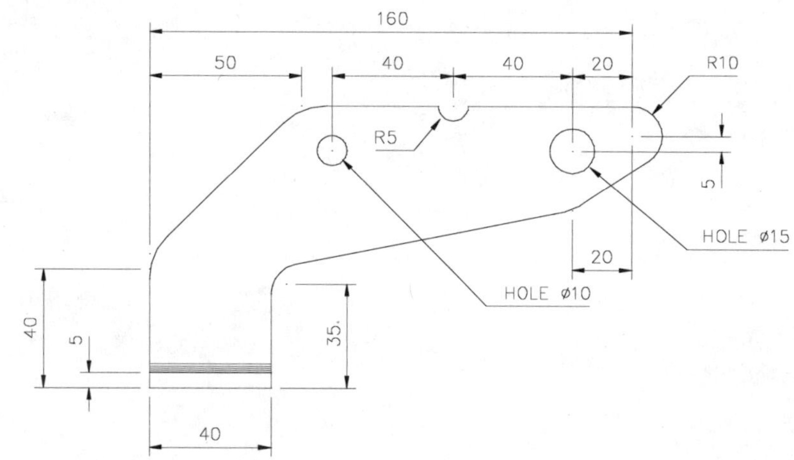

Fig. 5.31 Exercise 2 – dimensioned plan

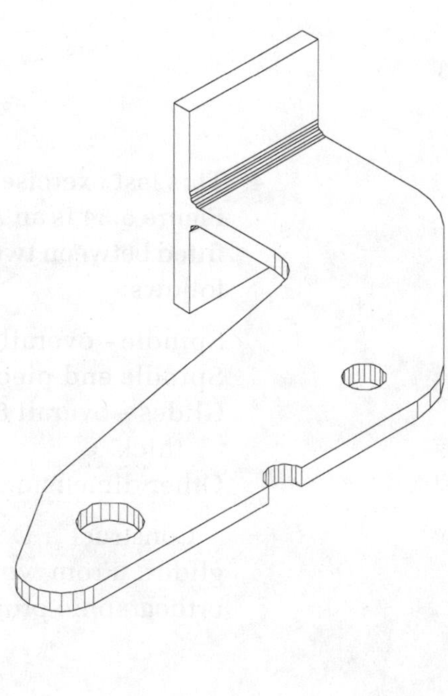

Fig. 5.32 Exercise 2 – AME solid model drawing

3. Figure 5.33 is an AME 3D solid model drawing of the footrest to which the clip shown in drawings Fig. 5.31 and Fig. 5.32 are to be fitted. The two pins of the footrest are meant to be removed so that the two holes of the clip (Fig. 5.31) fit under the heads of the pins when they have been replaced.

   No dimensions are included with Fig. 5.33. These are left to your own judgement, but remember that the two pins should fit into the two holes of the clip, after the clip has been changed by amending the distance between the two pins.

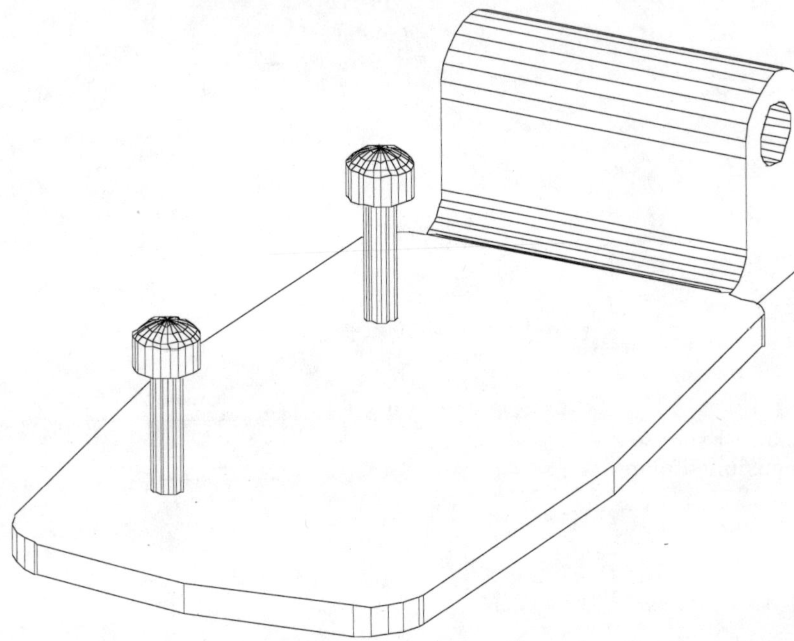

Fig. 5.33 Exercise 3

4. This last exercise is much more difficult than the previous three. Figure 5.34 is an AME 3D solid model drawing showing a spindle fitted between two glides. The dimensions for your drawing are as follows:

   Spindle – overall 150 long; diameter of spindle in its bearings 12.
   Spindle end pieces – each overall 25 long and diameter 16.
   Glides – overall 80 long; overall width 28; made from material 3 thick.
   Other dimensions are left to your own judgement.

   Construct a Designer 3D model drawing of the spindle in its glides. From your drawing **adview** a three-view third-angle orthographic projection.

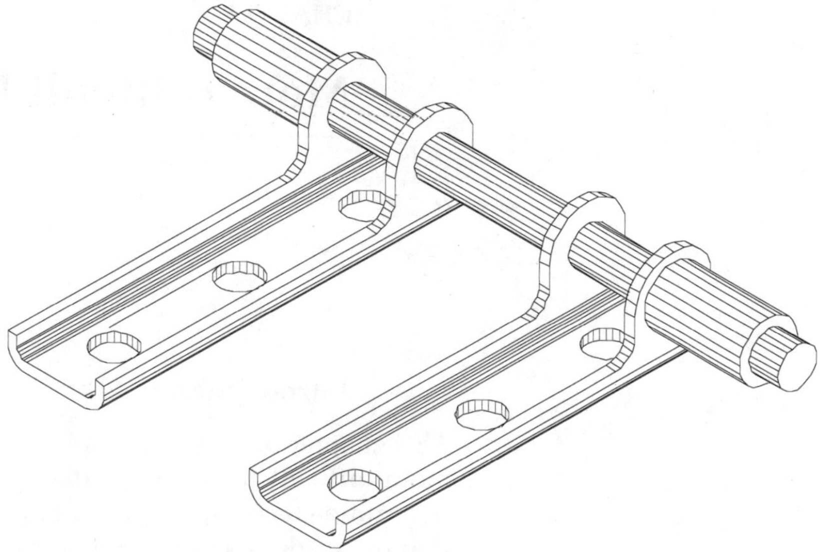

Fig. 5.34 Exercise 4

CHAPTER 6

More difficult Designer models

Introduction

This chapter describes a number of Designer 3D models which are more difficult to construct than those in previous chapters. The descriptions accompanying the drawings are short, on the assumption that the reader has worked many of the examples and exercises in previous chapters and, as a result, has had reasonable practice in constructing Designer models, obtaining orthographic views from them and has tested the parametric features of the software.

First example

This shows the construction of a support stand (Fig. 6.1) involving a number of supporting ribs. Frequent changes of work planes, work axes and sketch planes are required to complete the construction.

1. Draw the base outline (Fig. 6.2) – use the AutoCAD commands – **circle**, **pline**, **trim** and **array**.
2. With **adviewpart** call a pictorial view with the isometric option.
3. With **adprofile** change the outer part of the outline into a sketch profile.

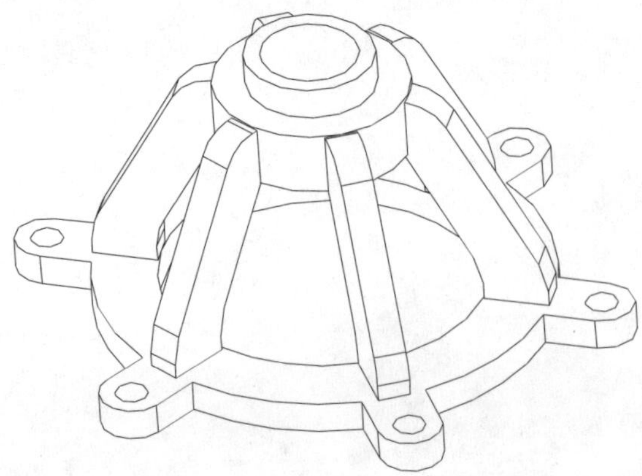

Fig. 6.1 First example. The completed 3D Designer model in an **adview** isometric view

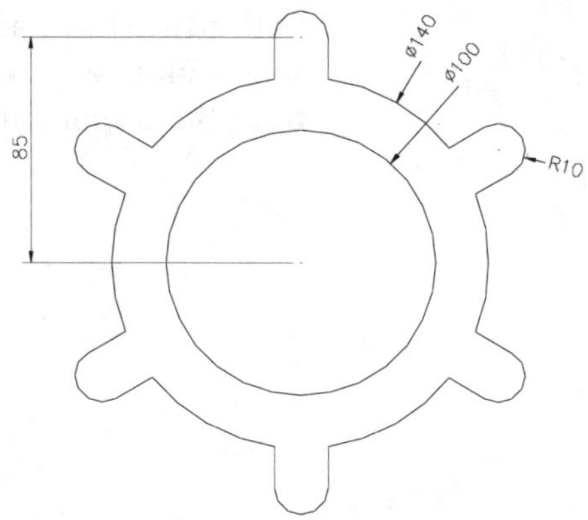

Fig. 6.2 First example. The outline for the base

4. With **adextrude – Base** option and height 10 – extrude the profile.
5. With **adprofile** change the inner circle into a sketch profile.
6. With **adextrude** – Cut and height 10 – extrude the circle.
7. Call **adworkaxis** and add a work axis to the view (Fig. 6.3)

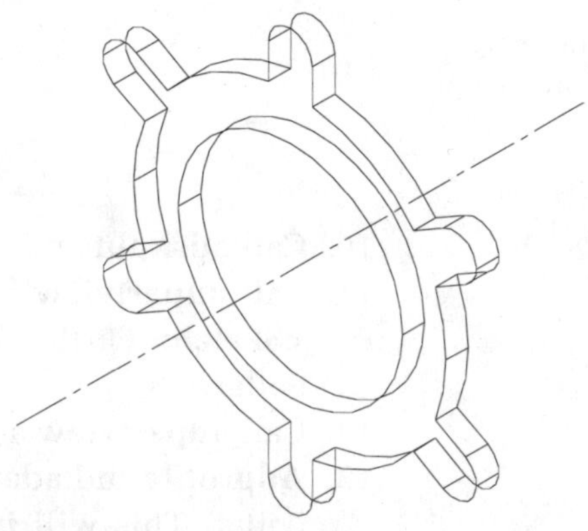

Fig. 6.3 First example. The extruded base with a work axis

8. With **adhole – Through**, **Diameter** 10 and **Concentric** set, add the holes in the lugs of the base (Fig. 6.4).

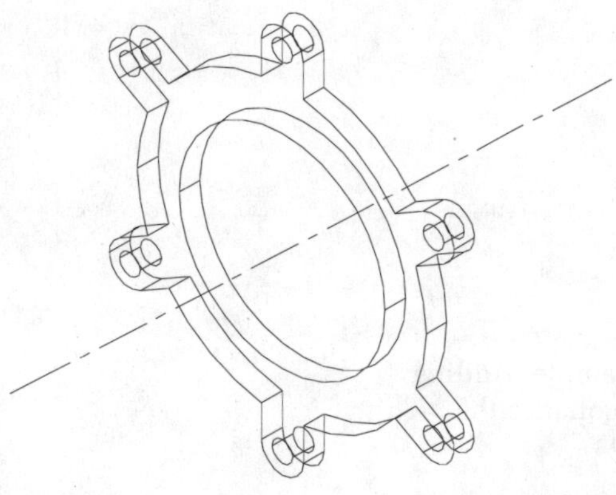

Fig. 6.4 First example. The holes added to the lugs in the base

9. Call **adworkpln** and in the **Designer work plane** dialogue box select **Planar Parallel** and **Offset**. Offset a work plane 50 units from the upper surface of the base (Fig. 6.5).

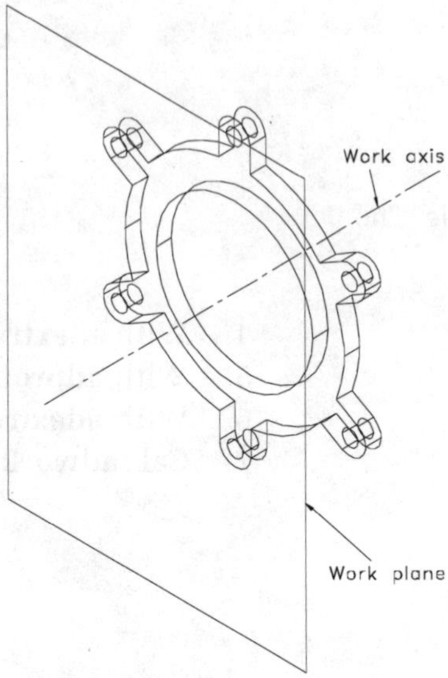

Fig. 6.5 First example. Work plane offset 50 from surface of base

10. Call **adskpln** and select an edge of a lug and the work plane.
11. Call **adpartview** followed by a *right-click* to accept the default **<Sketch>**. On the sketch plane draw three circles for the supporting collar.
12. Call **adpartview** and place the model in an isometric view.
13. **Adprofile** and **adextrude** the three circles to form the supporting collar. This will involve **Join** and **Cut** settings in the **Designer**

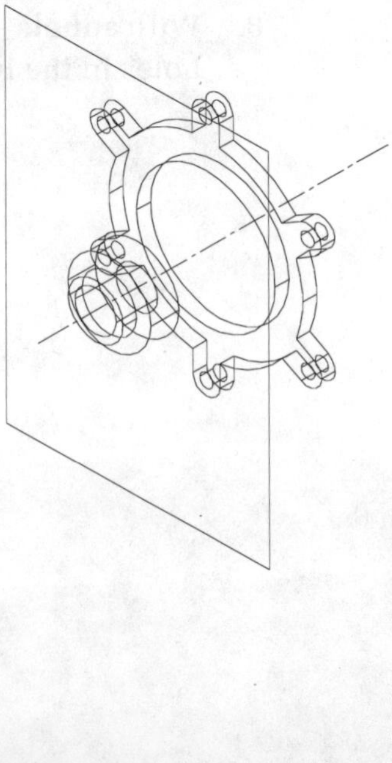

Fig. 6.6 First example. Adding the supporting collar to the model

Extrusion dialogue box – **Join** outer circle 20, **Join** middle circle 30, **Cut** inner circle 30 (Fig. 6.6).

14. Add work axes to two opposite holes in the base. With **adworkpln** use the two work axes to add another work plane (Fig. 6.7).

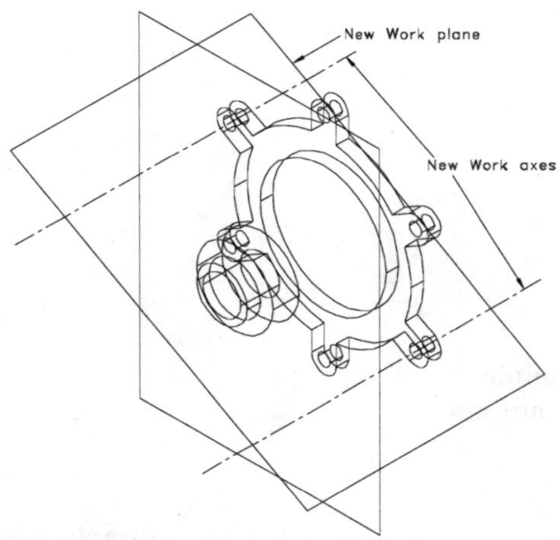

Fig. 6.7 Adding a work plane based on the two opposite work axes

15. With **adworkpln** add an **offset** work plane 5 units from the work plane in Fig. 6.7 (Fig. 6.8).

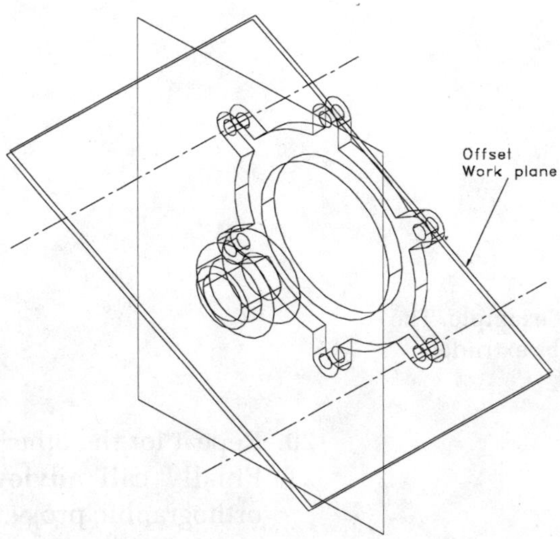

Fig. 6.8 First example. The offset work plane

16. Call **adskpln** and set a new sketch plane on the last work plane.
17. Call **adpartview**, followed by *right-click* to obtain the **<Sketch>** view.

18. On the sketch plane now on screen, draw the outlines of two ribs (Fig. 6.9).

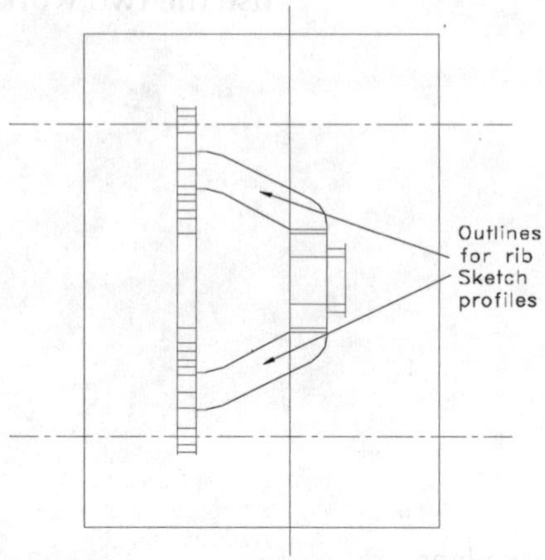

Fig. 6.9 First example. Drawing the rib outlines

19. Call **adpartview**, place in isometric view; call **adprofile** and **adextrude** one rib 10 units; repeat for the second rib (Fig. 6.10).

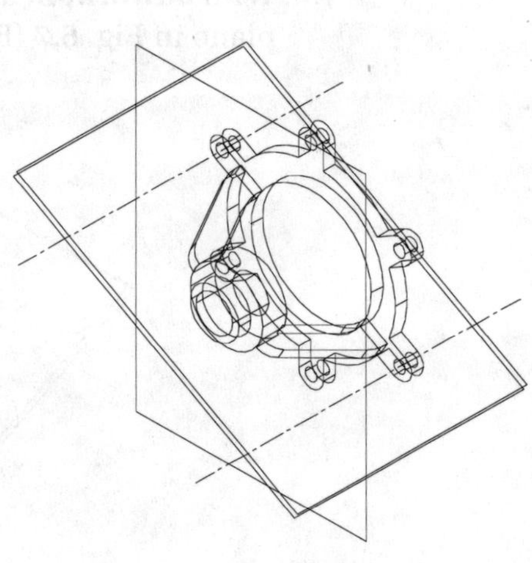

Fig. 6.10 First example. The first pair of ribs extruded

20. Repeat for the other two pairs of ribs (Fig. 6.11).
21. Finally call **adview** and produce the two-view third-angle orthographic projection given in Fig. 6.12.

Second example

This example (Fig. 6.13) is a Designer model of a handle for starting a generator motor. The model includes a sweep, a revolved solid and

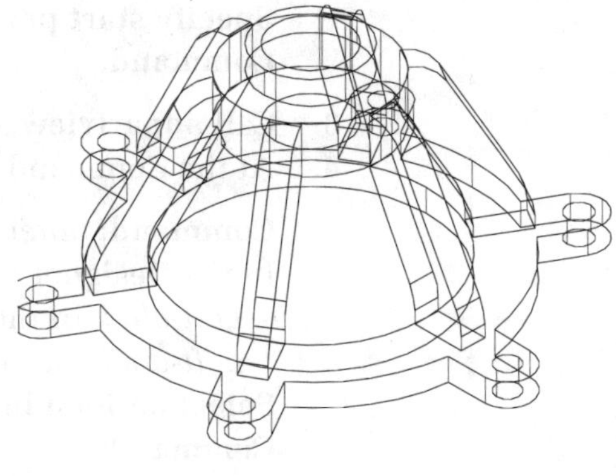

Fig. 6.11 First example. The completed Designer 3D model

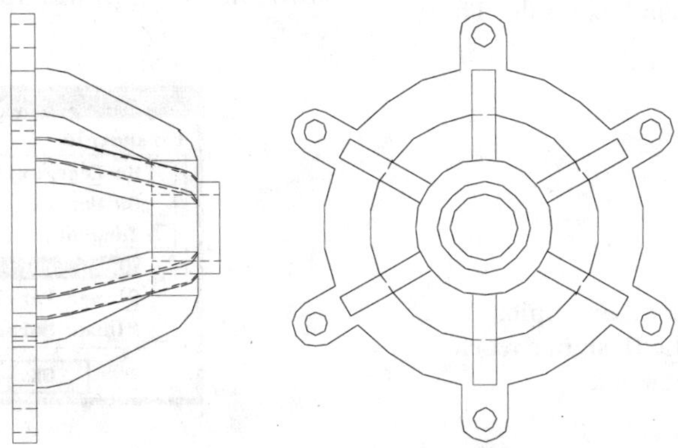

Fig. 6.12 First example. A two-view third-angle orthographic projection produced from the 3D model

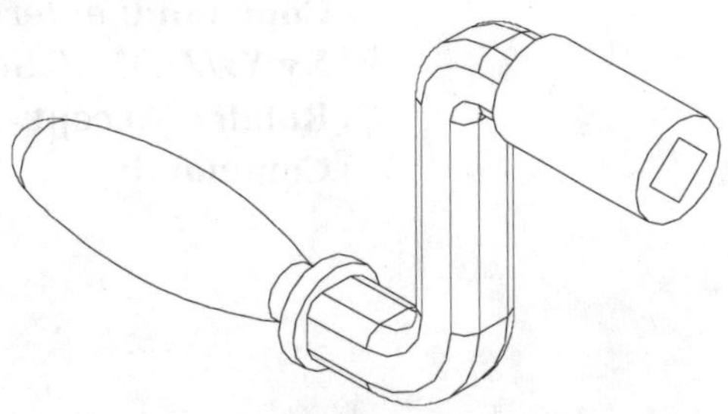

Fig. 6.13 Second example. An isometric drawing of the handle

an extruded solid. The sequence of working to construct the model was:

1. Draw the path profile (Fig. 6.14).
2. At the Command Line:

   Command: *enter* adpath *right-click*
   Select objects: *pick* the path profile
   Select objects: *right-click*
   Solved under constraints requiring 3 dimensions/constraints

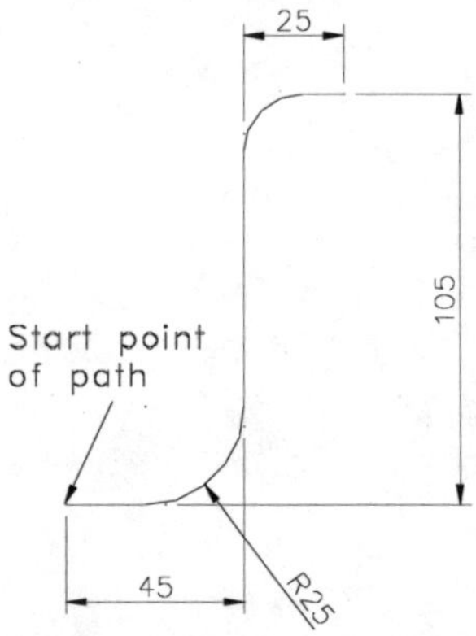

Fig. 6.14 Second example. The path profile

Specify start point of path: *pick* (Fig. 6.14)
Command:

3. Call **adpartview** and place the part in the isometric view.
4. At the Command Line:

Command: *enter* adworkpln *right-click*
In the **Designer work plane** dialogue box (Fig. 6.15):
Left-click in the **Sweep Profile** check box
Left-click on the **OK** button
Select an item in the path: *left-click* on the start point
Command:

And the work plane appears (Fig. 6.16)

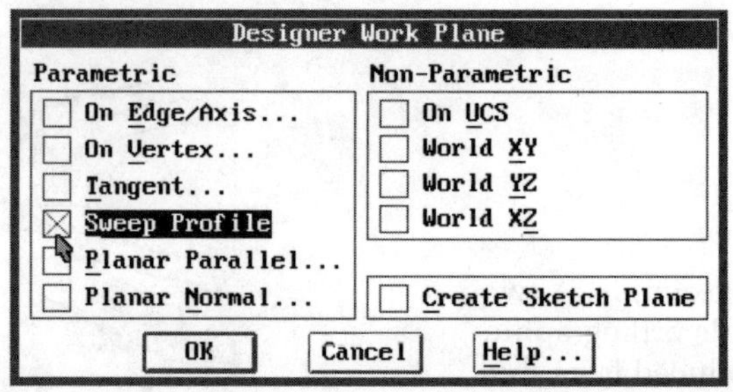

Fig. 6.15 Second example. Settings in the **Designer work plane** dialogue box

5. At the Command Line:

Command: *enter* adskpln *right-click*
Xy/Yz/Zx/Ucs/<Select work plane or planar face>: *pick* (Fig. 6.16)
Rotate/<Accept>: *right-click*
Command:

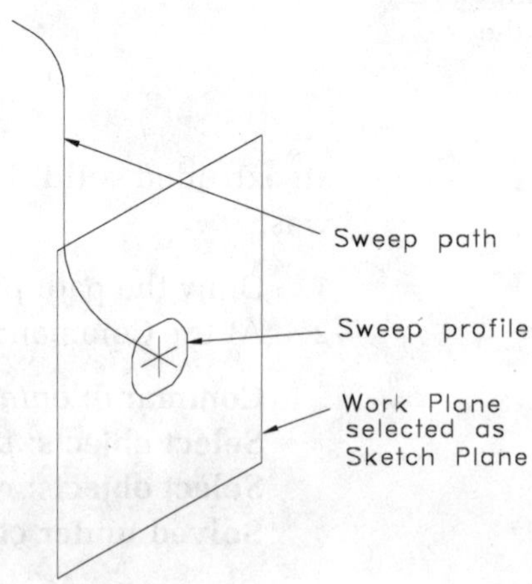

Fig. 6.16 Second example. The work plane on the path profile.

6. Call **adpartview** and *right-click* to accept the **Sketch** default view.
7. On the sketch plane draw the sweep profile outline.
8. Call **adprofile** and change the outline into a sketch profile.
9. Call **adpartview** and place the part in the isometric view.
10. At the Command Line:

Command: ***enter*** adsweep *right-click*
Select sweep path: *pick* the sweep path
Select sweep cross-section profile: *pick* the sweep profile
Command:

And the sweep constructs (Fig. 6.17).

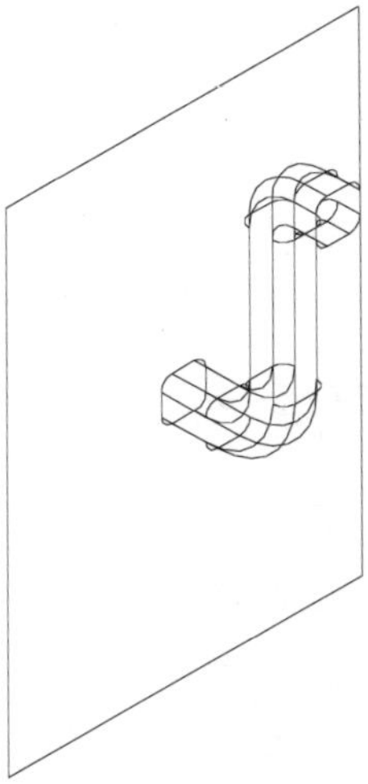

Fig. 6.17 Second example. The sweep

11. Call **adworkpln** and with **Planar Parallel** and **Edge/Axis** check boxes active in the **Designer work plane** dialogue box, add a work plane perpendicular to the existing work plane.
12. Call **adworkpln** again and add a second work plane **Offset** from the first by 10 units – centre of the sweep (Fig. 6.18).

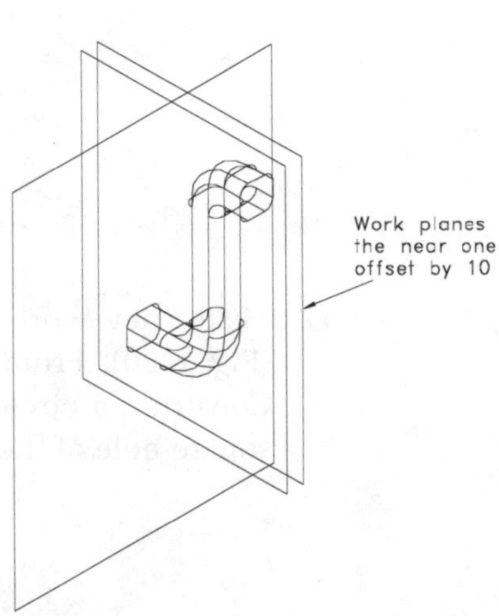

Fig. 6.18 Second example. Adding the work plane **Offset** by 10 from the first

13. Call **adskpln** and select the offset work plane.
14. Call **adpartview** and select the work plane as the required sketch plane.
15. On this new sketch plane construct the outline for the sketch profile for the solid of revolution of the handle. Call **adprofile** and make a sketch profile from the outline (Fig. 6.19).
16. At the Command Line:

Command: *enter* adrevolve *right-click*
In the **Designer Revolution** dialogue box which appears:
Left-click in the **By Angle** check box

Left-click in the **Base** check box
Enter 360 in the **Angle** box
Left-click on the **OK** button
Select axis of revolution: *pick* (Fig. 6.19)
Command:

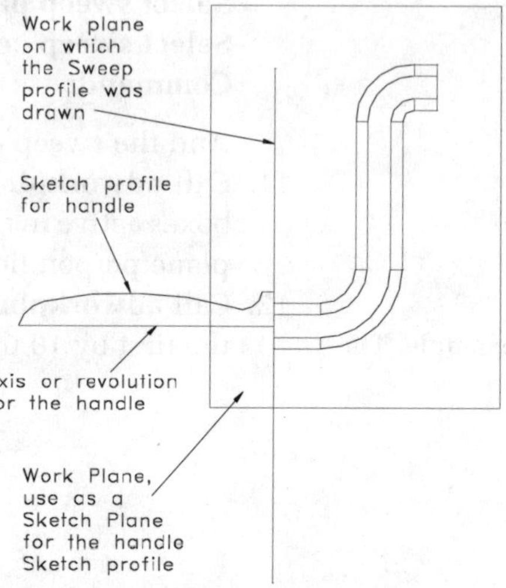

Fig. 6.19 Second example. The sketch profile for the handle on its sketch plane

17. Make a new work plane based on the top back surface of the sweep (Fig. 6.20). From this work plane, make a new sketch plane. Construct a circle and a square for the outer cylinder and the square hole of the boss.

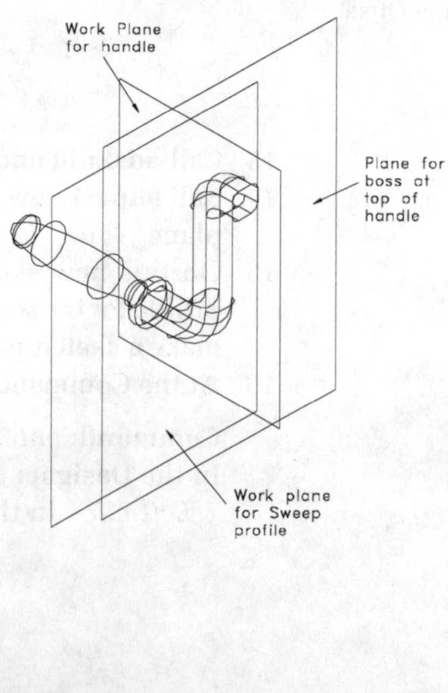

Fig. 6.20. Second example. The handle revolved with **adrevolve**, followed by setting a work plane for the boss

18. Call **adpartview** and place the model in the isometric view. **Adprofile** the circle and **adextrude** it by 50 units. **Adprofile** the square and **adextrude cut** by 50 units. The model is now complete (Fig. 6.21).

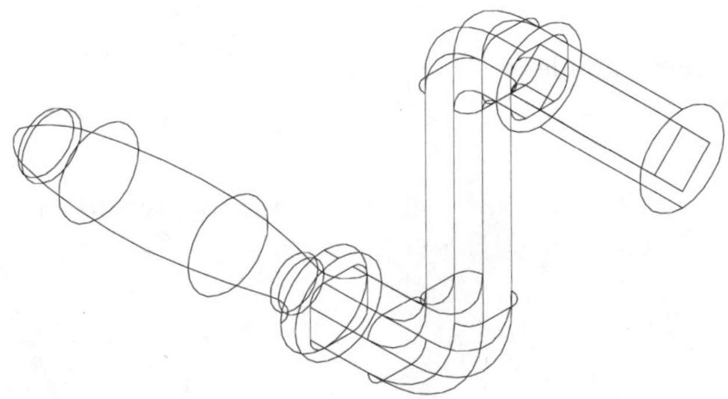

Fig. 6.21 The completed Designer 3D model

19. Call **adview** and construct a two-view third-angle orthographic projection of the model (Fig. 6.22).

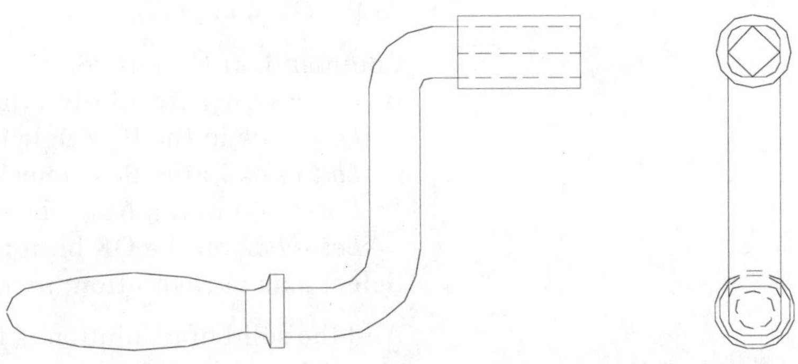

Fig. 6.22 Second example. An **adview** two-view orthographic projection

20. Call **adview** again and add an isometric view to the orthographic view. This is the view shown in Fig. 6.13 on page 91.

Third example

This example shows the construction of a Designer 3D model drawing of a mould from a pipe-bending machine. The construction involves an **adrevolve** and an **adextrude (Cut)**.

1. Construct the outline of the sketch profile for the solid of revolution (Fig. 6.23). Call **adprofile** and change the outline into a sketch profile.

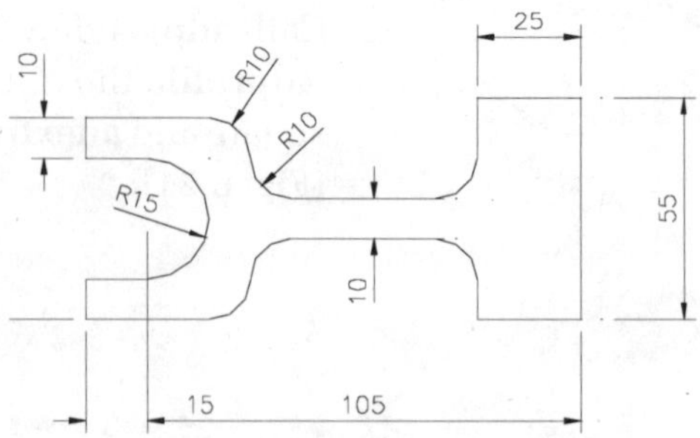

Fig. 6.23 Third example. Outline for sketch profile of the **adrevolve**

2. Call **adpartview** and set the isometric view (Fig. 6.24).

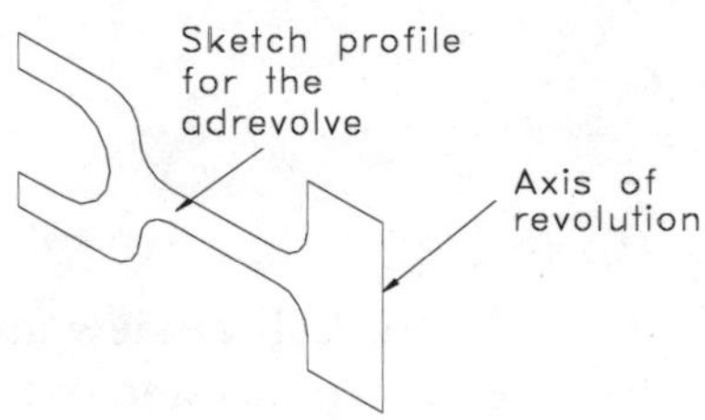

Fig. 6.24 Third example. The sketch profile in **adpartview** Isometric

3. At the Command Line:

Command: *enter* adrevolve *right-click*
In the **Designer Revolution** dialogue box:
Left-click in the **By Angle** check box
Left-click in the **Base** check box
Enter 360 in the **Angle** box
Left-click on the **OK** button
Select axis of revolution: *pick* (Fig. 6.24)

And the solid of revolution is formed (Fig. 6.25).

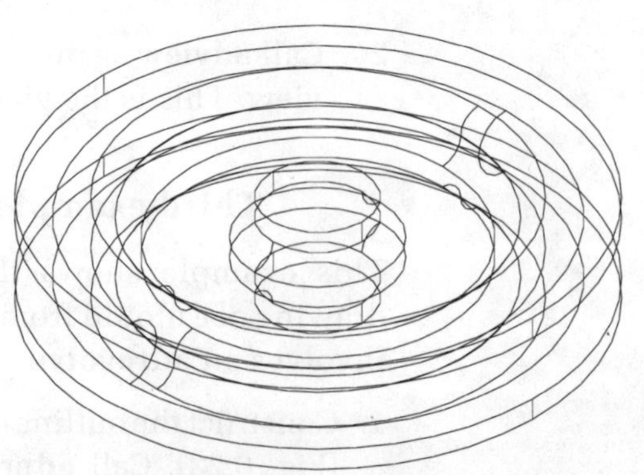

Fig. 6.25 Third example. The solid of revolution

4. Call **adworkaxis** and set the work axis through the centre of the solid. Call **adworkpln** and with **Edge/Axis** and **On Vector** place a work plane. Call **adworkpln** again and with **Plane Parallel** and **Offset** place a second plane 120 from the first. These three features are shown in Fig. 6.26.

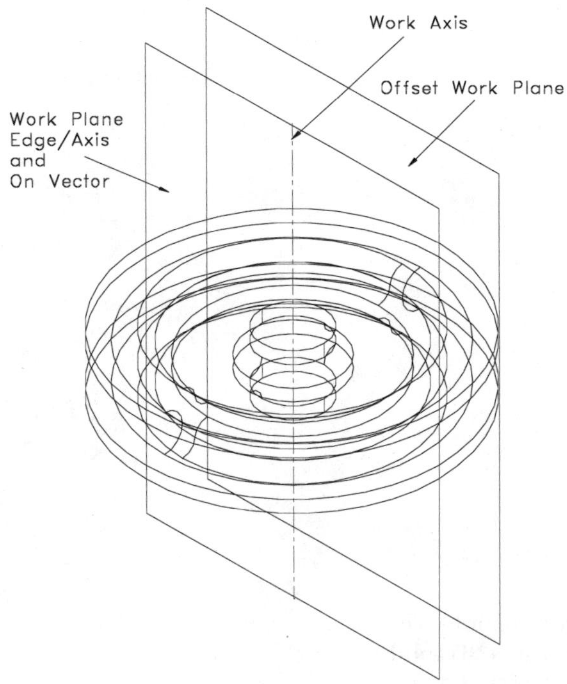

Fig. 6.26 Third example. The work axis and two work planes

5. Call **adskpln** and by selecting the offset work plane and the work axis, set the sketch plane on the offset work plane. With **adpartview**

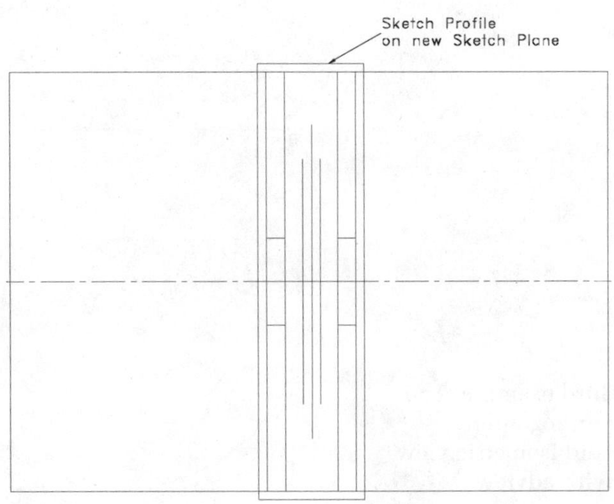

Fig. 6.27 Third example. The rectangle for the sketch profile for the extrusion

set to **Sketch**, draw a rectangular outline for the extrusion sketch profile (Fig. 6.27). Call **adprofile** and change it into a sketch profile.

6. Call **adpartview** and choose the isometric view.
7. Call **adextrude** and **Cut** extrude the rectangular sketch profile by 120 units (Fig. 6.28). The work axis and work planes can be erased now if thought necessary.

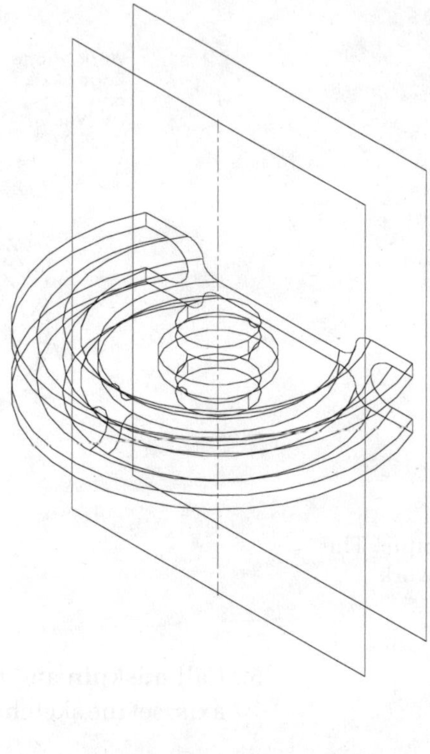

Fig. 6.28 Third example. The completed Designer 3D solid within its work planes and work axis

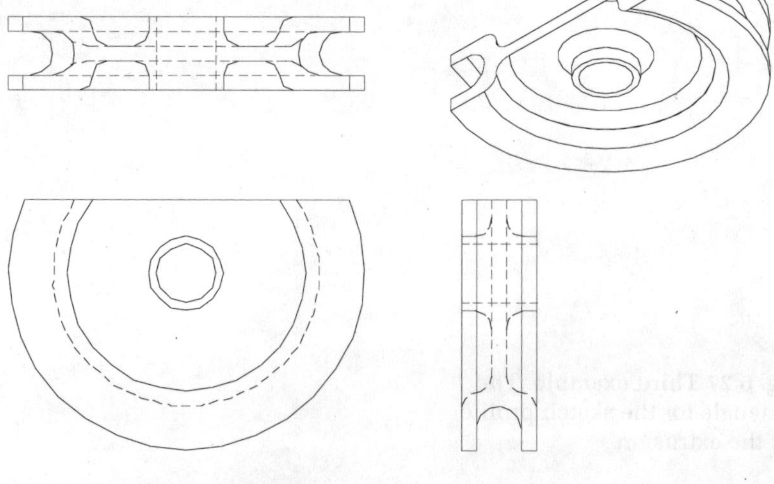

Fig. 6.29 Third example. The three-view orthographic projection and isometric view produced with **adview**

8. Call **adhole** and place a 40 diameter hole through the central boss.
9. With **adview** create a three-view orthographic projection and an isometric projection (Fig. 6.29).

Fourth example

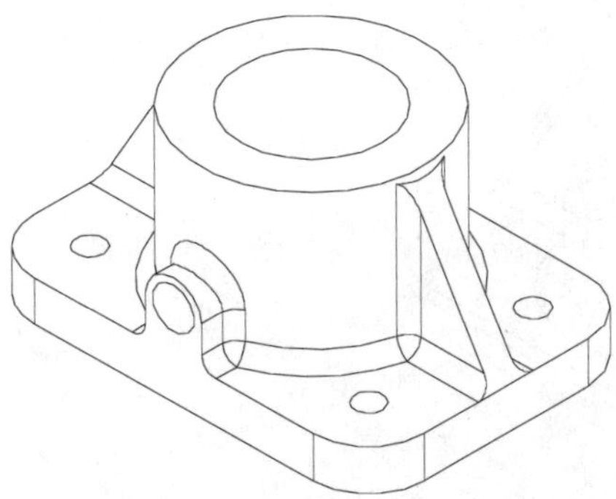

Fig. 6.30 An isometric view of the fourth example

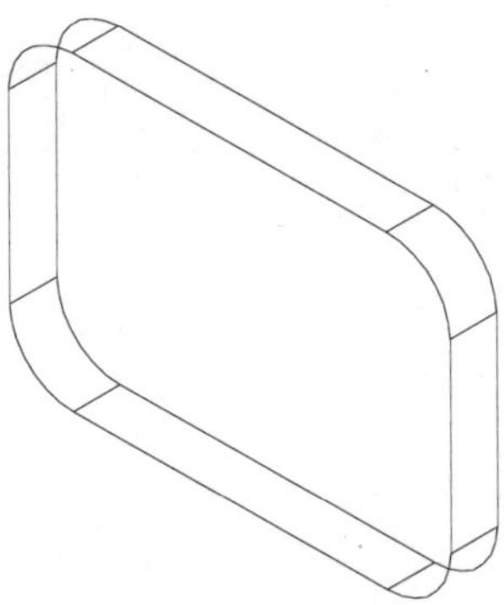

Fig. 6.31 Fourth example. The base after **adprofile** and **adextrude**

This final example includes a variety of work planes, with extrusions, together with some holes and fillets. An isometric view of the finished model is shown in Fig. 6.30.

1. Draw the outline of the base. Call **adprofile** and change it into a sketch profile. Call **adpartview** isometric. Call **adextrude** and **Base extrude** the profile 15 units (Fig. 6.31).
2. **Adpartview** into sketch view. Draw the circle for the upright cylinder. Call **adprofile** and change it into a sketch profile. **Adpartview** isometric. **Adextrude (Join) Distance:** 70 (Fig. 6.32).

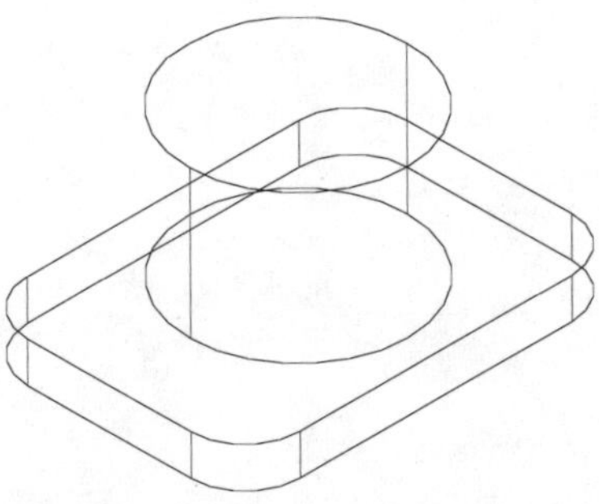

Fig. 6.32. Fourth example. The vertical cylinder **join extruded** to base

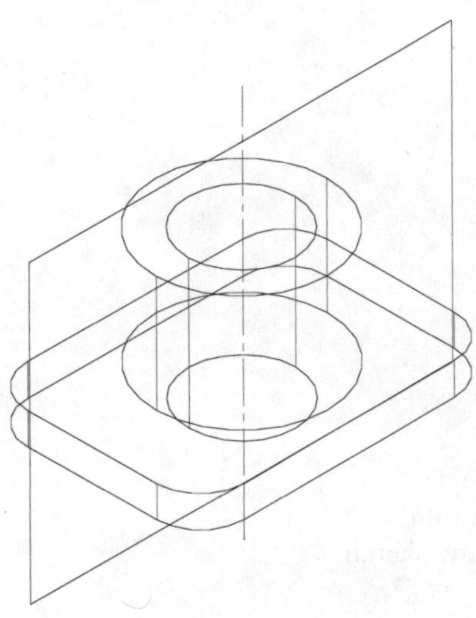

Fig. 6.33 Fourth example. Hole, work axis and work plane added

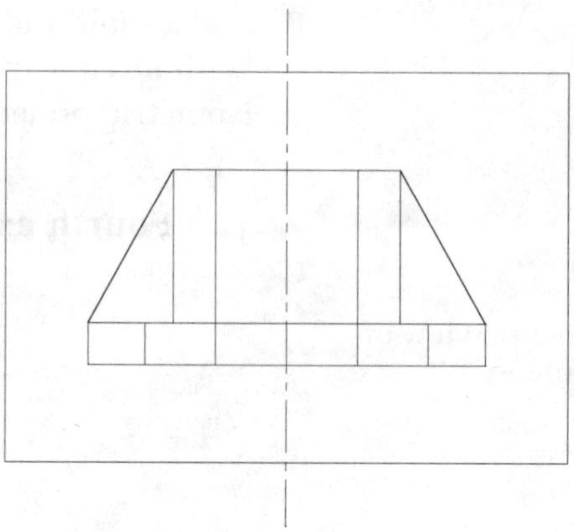

Fig. 6.34 Outline of webs on sketch plane

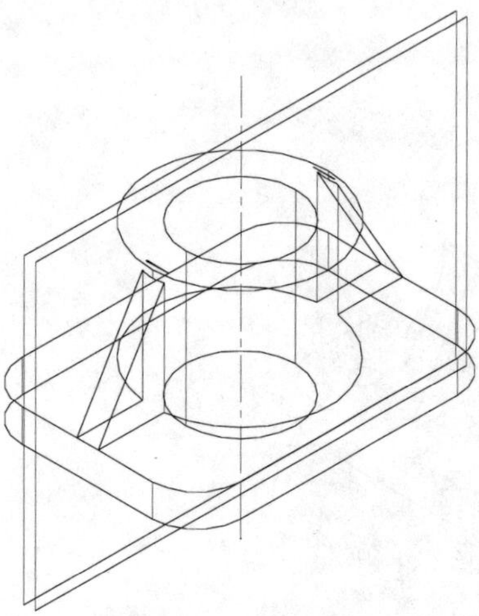

Fig. 6.35 Fourth example. Offset work plane

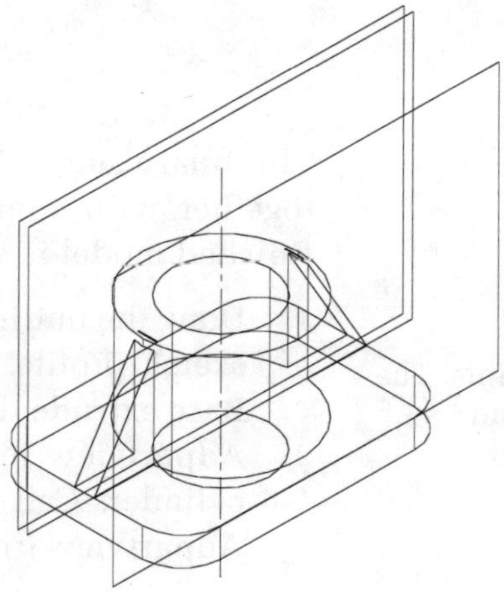

Fig. 6.36 Fourth example. Offset work plane at front of model

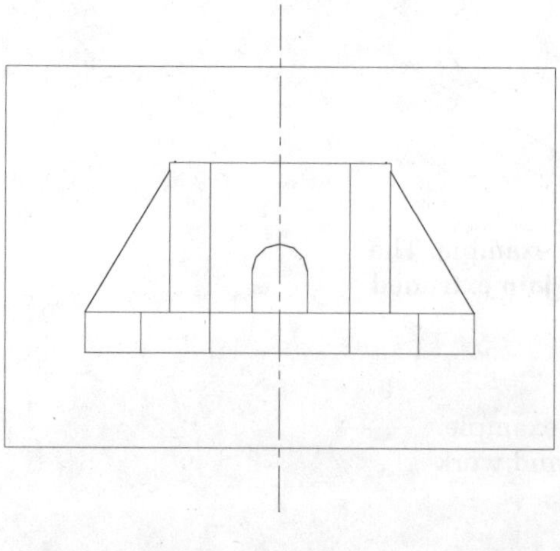

Fig. 6.37 Fourth example. Outline of boss on new sketch plane

3. **Adhole** a central hole **Through**, **Drilled** and **Dia:** 50. Add a work axis and a work plane (**Edge/Axis** and **On Vector**) – Fig. 6.33.
4. Offset another work plane 5 units from the first (see Fig. 6.35)
5. **Adskpln** based on the offset work plane. **Adpartview** sketch. Add outline of webs (Fig. 6.34).
6. **Adpartview** isometric. **Adprofile** and **adextrude** (**Join** 10 units) each web outline in turn (Fig. 6.35)
7. Offset a new work plane to the front of the model (Fig. 6.36). Call **adskpln** and make a new sketch plane based on the offset work plane. Call **adpartview** sketch and draw the front boss outline on the sketch plane (Fig. 6.37).
8. **Adpartview** isometric. **Adprofile** the boss outline. **Adextrude** (**Join**) the sketch profile. Call **adhole** and add the hole in the boss (Fig. 6.38).
9. Call **adfillet** and fillet edges as in Fig. 6.39 at a radius of 5 units.
10. Call **adview** and position three orthographic views as in Fig. 6.40.

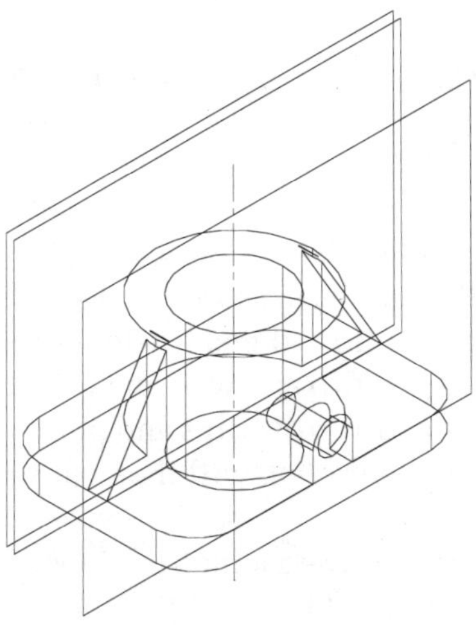

Fig. 6.38 Fourth example. The boss with its hole added to the model

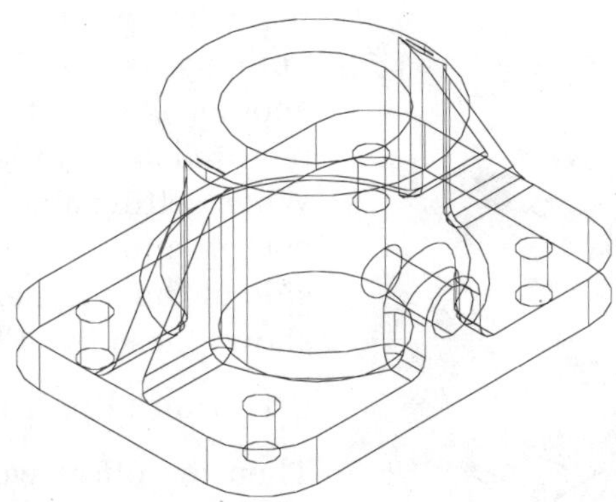

Fig. 6.39 Fourth example. Fillets added

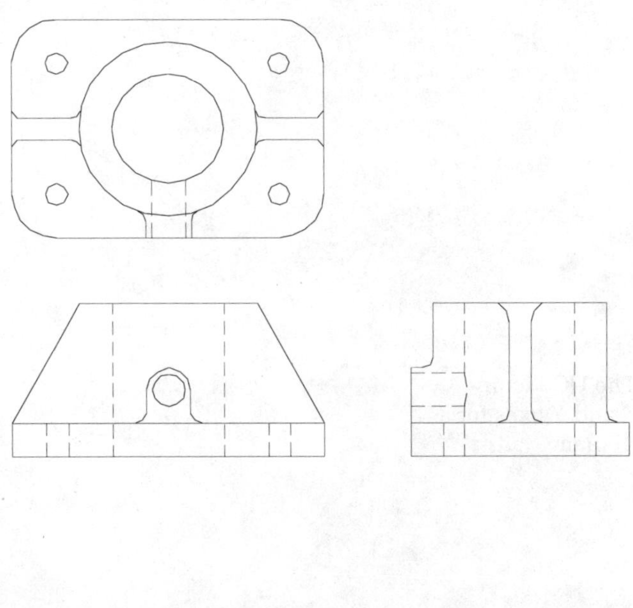

Fig. 6.40 Fourth example. Orthographic views of the model

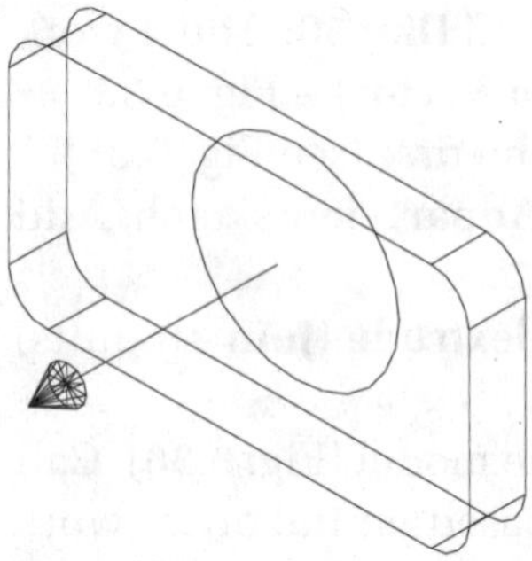

Fig. 6.41 The flip arrow

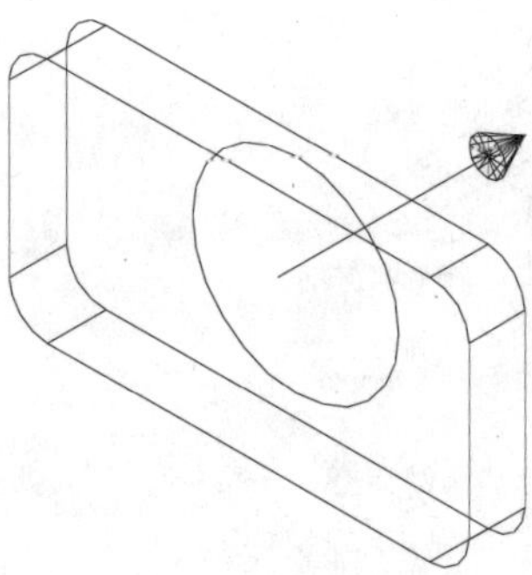

Fig. 6.42 Flipping the flip arrow

Notes

1. When calling **adextrude** to **Join** or **Cut** and extrusion, one of the options which may appear is:

   Direction Flip/<Accept>:

   Associated with the model a flip arrow will show indicating the direction in which the extrusion will take place, as in Fig. 6 41. If a *right-click* is given in response to the option, the extrusion will take place in the direction indicated by the flip arrow. If an f (Flip) is *entered* as a response to the option, the flip arrow flips and points in the opposite direction (Fig. 6.42). A *right-click* will then cause the extrusion to form in this new direction.
2. When setting a new sketch plane while in the isometric view of **adpartview**, the final option at the command is:

   Rotate/<Accept>:

   The UCS icon shows the direction of the X and Y axes of the sketch plane being set (Fig. 6.43). *Entering* r (Rotate) in response to the option causes the UCS icon to rotate through 90°. A second r causes another 90° rotation. To set the X and Y axes in relation to the required sketch plane, continuing *entering* r until satisfied.
3. When setting a new **Offset** work plane, Flip arrows appear at the corners and centre of the work plane to show the operator to which side of the original work plane the offset should be. Figure 6.44 shows these five Flip arrows. If an f (for Flip) is the response to:

   Direction Flip/<Accept>:

   Then the offset work plane appears on the opposite side of the original work plane with flip arrows pointing in the opposite direction.

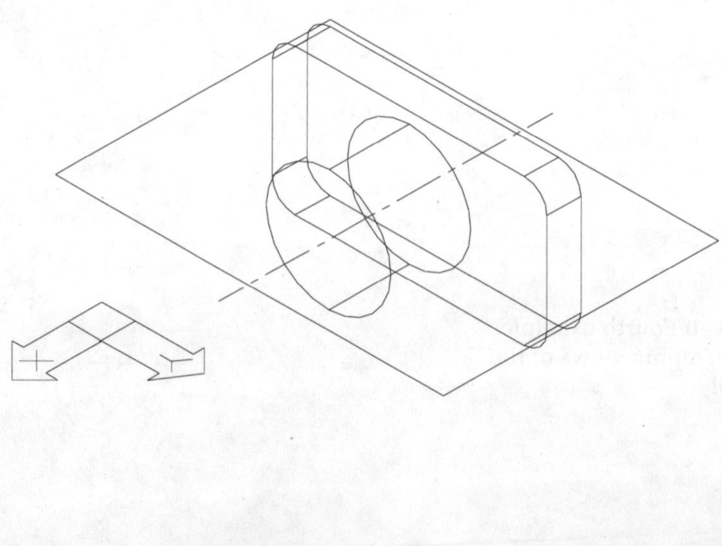

Fig. 6.43 The UCS icon showing X and Y axes for a new sketch plane

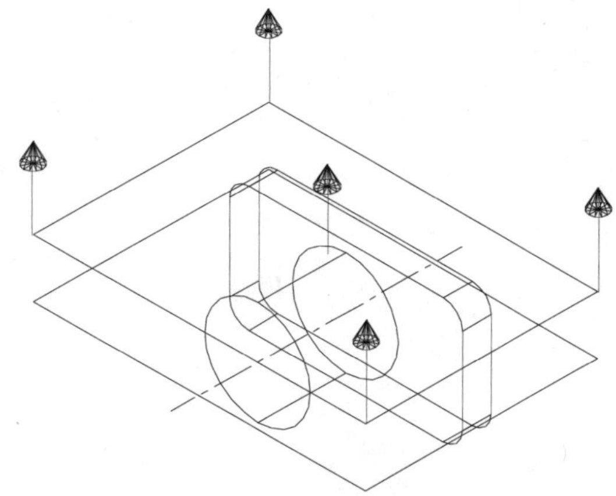

Fig. 6.44 Flip arrows on an offset work plane

4. If you find that one method of setting a new work plane does not work (a warning will appear at the Command Line), try another method from the **Designer work plane** dialogue box.
5. It is occasionally useful to use the AutoCAD command **vpoint** to place a Designer model in a good viewing position, rather than use the isometric option of the **adpartview** Designer command. The reader is advised to experiment.
6. It is occasionally useful to set the AutoCAD variable **ucsfollow** ON (1) when constructing Designer drawings. However, it may be found that sketch planes appear in unusual positions on screen when asked to **Rotate/<Accept>:**. Despite this, the setting of the variable may be found to be of value with some constructions. Again, the reader is advised to experiment.

Exercises

1. Figure 6.45 is a Designer third-angle orthographic projection, together with an isometric view, of an angle bracket. Construct a Designer 3D model of the bracket to the given dimensions. From your model set up a three-view first-angle orthographic projection of the bracket.

   Include a border and a title block with your orthographic projection. Fully dimension your drawing.
2. Figure 6.47 is a three-view third-angle orthographic projection, including an isometric view, set up from a Designer 3D model.

   In order to include the holes in the base, it was necessary to include work points at the hole centres on the original sketch plane from which the base was extruded. In order to place a work point, call the command **adworkpt** and place the point as required. Figure

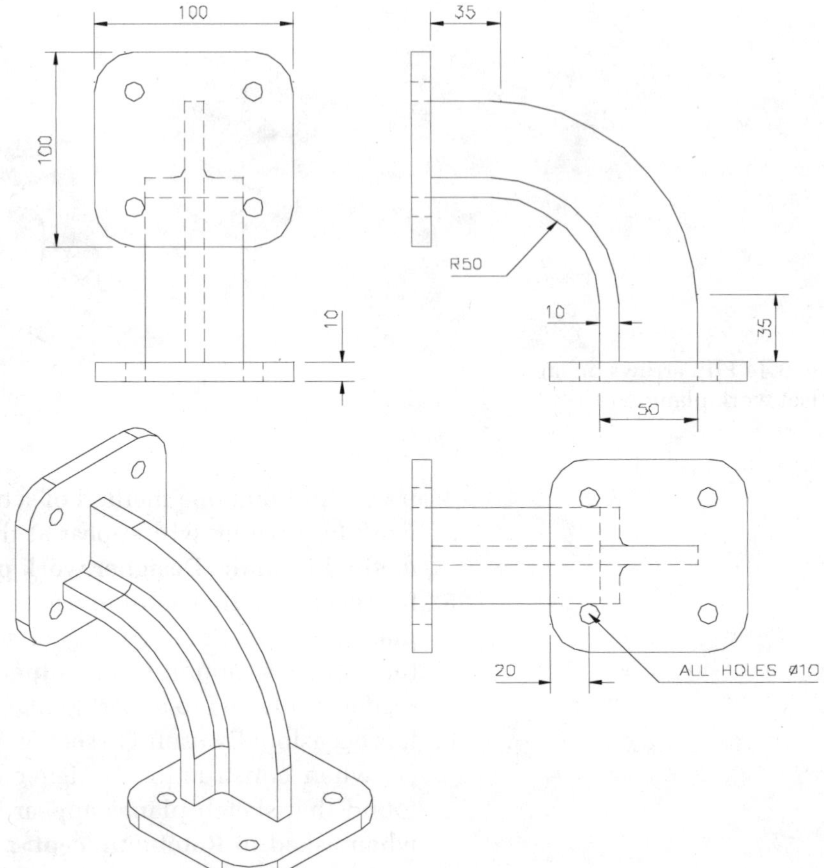

Fig. 6.45 Exercise 1

6.46 shows the Work Points added on the sketch plane for this exercise.

Construct the Designer 3D model of the support shown in the orthographic projection, working to the dimensions given. From your 3D model set up the third-angle orthographic projection and isometric view given in Fig. 6.47.

3. Working to dimensions of your own choice, construct the Designer 3D model shown in the two-view third-angle orthographic projection of Fig. 6.49. From your 3D model **adview** a two-view first-angle orthographic projection of your model.

   Note that the isometric view shown with Fig. 6.48 is an AutoCAD AME (Advanced Solid Modelling) model and not a Designer isometric.

4. Figure 6.49. The upper drawing shows the Designer 3D model from which the other two drawings were obtained. First construct the upper drawing to sizes given in the lower drawings; then **adchamfer** and **adfillet** as shown.

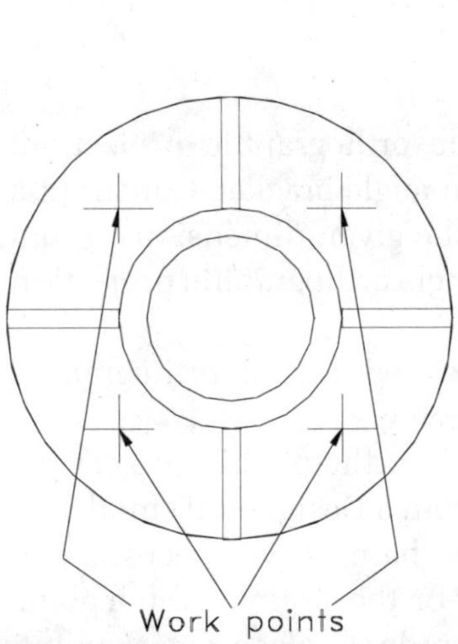

Fig. 6.46 Work points on the sketch plane for Exercise 2

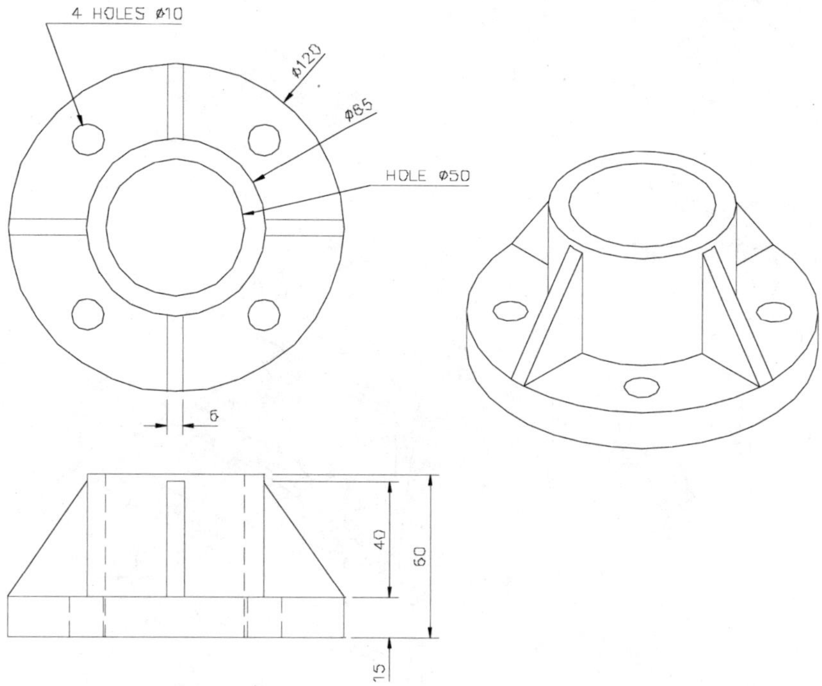

Fig. 6.47 Exercise 2

Fig. 6.48 Exercise 3

From your resulting 3D model set up the two-view third-angle orthographic projection shown in the lower drawing.

Fully dimension your orthographic projection.

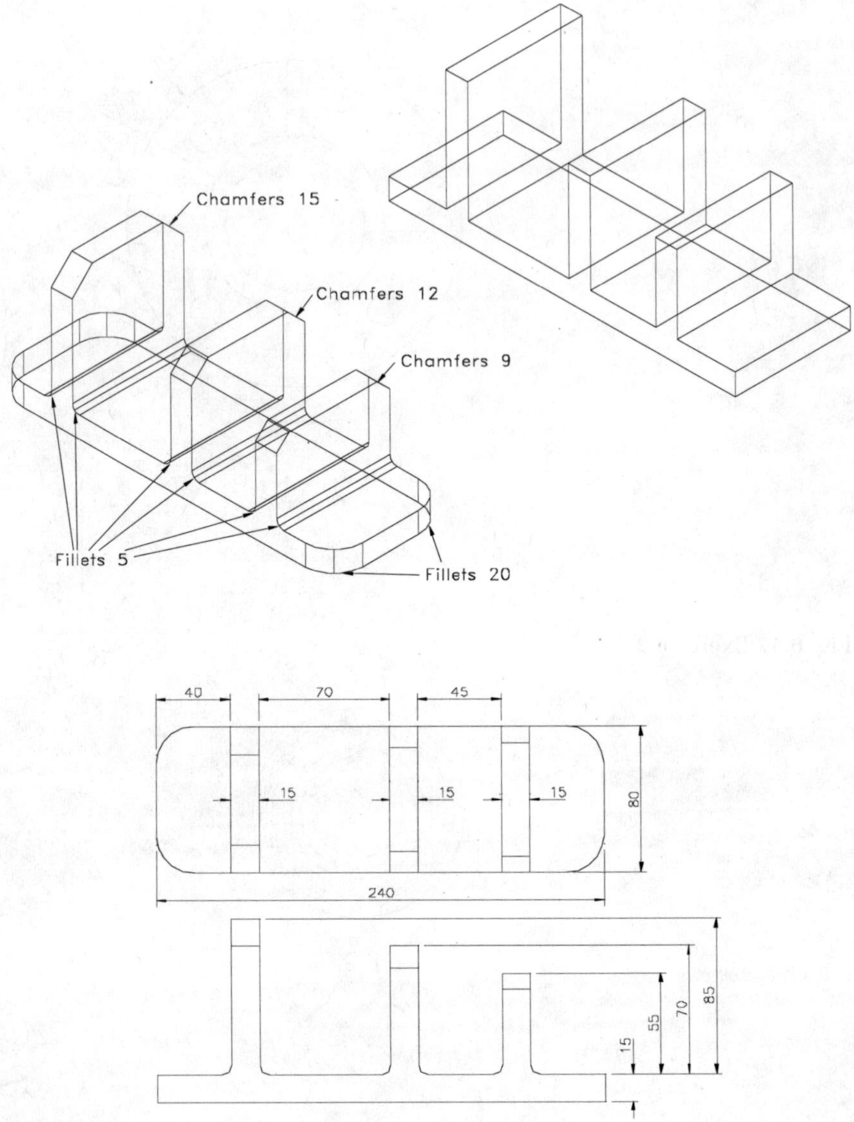

Fig. 6.49 Exercise 4

CHAPTER 7

Exploded Designer 3D models

Introduction

When constructing Designer 3D models as described in previous chapters, all details in the models have been included in a single part and the model responds as a single feature. In order to construct exploded 3D models in Designer, each part must have a separate identity. The example given in Fig. 7.1, which is a Designer **adview** isometric view of an exploded drawing, consists of three parts, each one separate from the other ones.

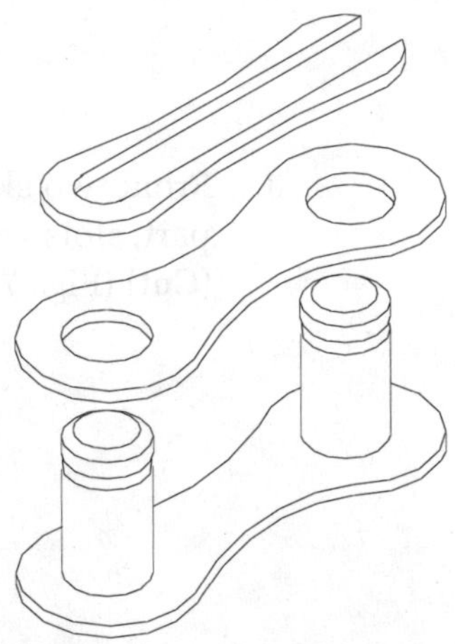

Fig. 7.1 A Designer exploded 3D model of a chain clip

Constructing the chain clip model in Fig. 7.1

The construction was carried out in the following sequence:

1. From the sketch profile (Fig. 7.2) the base of the first part (Part 0) was extruded with **adextrude.** Note the use of **Equation** dimensions. More about these later in this chapter.
2. The two pins of Part 0 were extruded from circles drawn on the sketch plane with the aid of **adextrude (Join)** (Fig. 7.3).

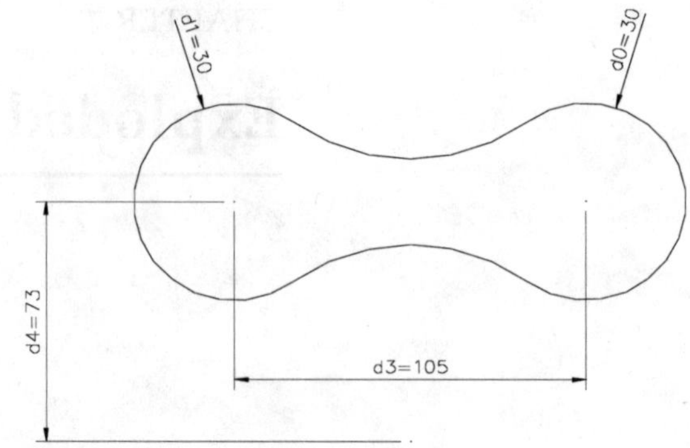

Fig. 7.2 The dimensioned sketch profile for Part 0

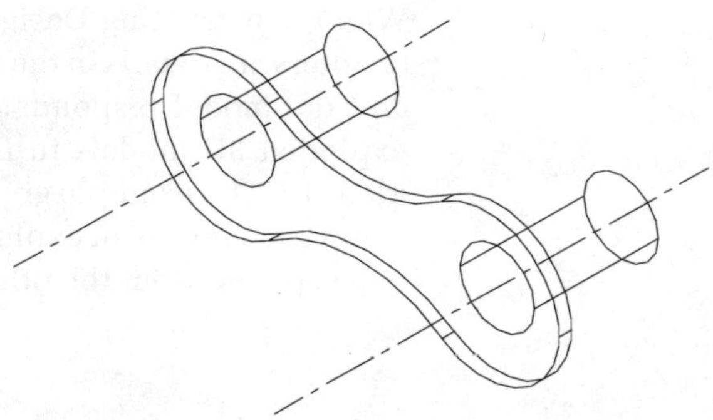

Fig. 7.3 Adding pins to the base for Part 0

3. From two sketch profiles drawn on a sketch plane central to the part, slots were constructed in the pins with the aid of **adrevolve (Cut)** (Figs 7.4 and 7.5).

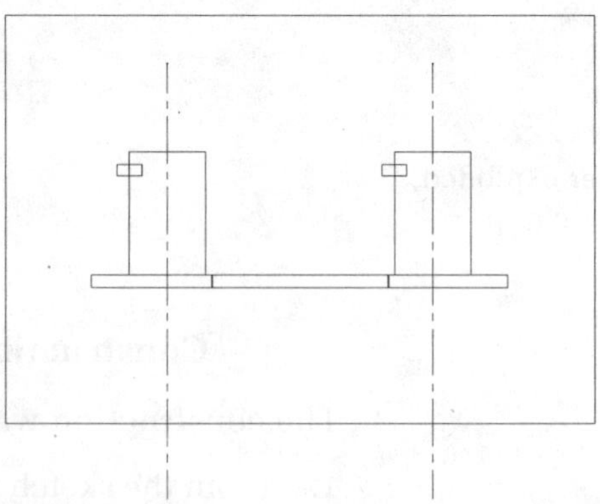

Fig. 7.4 The two sketch profile outlines for the slots in the pins of Part 0

4. Chamfers (distances 2) were added to the tops of the pins with the aid of **adchamfer**, as shown in Fig. 7.5.

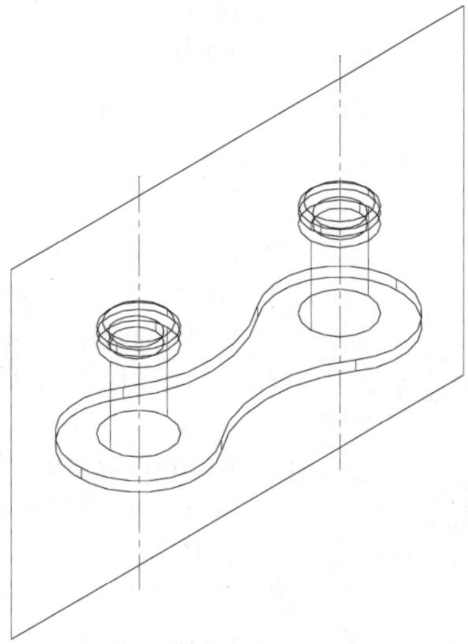

Fig. 7.5 The completed Part 0

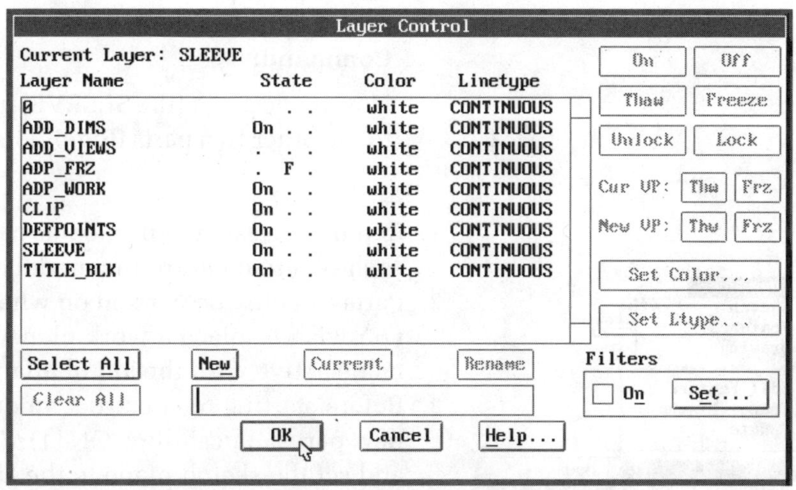

Fig. 7.6 The **Layer Control** dialogue box for this exploded model

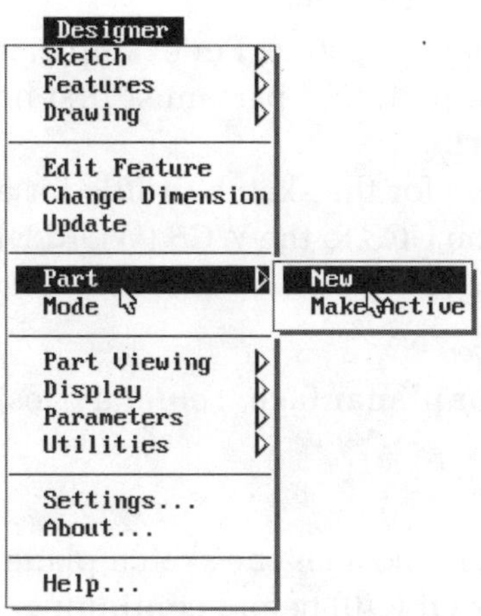

Fig. 7.7 Selecting **New Part** from the **Designer** pull-down menu

5. In the **Layer Control** dialogue box, turn **layer 0** off (on which Part 0 has been constructed) and make two new layers **SLEEVE** (for Part 1) and **CLIP** for Part 2 (Fig. 7.6). Now make **SLEEVE** the current layer.
6. At the Command Line:

Command: *enter* adnewpart *right-click*
Part 1 initialized.
Command:

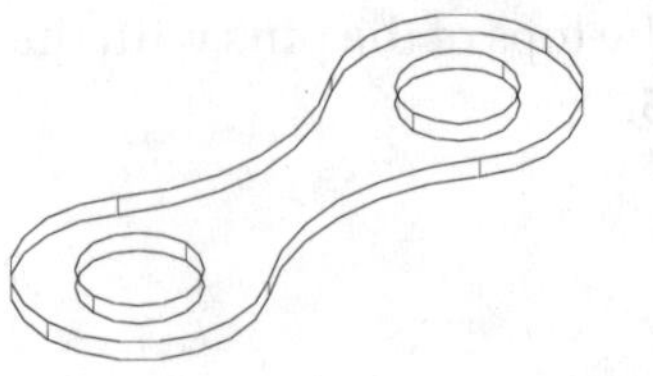

Fig. 7.8 The sleeve constructed on layer **SLEEVE**

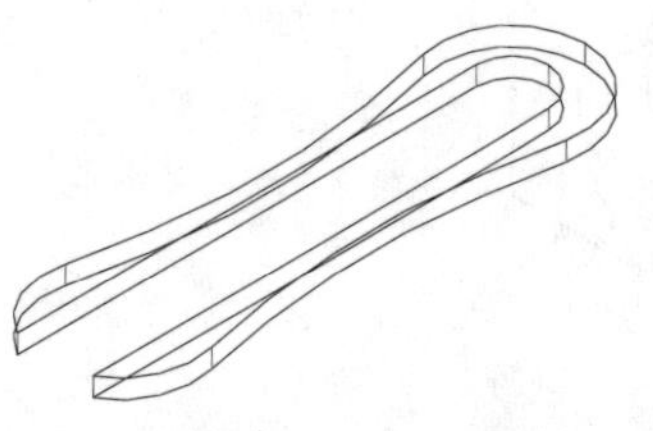

Fig. 7.9 The clip constructed on layer **CLIP**

7. Now construct the sleeve (Part 1) on the layer **SLEEVE** (Fig. 7.8).
8. In the **Layer Control** dialogue box, turn layer **SLEEVE** off (on which Part 1 has been constructed) and make **CLIP** the current layer.
9. At the Command Line:

Command: *enter* adnewpart *right-click*
Part 2 initialized.
Command:

10. Now construct the clip (Part 2) on the layer CLIP (Fig. 7.9).
11. In the **Layer Control** dialogue box turn layers 0 and SLEEVE back ON. All three parts now appear in the drawing editor.
12. Set **ucsfollow** ON (1). Place the parts in the UCS Preset Front. It may be found that the UCS Preset Right or Left may be better.
13. Remembering that Part 2 (the CLIP) is currently the active part, call the AutoCAD command **move** and move the clip into a suitable position with regard to Part 0.
14. At the Command Line:

Command: *enter* adactpart *right-click*
Select part: *pick* Part 1
Part 1 is now active.
Command:

Now move part 1 (the SLEEVE) into a suitable position with regard to the other two parts (Fig. 7.11 shows all three parts in position).

Notes

1. Exploded Designer 3D models can only be constructed by placing each separate part of the model on its own layer.
2. Parts can only be worked on when they are active. For example, if you wish to place a work plane on a part, that part must first be made active with the aid of **adactpart**.
3. Before starting to construct an outline for the sketch profile for a new part, set **ucsfollow** ON (1). Set the UCS to the WCS (WORLD) and set the sketch plane to the UCS by:

Command: *enter* adskpln *right-click*
Xy/Yz/Xz/UCS/<Select work plane or planar face>: *enter* u (Ucs) *right-click*
Command:

And the UCS (which will be the WCS) becomes the sketch plane. It is then advisable to turn **ucsfollow** OFF (0) before continuing.
4. When a part is active it can be acted upon by AutoCAD commands such as **move**. However, if you try commands such as **mirror** or **rotate**, the results may not be at all as expected.

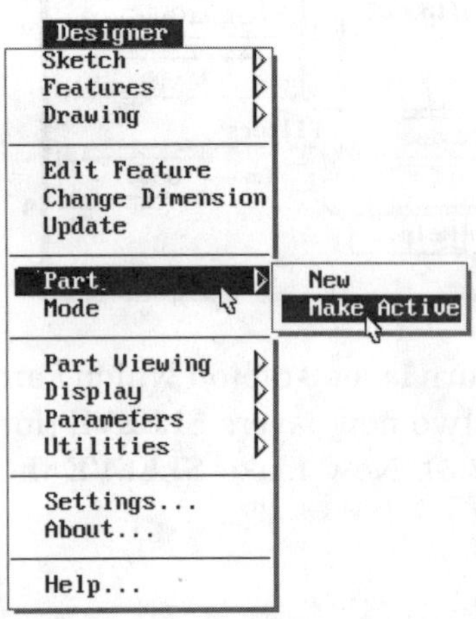

Fig. 7.10 Selecting **Make Active** from the **Designer** pull-down menu

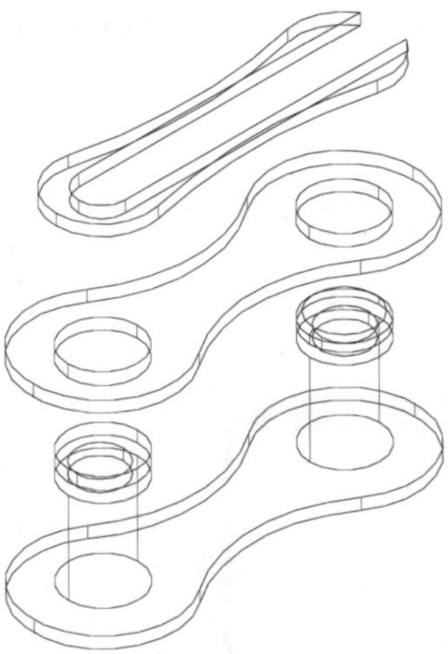

Fig. 7.11 All three Parts in their final exploded position

Parameters

Figure 7.2 on page 108 included **Equation** dimensions. In a Designer 3D exploded model, parts can be linked by using global parametric dimensions. Then when a change is made to a dimension in one part with **adeditfeat**, the parametric functions of Designer will apply the change to all parts of the model. Examples of this parametric functioning of Designer is beyond the scope of an introductory book of this nature, but the reader may wish to experiment with its use. The **Equation** dimensions were added to Fig. 7.2 with the aid of **adpardim**, but before the command was called:

Command: *enter* addimdsp *right-click*
Parameters/Equations/<Numerals>: *enter* e (Equations) *right-click*
Command:

And all dimensions added to a sketch profile will be in an equation form as shown in Fig. 7.2.

The dimensions of the whole drawing can be linked to the model with the aid of the command **adparam** as in the following example:

Command: *enter* adparam *right-click*
Create/Delete/List/Import/Export/>eXit>: *enter* c (Create) *right-click*
Enter equation: centreslength = 105 *right-click*
Enter equation: endradius = 30 *right-click*
Enter equation: mainradius = 200 *right-click*
Enter equation: radiusdimension = 73 *right-click*
Enter equation: *right-click*
Command: *right-click* to get back to the options
Create/Delete/List/Import/Export/>eXit>: *enter* e (Export) *right-click*

And the **Export Parameter File** dialogue box appears. *Enter* a suitable file name, followed by a *left-click* on the **OK** button of the dialogue box.

Parameter file E:\DESIGN/CHAP07\PART01.PRM created.
Create/Delete/List/Import/Export/>eXit>: *enter* i (Import) *right-click*

And the **Import Parameter File** dialogue box appears (Fig. 7.14)

Select the name **PART01** from the list box, followed by a *left-click* on the **OK** button.

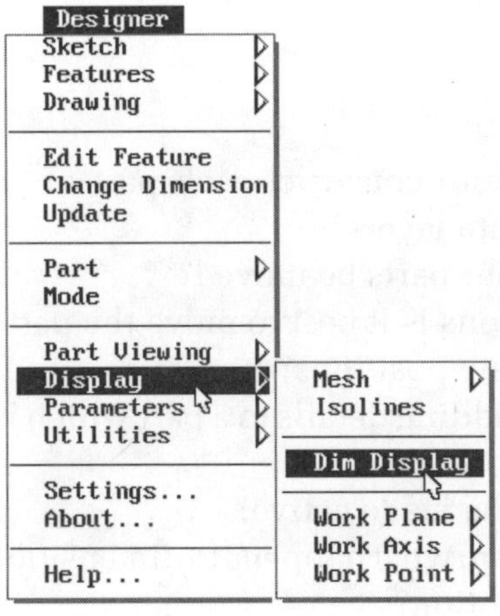

Fig. 7.12 Selecting **Dim Display** from the **Designer** pull-down menu

And the AutoCAD screen changes to an AutoCAD text screen with details of the **PART01.PRM** file showing (Fig. 7.15).

Further equations can be added if wished while in the AutoCAD text screen.

Note

Changes to a parameter file (extension *.prm) can be used to parametrically amend an exploded model drawing. Again, the reader is advised to experiment with parametric files.

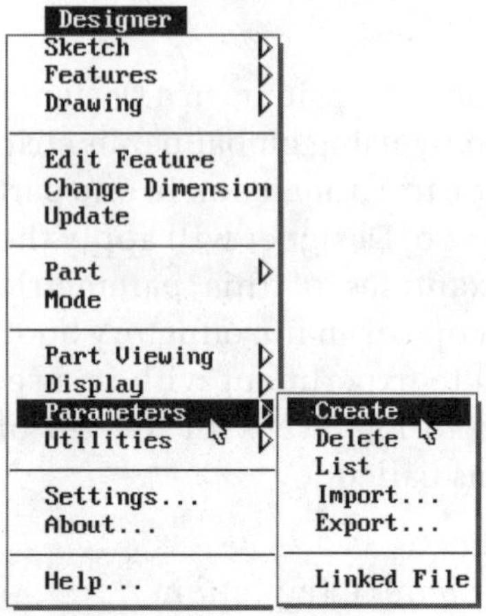

Fig. 7.13 Selecting **Create** form the **Parameters** sub-menu of the **Designer** pull-down menu

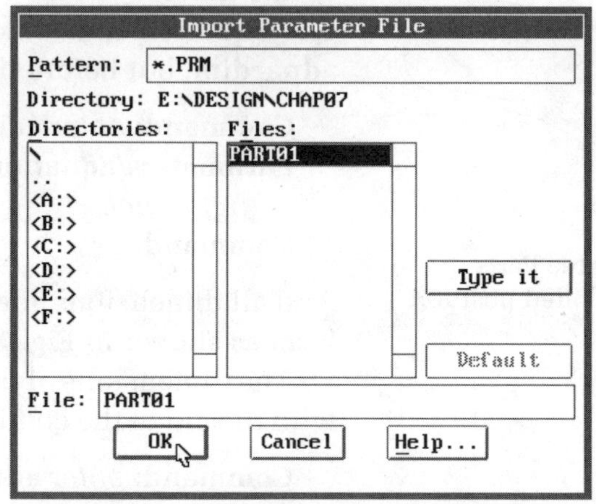

Fig. 7.14 The **Import Parameter File** dialogue box

```
   Parameter Name          Definitions

 1)       centreslength = 105
 2)           endradius = 30
 3)          mainradius = 200
 4)     radiusdimension = 73

Create/Delete/List/Import/Export/<eXit>:
```

Fig. 7.15 Details from the **PART01.PRM** file

Questions

1. Why do you think it is necessary to construct each part of an exploded Designer view on separate layers?
2. With which command can Designer parts be moved?
3. In which of the **adpartview** positions is it best to move the parts for an exploded view into their new positions?
4. What happens when you attempt adding details to a part which is not active?
5. With which command can a part be made active?
6. When using the command **addimdsp**, what happens to dimensions when you choose the **Numerals** option?
7. What is the purpose of using the command **addimdsp**?
8. What is a parameter file? What is the file extension for such files?

9. When do you think it is of value to have **ucsfollow** ON (1) when constructing a Designer 3D model?
10. Why must you never delete details on the layer **ADD_DIMS**?

Exercises

The only real differences between constructing a single part Designer model as described in earlier chapter from constructing an exploded model are:

The command **adnewpart** must be called before construction starts on each part.

Each part of an exploded drawing must be constructed on a new layer. It will probably be advisable to turn off those layers containing other parts.

When all parts have been constructed they can be moved into suitable positions for the exploded view with the aid of the AutoCAD command **move**.

When moving parts with the aid of **move**, set the viewing position by first setting **ucsfollow** ON (1). It is then likely that the best viewing position for this purpose is either the **UCS Presets** Front, Right or Left.

The constructions of each of the parts of an exploded view follow the descriptions given in earlier chapters. Because of this, it is thought that the single example given in this chapter, followed by two exercises, will be sufficient practice for the reader to be able to construct exploded Designer models.

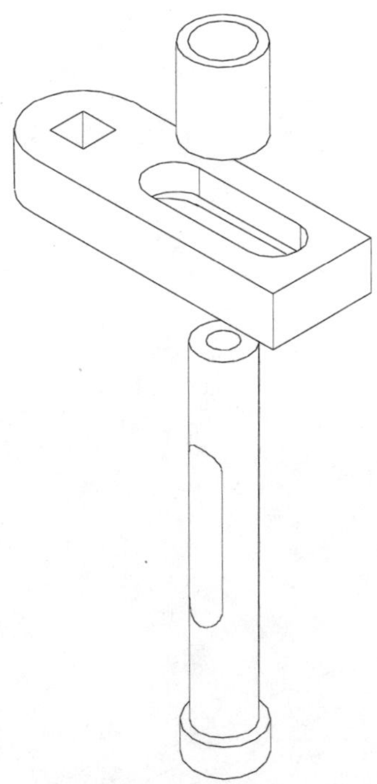

Fig. 7.16 Exercise 1. The Designer isometric drawing of the exploded 3D model

1. Figure 7.16 shows an exploded view of part of a sphere-turning attachment from an engineering lathe. Figure 7.17 is the Designer orthographic projection from which the exploded isometric drawing was obtained.

   Construct the three-part drawing of the attachment to the details given in Fig. 7.17, then in a UCS Preset Right move the parts so as to produce the isometric view of Fig. 7.16.
2. Figure 7.16 shows an exploded view of part of a pair of forks attached end to end via a coupling. Figure 7.19 is the Designer orthographic projection from which the exploded isometric drawing was obtained.

   Construct the three-part drawing of the attachment to the details given in Fig. 7.19, then in the UCS Preset Right move the parts so as to produce the isometric view of Fig. 7.18.

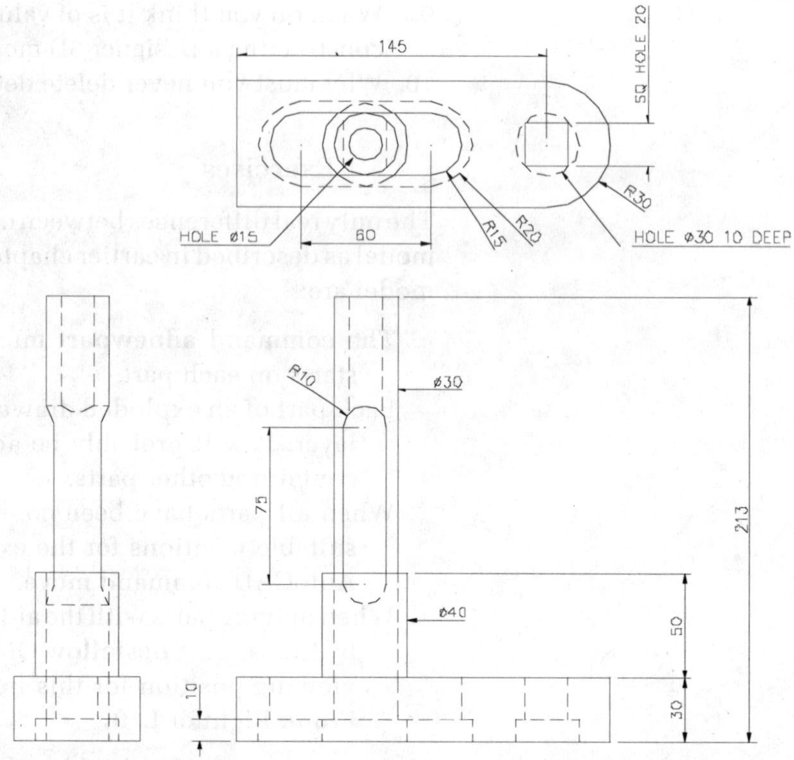

Fig. 7.17 Exercise 1. A Designer three-view third-angle orthographic projection

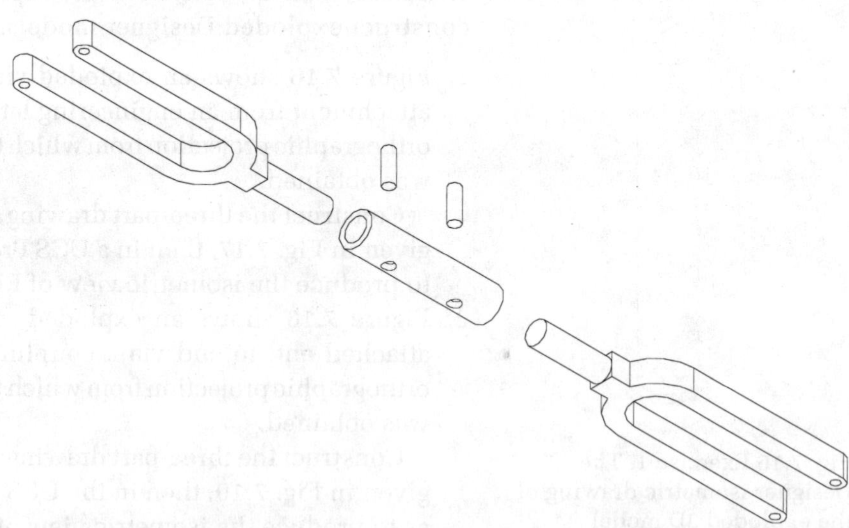

Fig. 7.18 Exercise 2. The Designer exploded drawing

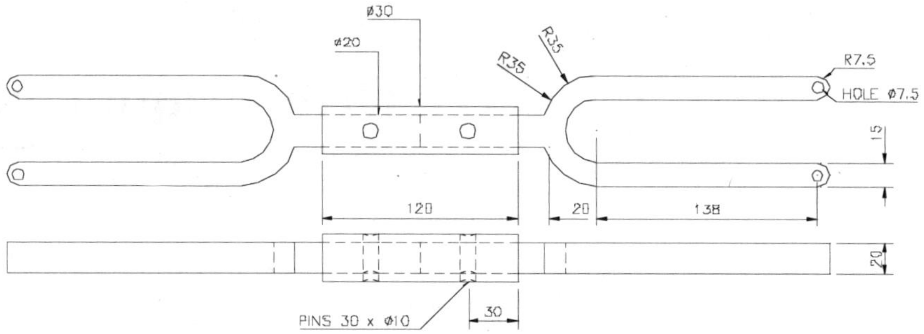

Fig. 7.19 Exercise 2. A Designer two-vew orthographic projection of a pair of forks attached end to end via a coupling

CHAPTER 8

Orthographic views

Introduction

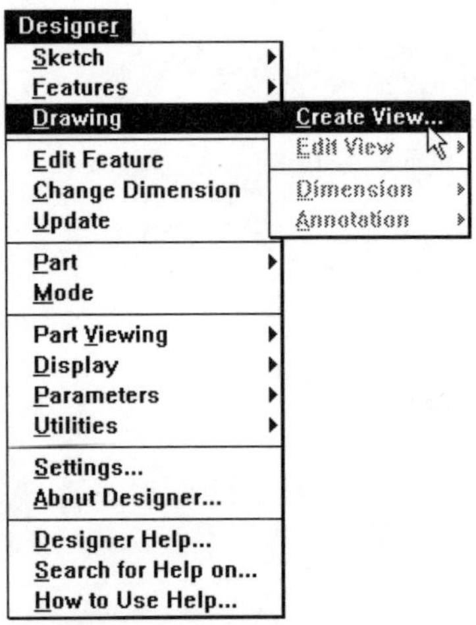

Fig. 8.1 Selecting **Create View...** from the **Designer** pull-down menu

Orthographic views obtained with the aid of the Designer command **adview** (**Create View...** in the **Designer** pull-down menu – Fig. 8.1) have been shown in earlier chapters. Fuller details of the different types of orthographic projections are described in this chapter. When **adview** is called, the **Designer Drawing View** dialogue box appears (Fig. 8.2) showing the settings available when placing orthographic views in the **Drawing Mode** screen of Designer. Most of the settings are made in check boxes, which show either diagonals or a button when ON and are empty when set OFF.

Types of view

Five types of orthographic view are possible as shown in the **Type** box of the dialogue box – **Base**, **Ortho**, **Aux**, **Isometric** and **Detail**:

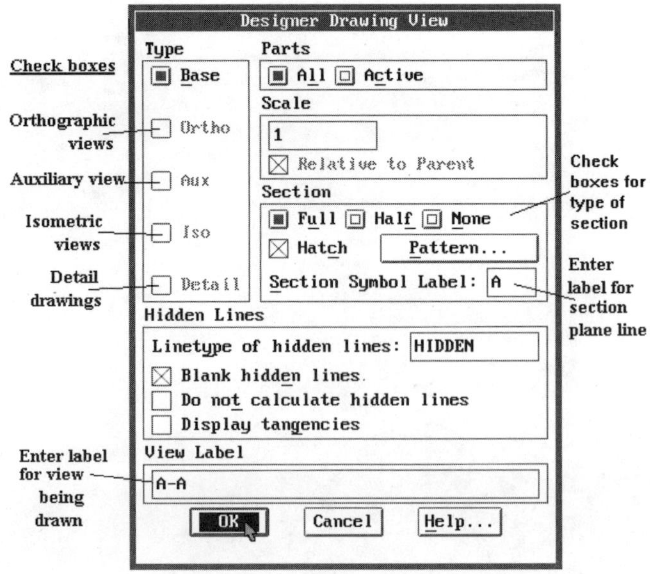

Fig. 8.2 The **Designer Drawing View** dialogue box

Base

A view obtained with **Base** active is regarded by Designer as the **Parent** view of all the views in the final orthographic drawing. When selecting the surfaces and edges for this view, care must be taken to ensure that the correct desired view is being obtained because other orthographic views will usually depend upon the parent view. Some examples from the Designer 3D model (Fig. 8.3) are shown in Fig. 8.4.

Command: *enter* adview *right-click*

In the **Designer Drawing View** dialogue box select **Base**, **All** and accept **Scale** as **1**. *Left-click* on **OK**.

Xy/Yz/Zx/Ucs/<Select work plane or planar face>: *enter* x (Xy) *right-click*
X/Y/Z/<Select work axis or straight edge>: *pick*
Rotate/<Accept>: *enter* r (Rotate) until UCS icon as wished

In the **Drawing Mode** screen which now appears:

View Center: *pick*
View Center: *right-click*
Command:

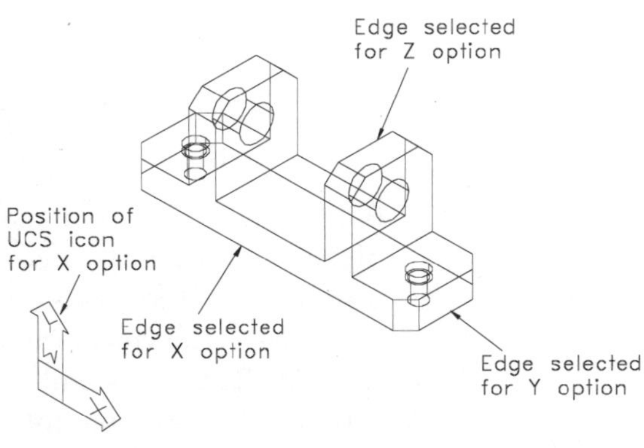

Fig. 8.3 Edges selected for **Xy**, **Yz** and **Zx Base** views

Notes

1. As can be seen in Fig. 8.4, the three views placed under the **Xy**, **Yz** and **Xz** options are **NOT** in orthographic projections – they are all **Base** views placed at random.
2. Probably the most common method of responding to the **adview** option prompts is to accept the two defaults **<Select work axis or straight edge>:** and **<Select work plane or planar face>:**. Figure 8.5 shows the highlighting of the planar face and the straight edge selected in response to the default options to obtain a front view.

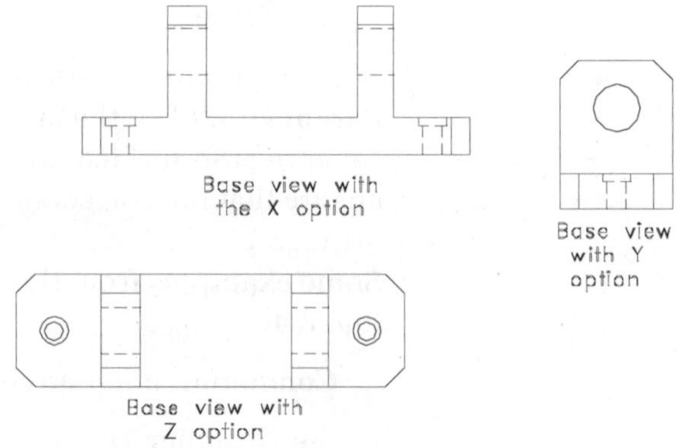

Fig. 8.4 The results of the **Base Xy**, **Yz** and **Zx** options

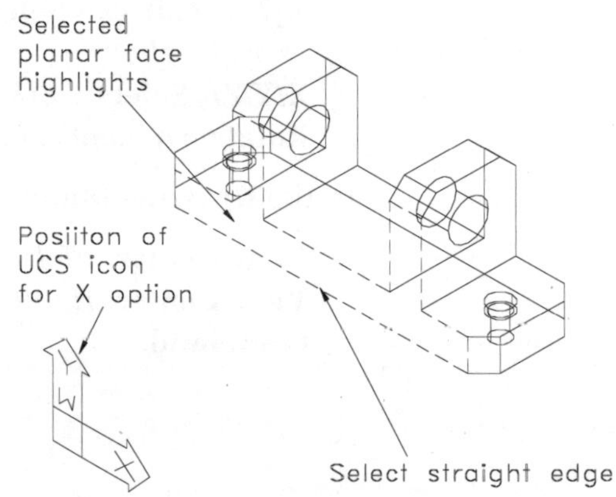

Fig. 8.5 Selecting a planar face and a straight edge in response to the default option of **adview** command

Ortho

Before being able to place an **Ortho** view, a **Base** view must first be placed as a **Parent** view. Once a parent view has been placed, any number of orthographic views may be positioned from the parent. Note that **Ortho** views are vertically or horizontally in line (orthogonal) with the **Base** view and cannot be placed in positions which are not orthogonal to the parent. Figure 8.6 shows an End view and a Plan placed othogonally to a parent view with the **Ortho** check box active. This example shows the three views in first-angle projection. In the **Designer Drawing Variables** dialogue box of the **Drawing Settings** dialogue box the **First Angle** had been selected.

Note

Hidden lines are automatically shown in all views unless the **Blank Hidden Lines** check box is ON (diagonals crossing the check box). *Left-clicks* in the check box turn it ON or OFF.

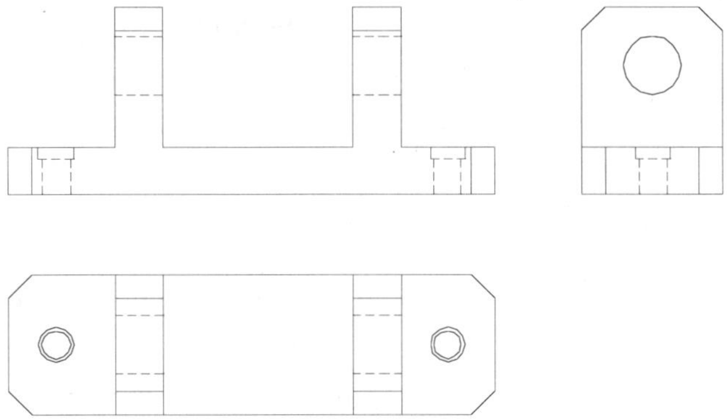

Fig. 8.6 An end view and a plan placed orthogonally to the parent (front) view with **Ortho** set

Aux

Figure 8.7 shows a two-view first-angle orthographic projection with the addition of an auxiliary view showing the true shape of the sloping face. The auxiliary view was placed after selecting **Aux** from the **Designer Drawing View** dialogue box. The Command Line shows:

Command: *enter* adview *right-click*

In the **Designer Drawing View** dialogue box

Left-click in the **Aux** check box to make **Aux** active. *Left-click* on the **OK** button.
Select a straight edge in the parent view: *pick*
Select a second point or <RETURN> to use the selected edge: either *right-click* or *pick* a second point
Location for auxiliary view: *pick* a position *right-click*
Location for auxiliary view: *right-click*
Command:

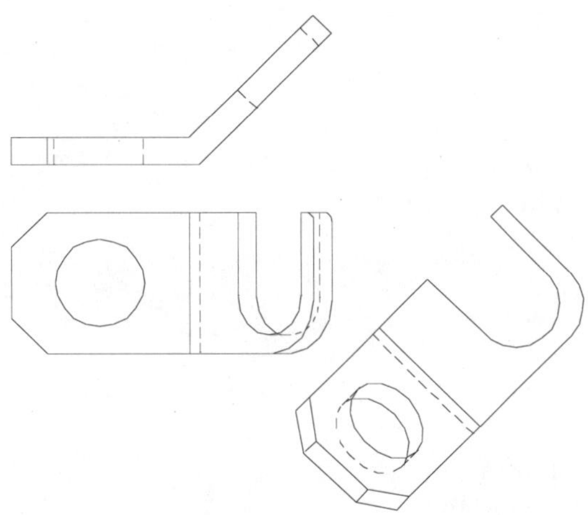

Fig. 8.7 A first-angle orthographic projection which includes an auxiliary view

Isometric

Left-click in the **ISO** check box of the **Designer Drawing View** dialogue box, followed by a *left-click* on the **OK** button. Then at the Command Line:

Select parent view: *pick*
Location for isometric view: *pick* a suitable position
Location for isometric view: *right-click*
Command:

Figure 8.8 shows an isometric view added to a three-view first-angle orthographic projection.

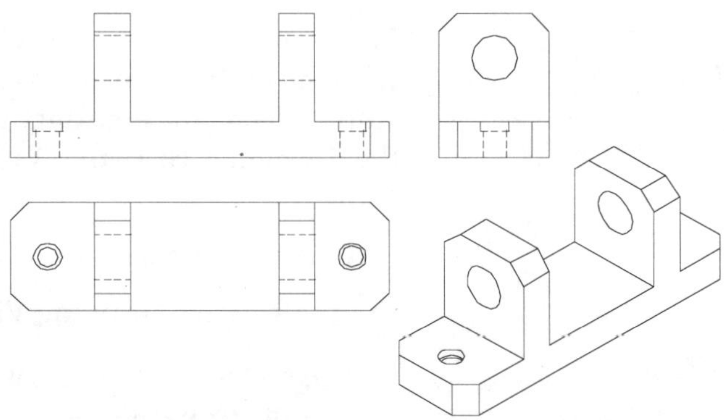

Fig. 8.8 An orthographic projection with an added isometric view

Detail

Left-click in the **Detail** check box of the **Designer Drawing View** dialogue box, followed by a *left-click* on the **OK** button. Note that the **Blank Hidden Lines** check box is checked. Then at the Command Line:

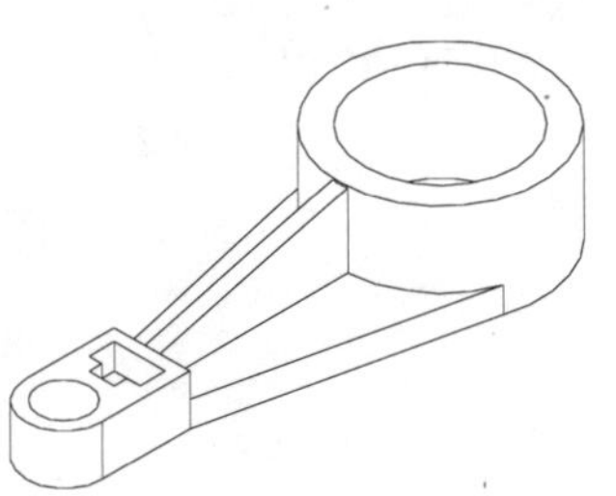

Fig. 8.9 An isometric view of the example given in Fig. 8.10

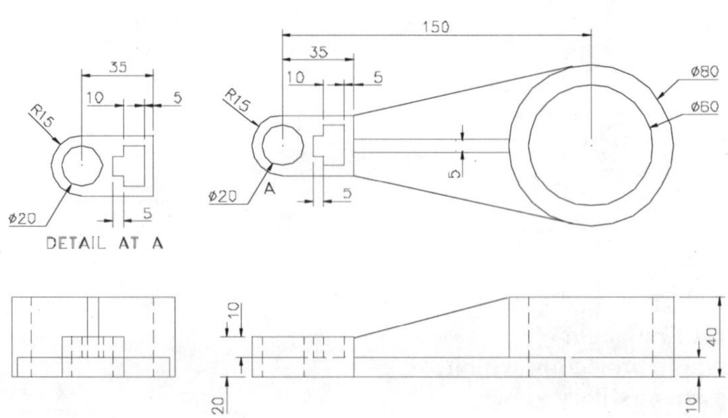

Fig. 8.10 A detail from a view in an orthographic projection

Command: *enter* adview *right-click*
Select vertex in parent for detail center: *pick*
Drag rectangle around detail: *drag* the rectangle
Location for detail part: *pick*
Location for detail part: *right-click*
Command:

Sectional views

Call **adview** and in the **Designer Drawing View** dialogue box (Fig. 8.11):

Left-click in the **Full** check box of the **Section** area
Left-click in the **Hatch** check box to set hatch ON
Left-click on the **Pattern...** button

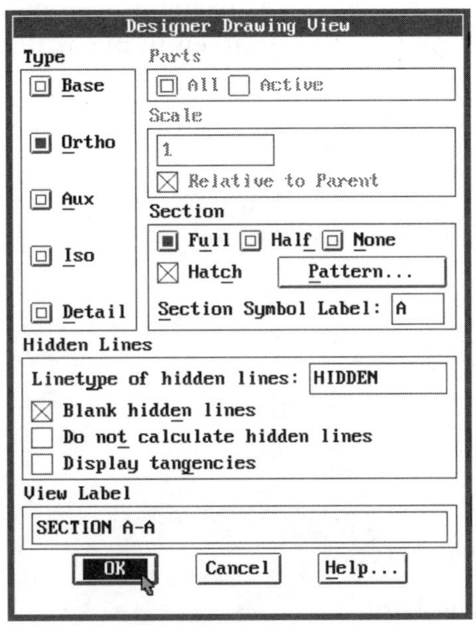

Fig. 8.11 The **Designer Drawing View** dialogue box showing the settings for a sectional view

The AutoCAD **Hatch Options** dialogue box appears (Fig. 8.12)

Make the required settings in this dialogue box. *Left-click* on the **OK** button. At the Command Line:

Command: *enter* adview *right-click*
Select parent view: *pick*
Location for orthographic view: *pick*
Location for orthographic view: *right-click*
Section through Point/<work plane>: *right-click* in parent view

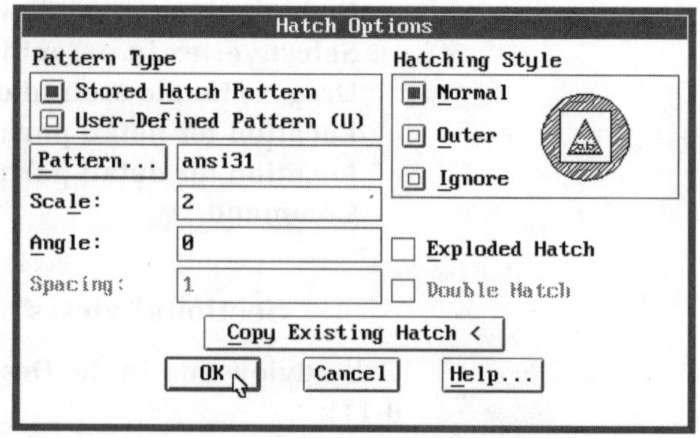

Fig. 8.12 The **Hatch Options** dialogue box showing the settings for the sectional view in Fig. 8.13

Select work plane in parent view for the section *pick* the edge of the central work plane
Command:

An example of a sectional view included in an orthographic projection is given in Fig. 8.13.

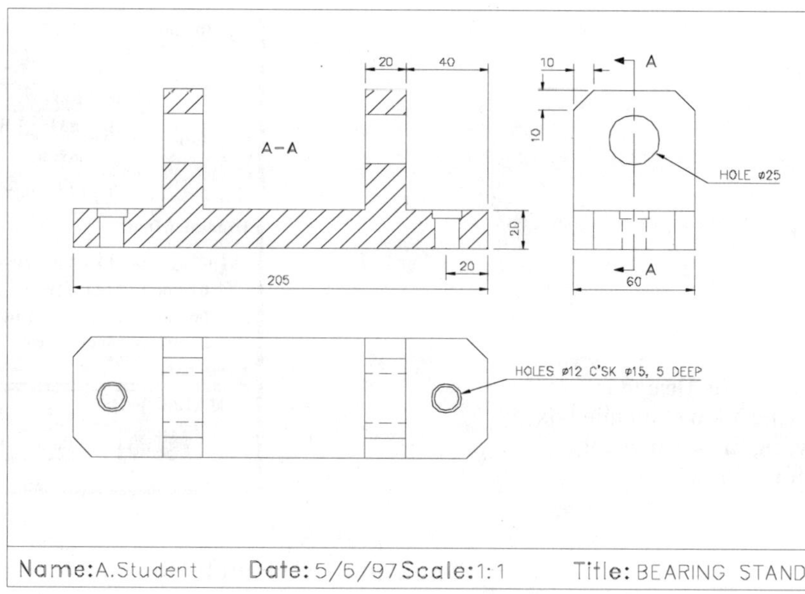

Fig. 8.13 A three-view first-angle orthographic projection which includes a sectional view

A Half section

It will have been noted in Fig. 8.11 that one of the possibilities under **Section** is **Half**. *Left-click* in the **Half** check box. At the Command Line:

Command: *enter* adview *right-click*
Select parent view: *pick*

Select work plane in parent view for the section: *right-click* in parent view, followed by *picking* the plane
Select second work plane in parent view for the section: *pick*
Side of half section Flip/<Accept>: *right-click*
Command:

An example is given in Fig. 8.14, which includes an isometric view of the **half** section, in which it must be noted it is the half section which shows, not a full view.

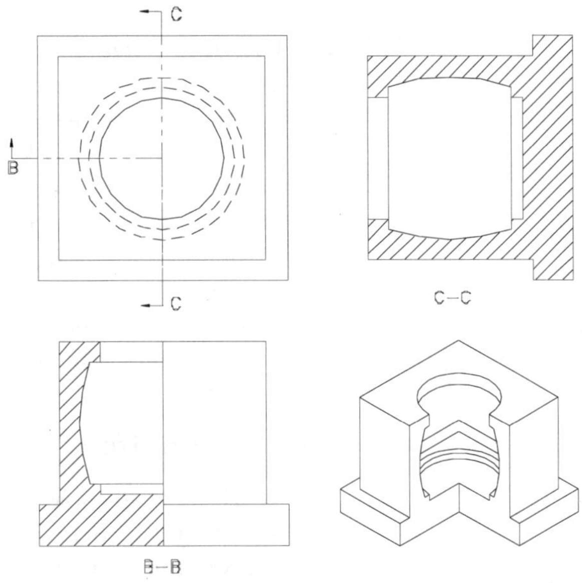

Fig. 8.14 A half sectional view. An isometric drawing is included taken from the half section

Notes

1. So far in this chapter we have been dealing largely with orthographic projections which do not include dimensions. It must be remembered that one of the more important features of Designer is its ability to use parametric dimensioning and changing all sizes of a part to fit in with changes in parametric dimensions. More about dimensions as they affect orthographic projections will be given later in this chapter.
2. Dimensions added to Designer orthographic drawings with the aid of the AutoCAD command **dim** are not parametric dimensions. Thus any change in the part made with **adeditfeat** will show a change in those dimensions included when constructing the sketch profile or extruding a profile in the orthographic projection when **adeditfeat** is used to change a parametric dimension in the part. The added AutoCAD dimensions will remain unchanged. This is because the AutoCAD dimensions are static – they are not parametric.

3. Centre lines as such are not included in Designer orthographic projections. The operator can, if desired add them using the AutoCAD Command **Line** or **pline** and changing the line to a centre line with the aid of the AutoCAD command **change**.
4. Hidden lines are automatically included in Designer orthographic views, unless the **Blank Hidden Lines** check box is ON in the **Designer Drawing View** dialogue box, in which case hidden lines will not be included with the view.
5. The default angle of projection in Designer is third-angle. If you wish to work in first-angle, remember to set **First Angle** ON in the **Drawing Variables** dialogue box of the **Designer Settings** dialogue box.
6. When including a section in an orthographic drawing, it is probably best to include work planes and work axes with the 3D model. These will be of value when selecting the sectioning plane.
7. When a section is included, a section plane line showing the edge of the section plane is automatically placed on the view from which the section is derived. If a label is required for the section plane, it is entered in the appropriate box in the **Designer Drawing View** dialogue box (Fig. 8.2).

Exercises

1. Working to any sizes you think suitable, construct the Designer part shown in Fig. 8.15. Include both a central work axis and a central work plane. From your part drawing, produce the three-view third-angle orthographic projection, which includes a sectional view given in Fig. 8.16.

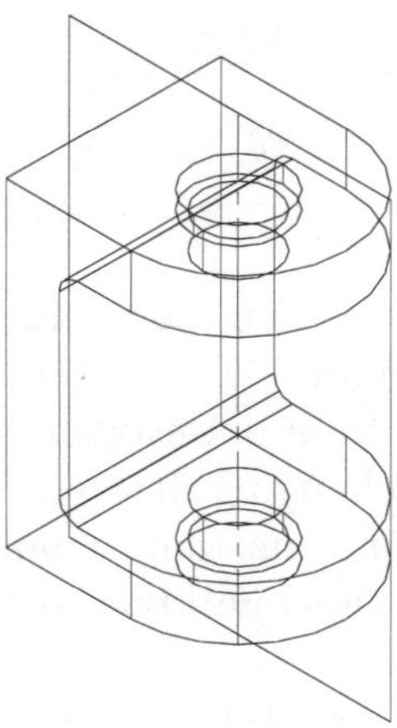

Fig. 8.15 The 3D Designer model part for Exercise 1

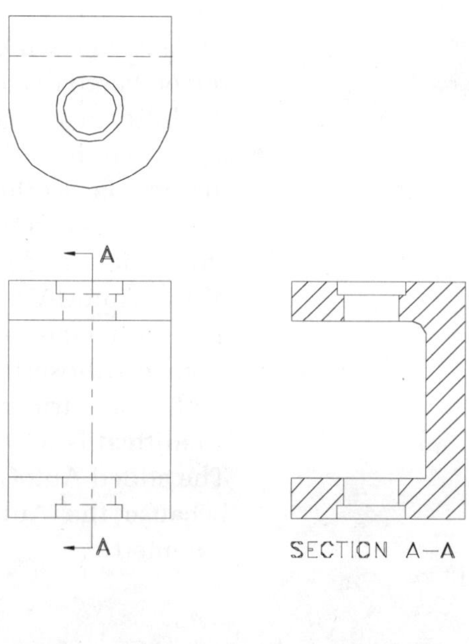

Fig. 8.16 Exercise 1

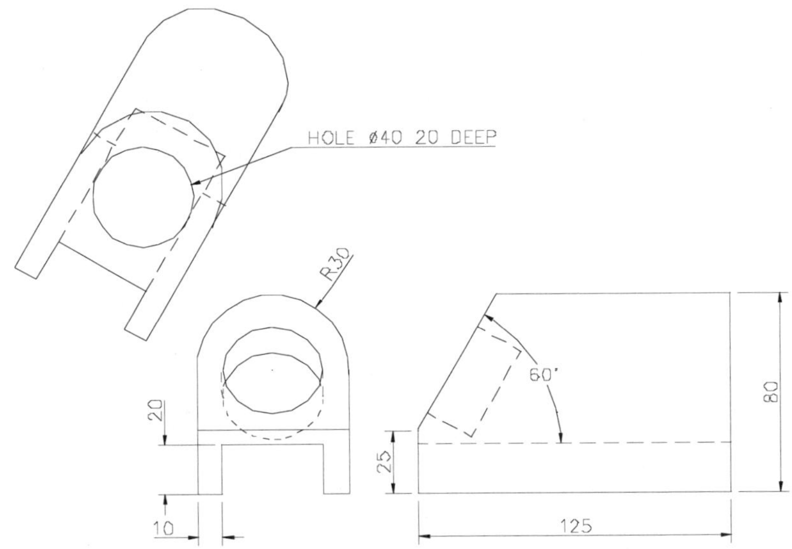

Fig. 8.17 Exercise 2

2. Construct a Designer 3D model part of the component given in Fig. 8.17 to the given dimensions. Include dimensions with the sketch profile with **adpardim**. From your 3D model produce the given orthographic views. Attempt changing dimensions in the 3D model with **adeditfeat**. Call **update** and check changes in your orthographic views.
3. Construct a Designer 3D model part to the dimensions given in the orthographic views of Fig. 8.18. When you construct the part, include dimensions in the sketch profile with **adpardim**. When the orthographic views are complete, change a dimension in the 3D

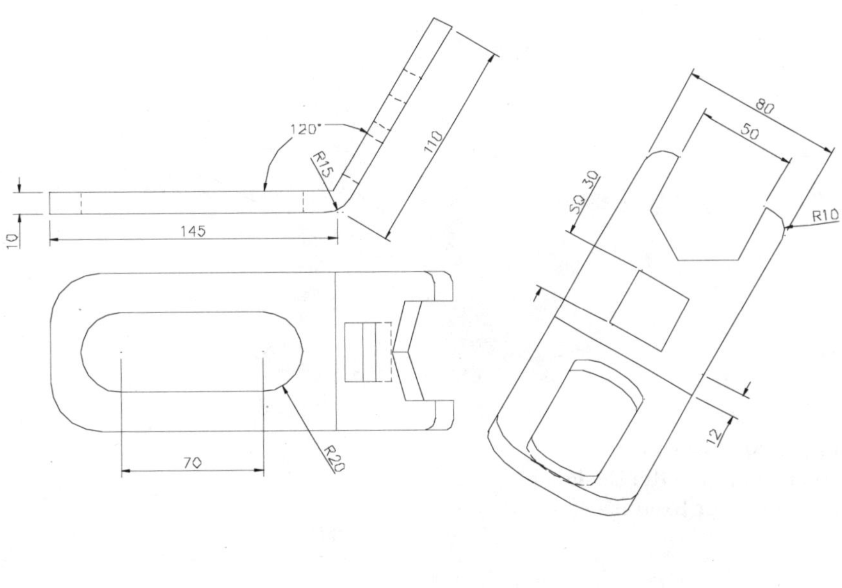

Fig. 8.18 Exercise 3

model with **adeditfeat.** Note changes in the orthographic views after **update**.

4. Figure 8.19 is a Designer orthographic projection in third-angle showing a front view in section, an end view and a plan. Stages in constructing the Designer 3D model part are shown in Fig. 8.20. Construct the part and from it the orthographic views given in Fig. 8.19. An isometric view of the model is given in Fig. 8.21.

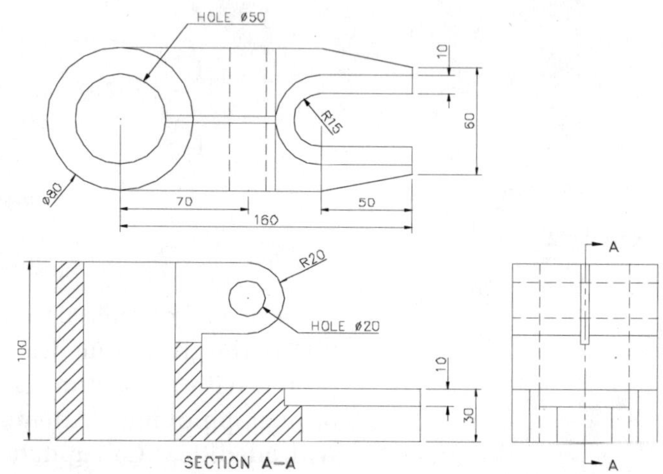

Fig. 8.19 Exercise 4

Editing dimensions in Designer drawings

Dimensions added to Designer orthographic projections with the aid of the AutoCAD command **dim** are not parametric. Designer parametric

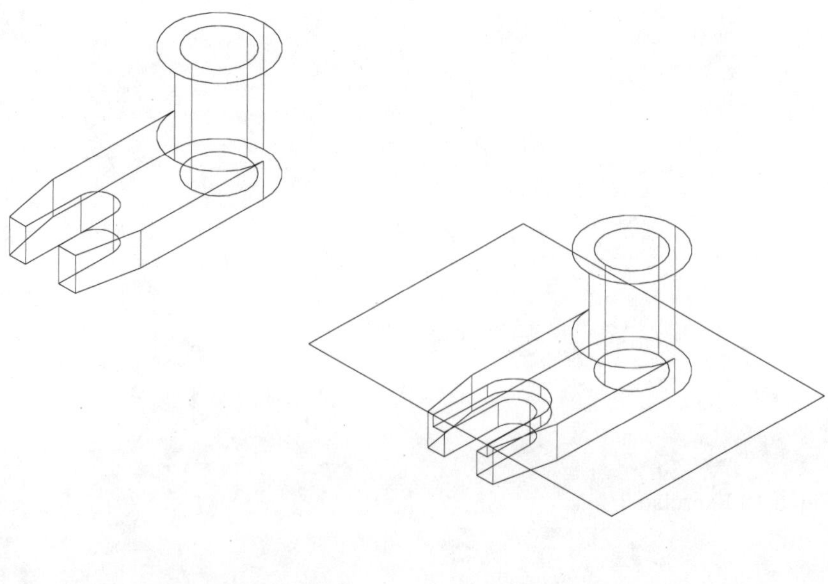

Fig. 8.20 Stages in the construction of the Designer 3D model for Exercise 4

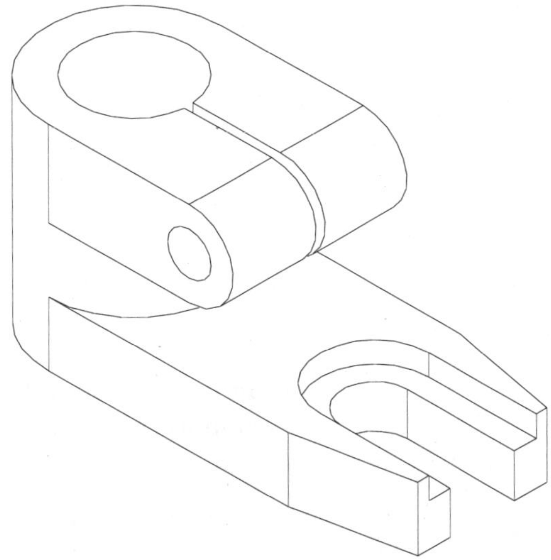

Fig. 8.21 Exercise 4. An isometric of the completed Part

dimensions can be edited with the aid of Designer commands. When so edited, the dimensions are parametric. To demonstrate the methods of editing Designer commands the simple 3D Designer model, as shown in Fig. 8.22, will be used.

The 3D model was derived from the dimensioned sketch profile, illustrated in Fig. 8.23, in which the dimensions are in numeric form.

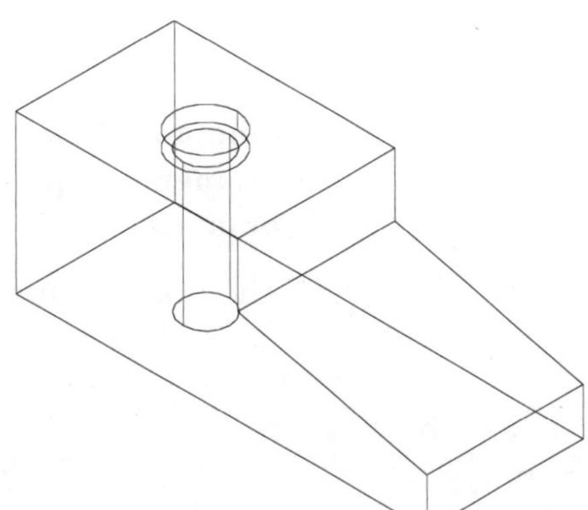

Fig. 8.22 The simple 3D model for demonstrating Designer dimension editing commands

The command *addimdsp*

The dimensions on the sketch profile can be amended to parametric dimensions, related each to the other with the aid of the Designer command **addimdsp**:

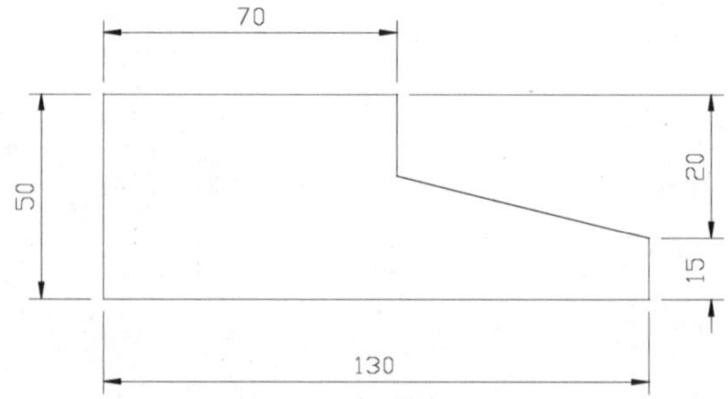

Fig. 8.23 The sketch profile for the demonstration model

Command: *enter* addimdsp *right-click*
Parameters/Equations/<Numeric>: *enter* e *right-click*
Command:

And the dimensions change to the form shown in Fig. 8.24.

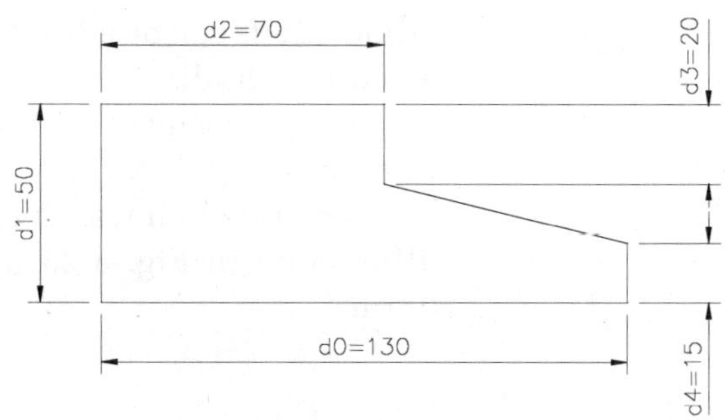

Fig. 8.24 The dimensions of the sketch profile changed to **Equation** form

Command: *enter* addimdsp *right-click*
Parameters/Equations/<Numeric>: *enter* p *right-click*
Command:

And the dimensions change to the form shown in Fig. 8.25.

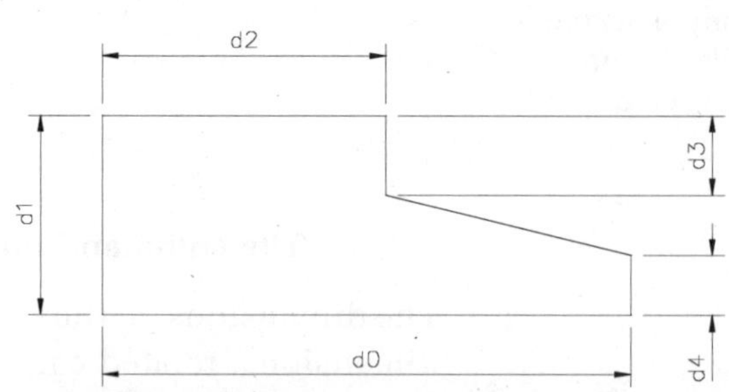

Fig. 8.25 The dimensions of the sketch profile changed to **Parametric** form

The command *adholenote*

Change the dimensions into numeric and **adview** the part to obtain the three-view orthographic projection shown in Fig. 8.26. It will be seen that the hole is not dimensioned. This can be remedied by calling the Designer command **adholenote**:

Command: *enter* adholenote *right-click*
Select arc or circle of hole feature: *pick* the circle of the hole
Location for hole note: *pick* a suitable position
Command:

And the note automatically appears in the selected position. Its sizes are based upon the entries made in the **Designer Hole** dialogue box

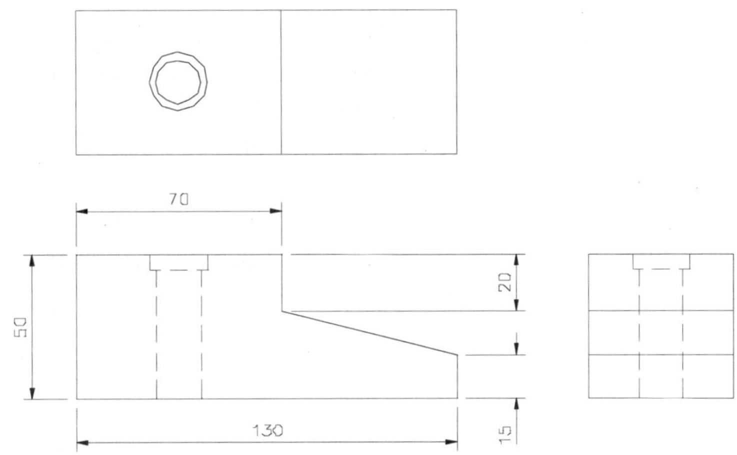

Fig. 8.26 Three orthographic views from the part with **Numeric** dimensions

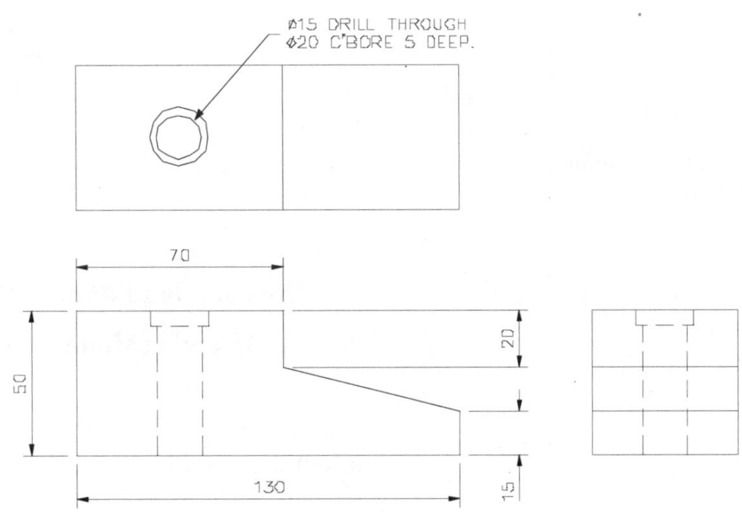

Fig. 8.27 The orthographic projection of Fig. 8.26 with the hole dimensions added with **adholenote**

when the hole was placed in the 3D model of the part as it was being constructed (Fig. 8.27).

Changing dimensions with *adeditfeat*

Go back to the original 3D model part with the aid of **admode**. Call **adeditfeat**:

Command: *enter* adeditfeat *right-click*
Sketch/<Select feature>: *pick* the 3D model part
Select dimensions to change: *pick* the 130 dimension
New value for dimensions <130>: *enter* 100 *right-click*
Select dimensions to change: *right-click*
Command:

The 3D model must now be updated as follows:

Command: *enter* adupdate *right-click*
Updating feature 20 of 20 (type: DatumOrientatedPlane)
Regenerating drawing.
Command:

And not only does the 3D model part update to the new dimension (Fig. 8.28), but so also does the orthographic drawing as can be seen when **admode** is called and the **Drawing** option accepted (Fig. 8.29).

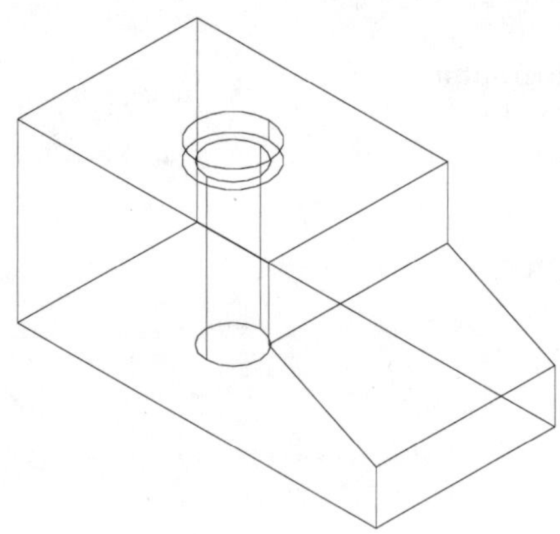

Fig. 8.28 The updated 3D model part

The command *addimatt*

While in the **Drawing Mode** of Designer, call the command **addimatt** as follows:

Command: *enter* addimatt *right-click*
Select dimensions to edit: *pick* any dimension

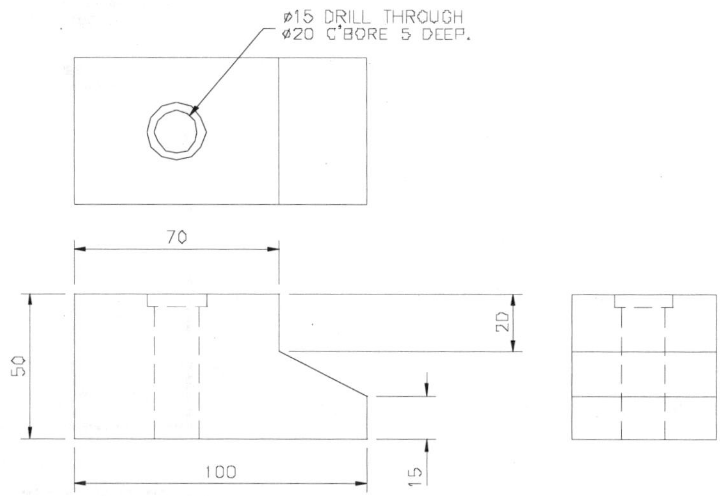

Fig. 8.29 The updated orthographic projection

The **Designer Dimension Options** dialogue box appears (Fig. 8.30) In the dialogue box, *left-click* on **Tolerance...** and the **Dimension Tolerances** dialogue box comes up on screen (Fig. 8.31). Make entries as desired and *left-click* on the **OK** button.

The **Designer Dimension Options** dialogue box reappears. *Left-click* on the **Extension Line Suppression...** button to bring up the **Extension Line Suppression** dialogue box (Fig. 8.32), in which changes can be made as required.

As can be seen from an examination of the contents of these three dialogue boxes, dimensions can take any form as set by the operator within the boxes.

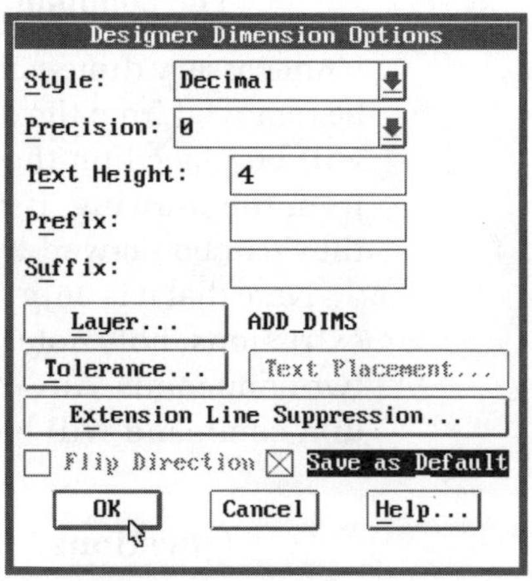

Fig. 8.30 The **Designer Dimension Option** dialogue box

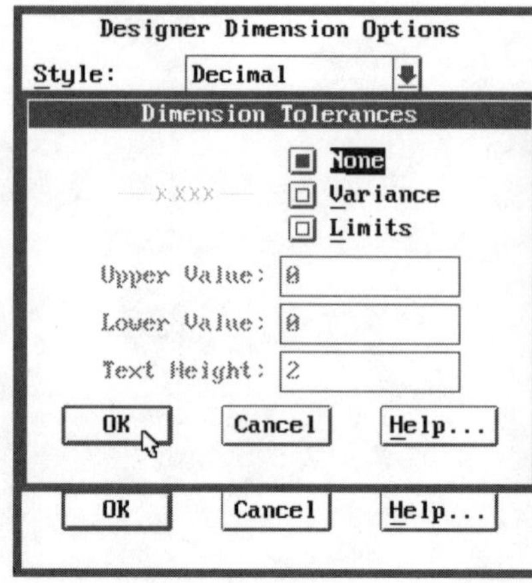

Fig. 8.31 The **Dimension Tolerances** dialogue box

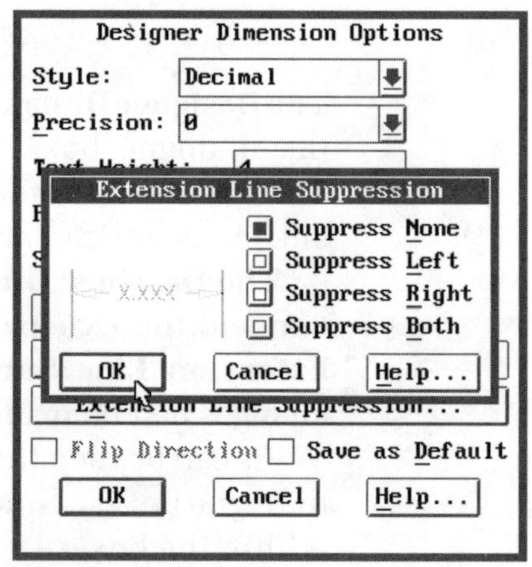

Fig. 8.32 The **Extension Line Suppression** dialogue box

The commands *adfrzdim* and *adthawdim*

Unnecessary dimensions in a Designer orthographic projection can be removed from the drawing with **adfrzdim**. The frozen dimension will be placed on the layer **ADP_FRZ** (a frozen layer) and hidden from the drawing. If required to be brought back into the drawing they can be thawed with the aid of the command **adthawdim**.

Note that it is only true Designer dimensions from sketch profiles, extrusions, hole notes, etc., that can be frozen or thawed with these two commands. Any dimensions placed with the aid of the AutoCAD **dim** command will be ignored by these commands.

Questions

1. How many types of orthographic view are possible in Designer when using the command **adview**?

2. What is meant by the term check box?
3. What is a parent view in a Designer orthographic projection?
4. What is the purpose of an auxiliary view in an orthographic projection?
5. How many types of sectional view are possible with Designer?
6. Why is it better to edit dimensions in a Designer orthographic projection with Designer commands rather than add AutoCAD dimensions to the view?
7. When is it necessary to freeze a Designer dimension?
8. It is sometimes necessary to move dimensions from one view to another in a Designer orthographic projection. Why should this be so?
9. How are the settings for Designer dimensions made?
10. What are the differences between a **Numeric**, a **Parametric** and **Equation** dimensions?

Further exercises

1. Figure 8.33 is a third-angle Designer orthographic projection which includes a redundant dimension and holes which are not dimensioned.

   Working to the given dimensions, construct a Designer 3D model from dimensioned sketch profiles. From your 3D drawing produce the given orthographic projection and the isometric view.

   Add hole dimensions and freeze the redundant dimension.

   The central part of the feature is too close to the holes. With **adeditfeat**, change the 120 dimension to 140 and check that the change has taken place in the orthographic projection.

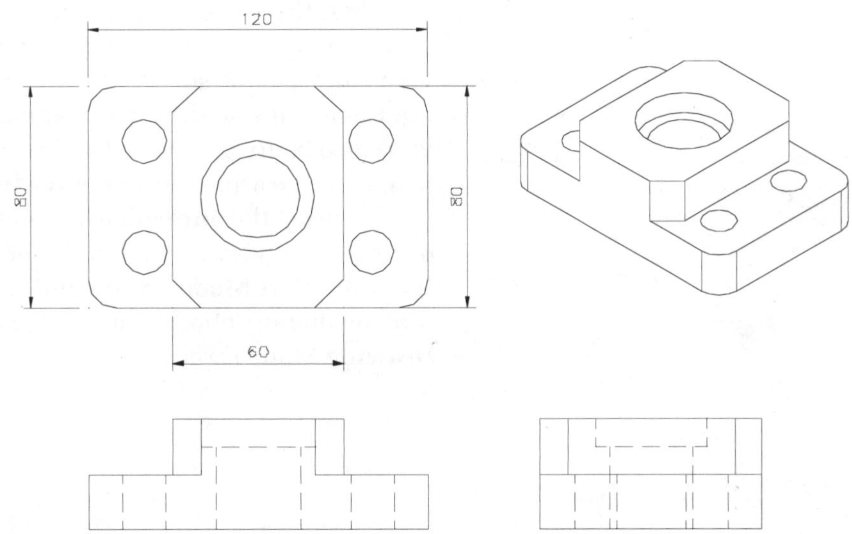

Fig. 8.33 Exercise 1

2. Figure 8.34 is a Designer third-angle orthographic projection derived from a 3D model based on a Sweep.

   Construct the sweep from a dimensioned path profile to the given dimensions. Produce. With the aid of **adeditfeat** change the 20 dimension of the sweep path to 30 and note the changes in **Drawing** screen.

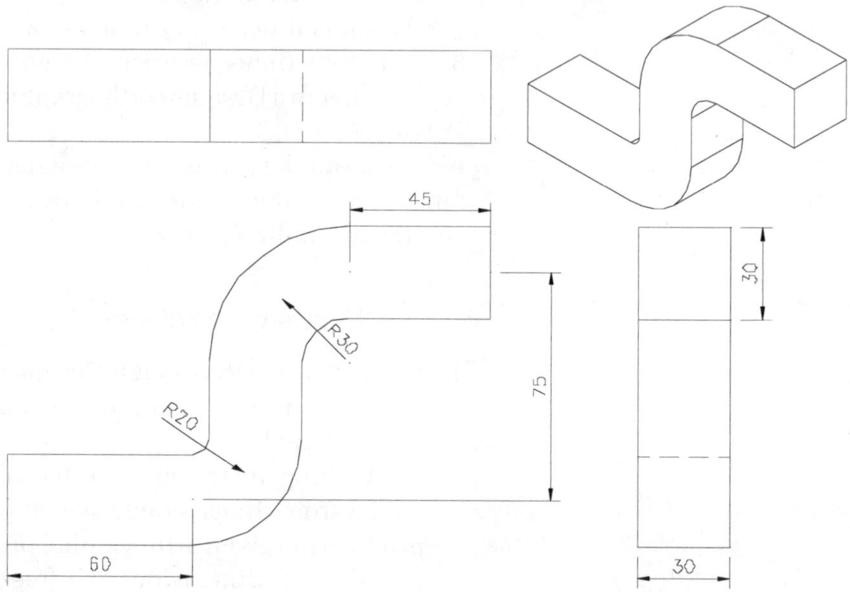

Fig. 8.34 Exercise 2

3. Figure 8.35 is a first-angle orthographic projection derived from a revolved 3D model.

   When the projection was produced, it was found that all the dimensions from the original sketch profile were on the left-hand view. In Fig. 8.35, some of the dimensions have been moved to the right-hand view with the aid of **admovedim**. Some of the dimensions were also badly positioned and were moved on the left-hand view to a better position with **admovedim**.

   Construct the **adrevolve** 3D model and from it produce the two orthographic views. Amend dimensions as shown in Fig. 8.35.

   In the **Part Mode** screen and using **adeditfeat** edit the radius dimensions and check that the changes have taken place within the **Drawing Mode** screen.

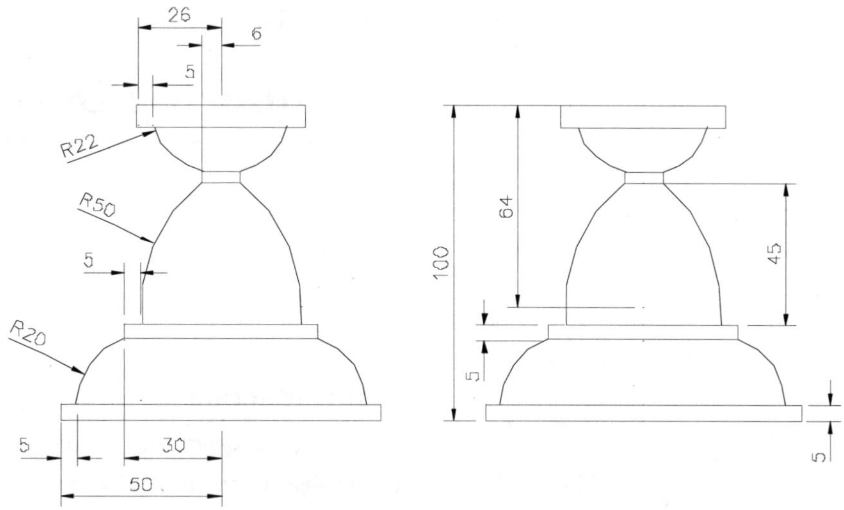

Fig. 8.35 Exercise 3

CHAPTER 9

Rendering Designer 3D models

Introduction

A newly constructed Designer 3D model cannot be rendered because it is in wireframe format with no surface meshes. Before the model can be rendered or acted upon by the AutoCAD commands **Hide** or **Shade** the wirefame must have surface meshes applied (Fig. 9.1). When the surface meshes have been formed, a 3D model can be rendered, either with the AutoCAD command system **Render** or in Autodesk **AutoVision**. Surface meshes are applied with the Designer command **admesh**.

The Designer command *admesh*

At the Command Line:

Command: *enter* admesh *right-click*
ON/OFf: *enter* on *right-click*
Select parts to mesh.
Select objects: *pick* the 3D model
Select objects: *right-click*
Allowable deviation between facets and model <0.1>: *enter* a figure *right-click*
After a period of time, depending upon the figure entered, the surface meshing lines appear on the 3D model
Command:

Notes

1. Figures 9.2 to 9.4 show the results of entering different meshing deviation figures.
2. The lower the figure the longer it takes for the meshes to form.
3. The level of the deviation figure will also affect the quality of rendering.
4. Surface meshed Designer 3D models can be acted upon by the AutoCAD commands **Hide** and **Shade**.

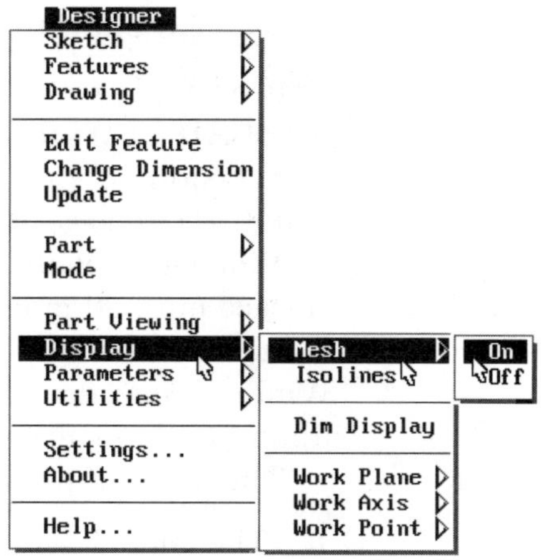

Fig. 9.1 Selecting **Mesh** from the **Designer** pull-down menu

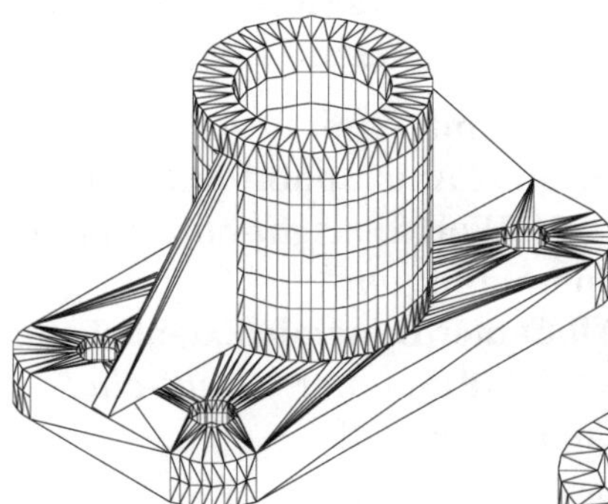

Fig. 9.2 **Admesh** of 0.1

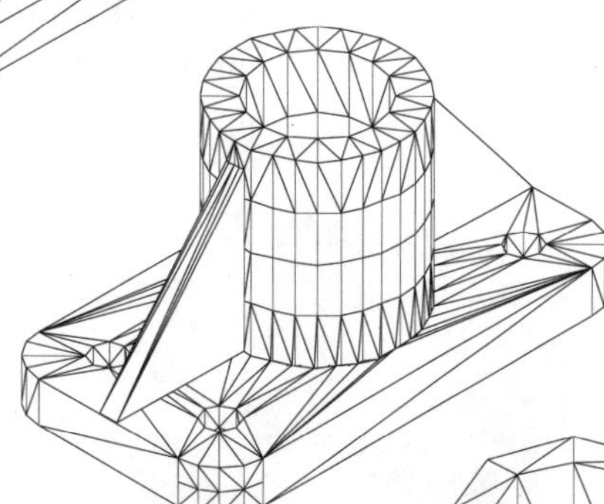

Fig. 9.3 **Admesh** of 0.5

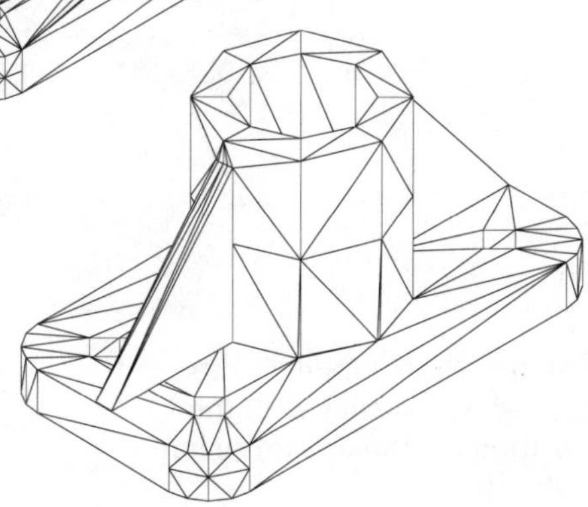

Fig.9.4 **Admesh** of 4

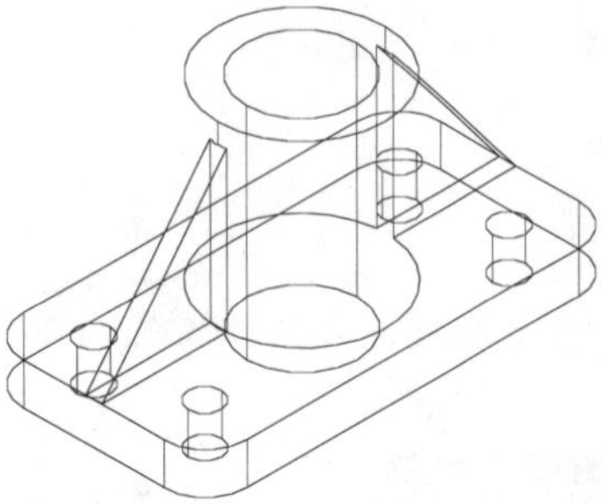

Fig. 9.5 The 3D Designer model to be rendered in AutoVision

An example of rendering in Autodesk AutoVision

This example – Figs 9.5 and 9.6 – was rendered in **AutoVision** in AutoCAD for Windows. It could just as well have been rendered in AutoVision in the DOS version of AutoCAD Release 12, or in AutoCAD Release 13 (DOS or Windows using AutoVision Release 2). When a Designer 3D model has been acted upon by **admesh**, the surface meshed model can be loaded into any of these releases. In fact, the reason why this example is being rendered in AutoCAD for Windows is to demonstrate that Designer 3D models can be worked upon in other software packages.

The order of procedure for rendering the example was:

1. The model was constructed in Designer and acted upon by **admesh** with the default derivation figure of 0.1 accepted.
2. The drawing was saved to file.
3. In AutoCAD for Windows the drawing file was loaded into the AutoCAD drawing editor.
4. The variable **ucsfollow** was set ON (1).
5. At the Command Line:

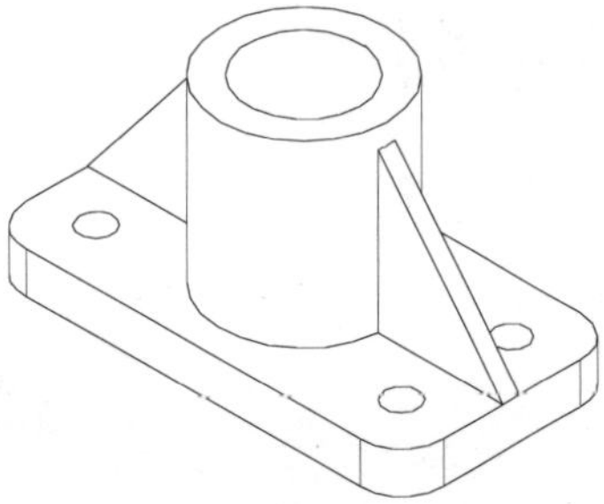

Fig. 9.6 An isometric view of the 3D model

Command: *enter* ucs *right-click*
Origin/ZAxis/3point/Entity/View/X/Y/Z/Prev/Restore/Save/Del/?/<World>: *right-click* to place the model in the **World UCS**
Command: *enter* z (Zoom) *right-click*
All/Center/Dynamic/Extents/Left/Previous/Vmax/Window/<Scale (X/XP)>: *enter* 1 *right-click*
Command:

The meshed 3D model is now in a plan view as indicated in

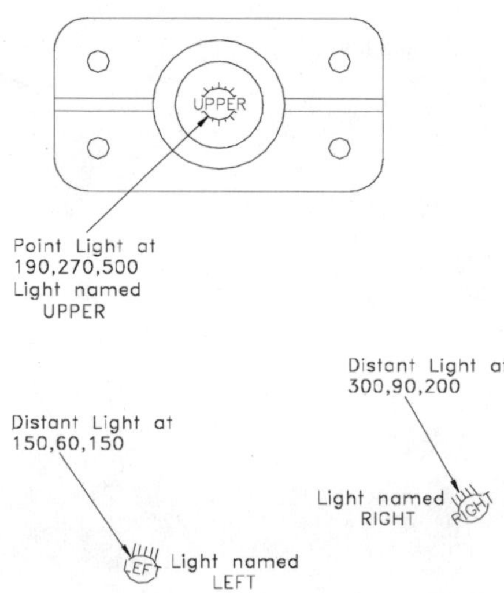

Fig. 9.7 The 3D model in its plan view together with the positions of three AutoVision lights

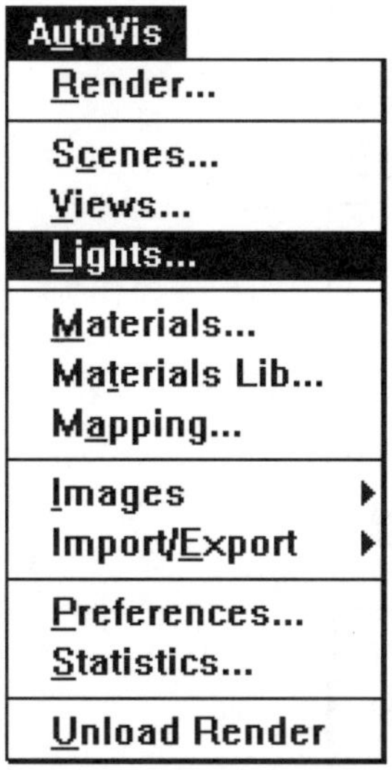

Fig. 9.8 Selecting **Lights...** from the **Autovis** pull-down menu

Fig. 9.7. If the plan is not in a suitable position, move it with the aid of the AutoCAD command **move**.

6. *Left-click* on **AutoVis** in the menu bar and again on **Lights...** in the **AutoVis** pull-down menu which appears (Fig. 9.8). In the **Lights** dialogue box which appears *left-click* on the **New...** button (Fig. 9.9).

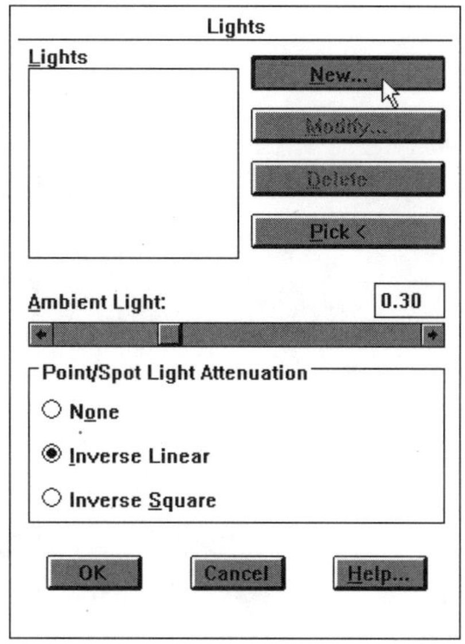

Fig. 9.9 The **Lights** dialogue box of **AutoVision**

7. In the **New Light Type** dialogue box, *left-click* on **Point Light** (Fig. 9.10). *Left-click* on the **OK** button. The **New Point Light** dialogue box appears. In this dialogue box, set the **Intensity** slider to about 100 and *left-click* on the **Modify<** button.
8. At the Command Line:

Command: _light
Enter light location <current>: *enter* .xy *right-click*
of *enter* 190,270 *right-click* or *pick* the point on screen
(need Z) *enter* 500 *right-click*
Command:

And a symbol for the point light appears in the indicated position.

9. In a similar manner place the two Distant Lights (Fig. 9.7).
10. *Left-click* on **Materials...** in the **AutoVis** pull-down menu (Fig. 9.12).
11. In the **Materials Library** dialogue box *left-click* on **BRASS GIFMAP** and also on the **Preview** button. A preview sphere of the chosen material appears in the **Preview** box (Fig. 9.13). *Left-click* on the

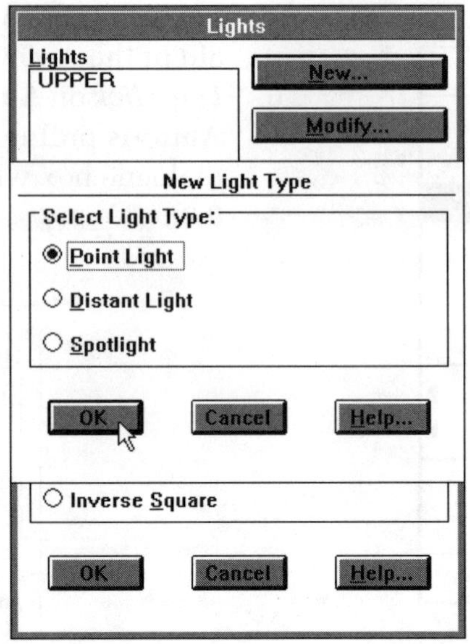

Fig. 9.10 Selecting **Point Light** from the **New Light Type** dialogue box

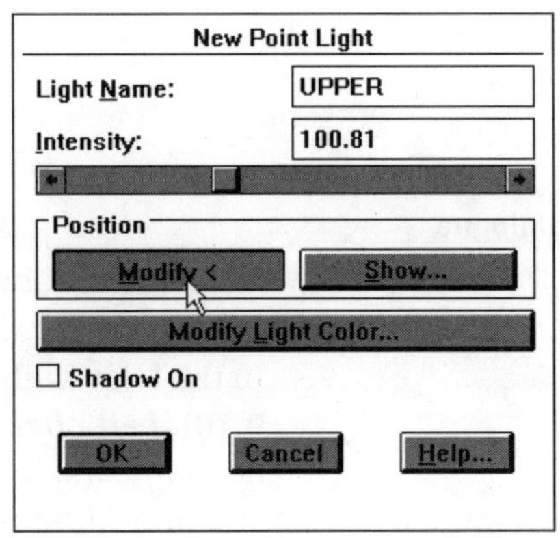

Fig. 9.11 Modifying the position of the **Point Light**

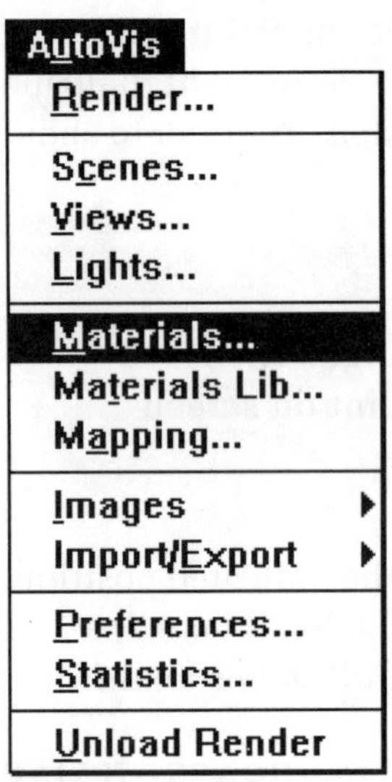

Fig. 9.12 Selecting **Materials...** from the **AutoVis** pull-down menu

Import button and the name of the chosen material appears in the **Materials List** box.

12. *Left-click* on the **OK** button and the **Materials** dialogue box appears. *Left-click* on **BRASS GIFMAP** and again on **Attach**. The Command Line requests that the feature to which the material is to be attached is selected. *Pick* the 3D model. The model is now ready to be rendered.
13. *Left-click* on **Render...** in the **AutoVis** pull-down menu. The **Render** dialogue box appears (Fig. 9.15). Accept the default settings – **AutoVision**, **Best Map**, **Smooth Shading** and **Apply Finishes** and *left-click* on the **OK** button. The model renders (Fig. 9.16).

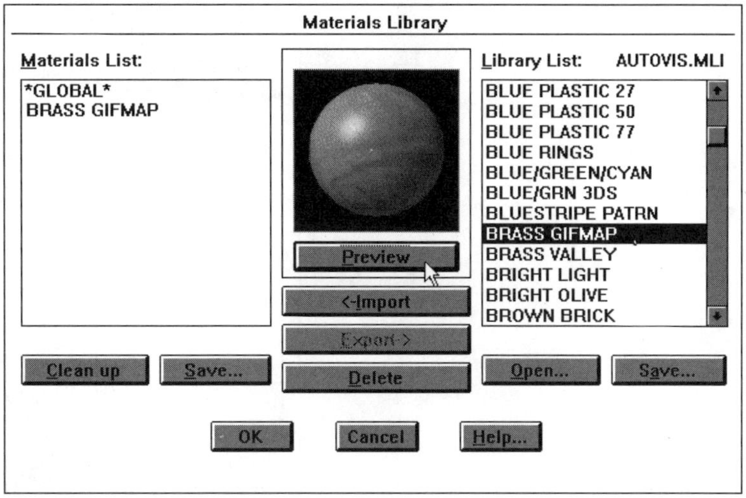

Fig. 9.13 Previewing the selected material in the **Materials Library** dialogue box

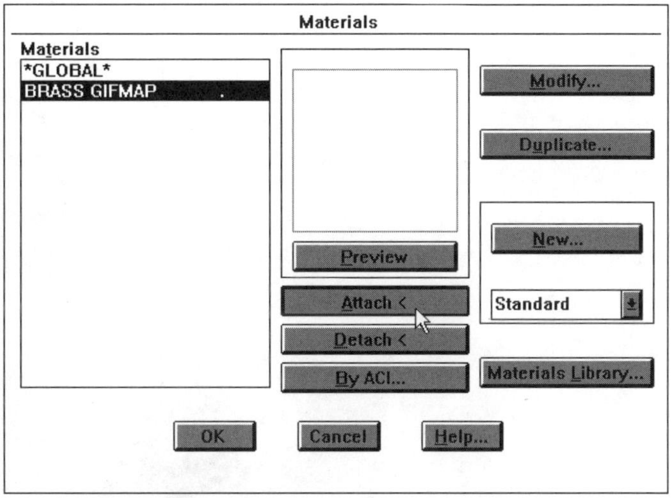

Fig. 9.14 Preparing to **Attach** a chosen material to the 3D model in the **Materials** dialogue box

Further examples of rendered Designer 3D models

Three further examples of rendered 3D models constructed in Designer are given in Figs 9.17 to 9.19. Figure 9.17 is a rendering of the model from Fig. 7.16 (page 113). Figure 9.18 is a rendering of the model from Fig. 8.9 (page 120). Figure 9.19 is a rendering of the model from Fig. 7.18 (page 114). The figures for lighting given below were the results of experimentation to obtain the best effects. In some of the lighting shadows were not included. In others, shadows were included.

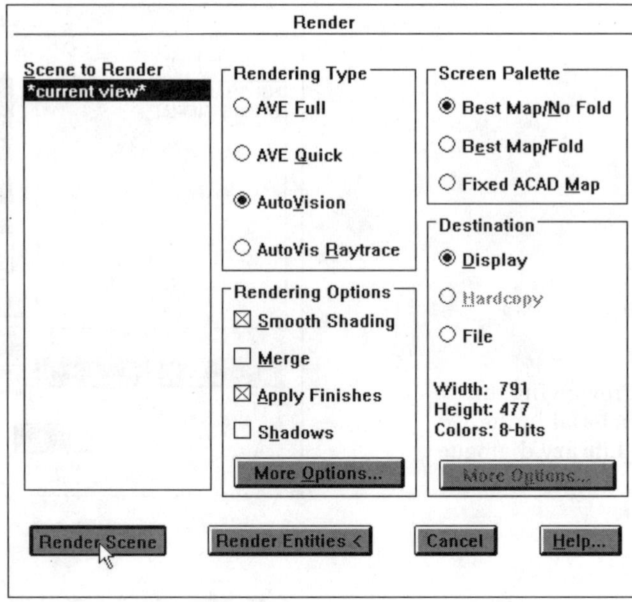

Fig. 9.15 The **Render** dialogue box with default settings

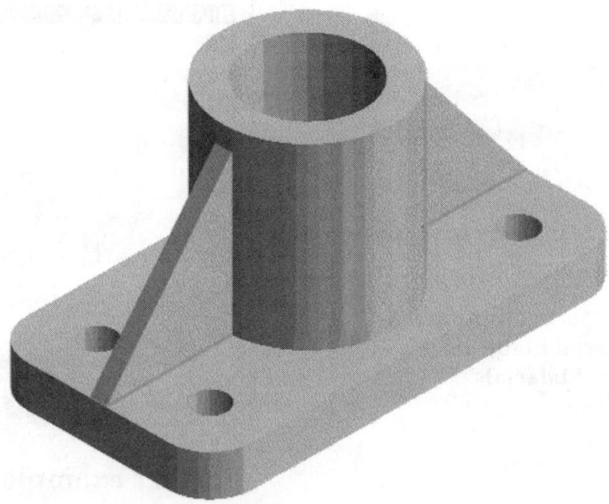

Fig. 9.16 The rendered 3D model

Rendering for Fig. 9.17

Each of the parts of this Designer 3D model had different materials attached from the AutoVision materials library as follows:

The tool ring (uppermost part): Copper
The tool body (central part): Blue plastic
The tool post (bottom part): Brass gifmap

The lighting for the rendering was as follows:

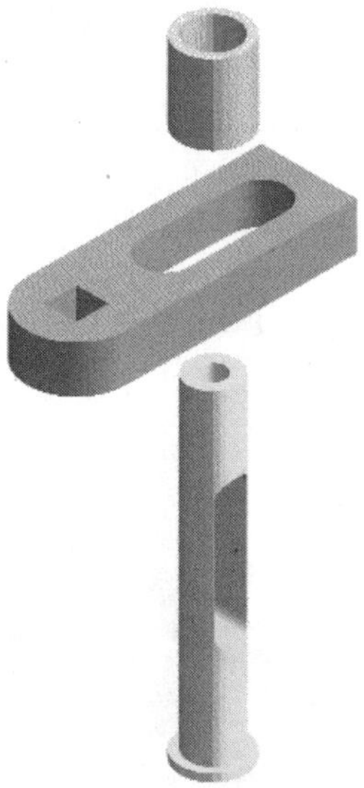

Fig. 9.17 Rendering of Fig. 7.16

UPPER:	Point light above the model. Strength approximately 100.
RIGHT:	Distant light in front of, above and to the right of the model. Strength 90.
RIGHT01	Distant light in front of, central to and to the right of the model. Strength 90.
LEFT:	Distant light in front, central to and slightly to the left of the model. Strength 50.

Rendering for Fig. 9.18

The material attached to this rendering was Copper. Lighting was similar to that for Fig. 9.18, except that there were only three lights – RIGHT01 not being included.

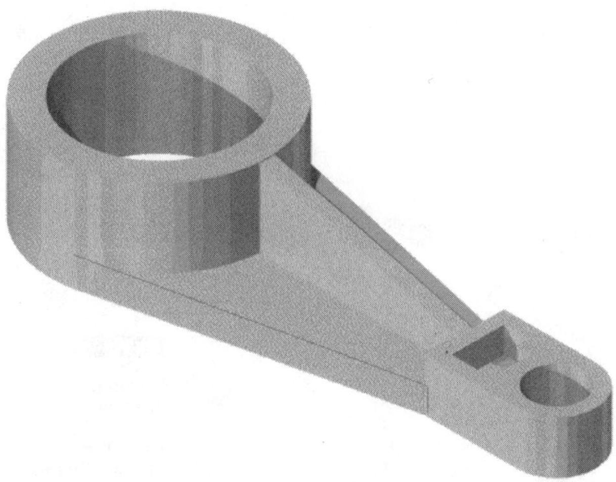

Fig. 9.18 Rendering of Fig. 8.9

Rendering for Fig. 9.19

The parts of this Designer 3D model had only two materials attached from the AutoVision materials library as follows:

The forks and the collar:	Copper
The pins:	Red plastic

The lighting for the rendering was as follows:

UPPER:	Point light above and to the right of the model. Strength about 100.
UPPER01:	Point light above and to the left of the model. Strength about 100.

RIGHT:	Distant light in front of, above and to the right of the model. Strength 100.
RIGHT01	Distant light in front of, central to and to the right of the model. Strength 80.
LEFT:	Distant light in front, central to and slightly to the left of the model. Strength 60.
LEFT01:	Distant light in front, above and to the left of the model. Strength 60.

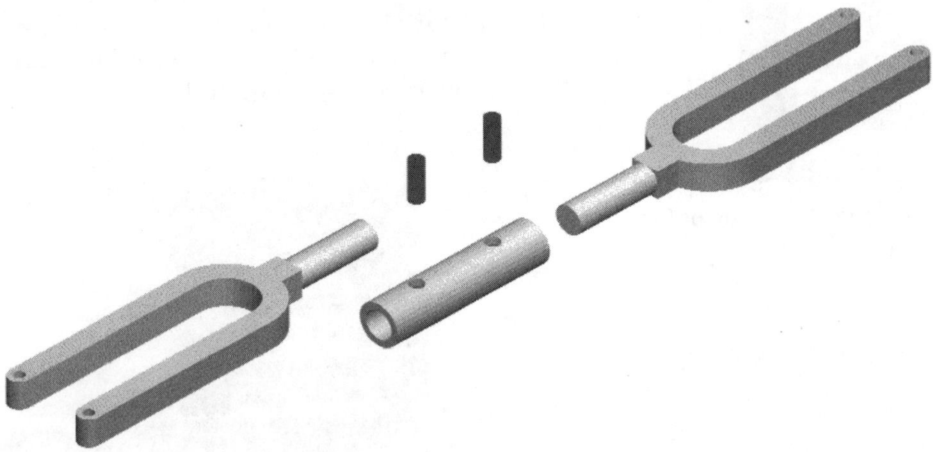

Fig. 9.19 Rendering of Fig. 7.18

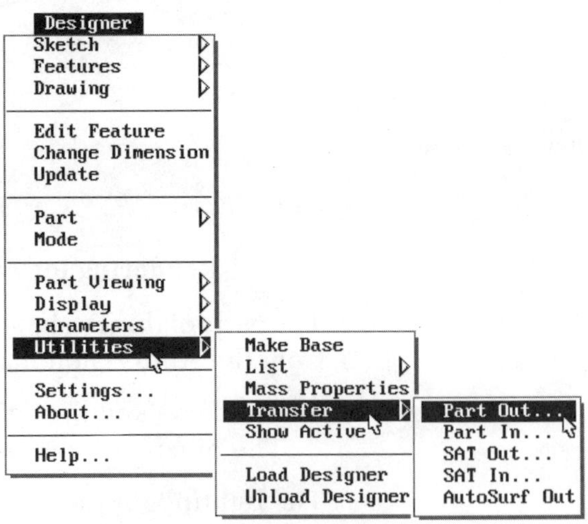

Fig. 9.20 Selecting **Part Out** from the **Designer** pull-down menu

Exporting and importing Designer files

As has already been shown in this chapter, Designer files containing 3D data, both wireframe and surface meshes, can be loaded into other AutoCAD releases. However, the Designer data will not be available unless the Designer software is already loaded into the AutoCAD being used. Despite this, and although it is not possible to load Designer into AutoCAD for Windows as has already been shown, a Designer model – and indeed a Designer orthographic projection – can be loaded into AutoCAD for Windows. However, the parametric information will not be available and some corruption will occur if editing of the Designer drawing takes place in AutoCAD for Windows.

Designer 3D models can also be loaded into Autodesk software packages such as AutoSurf and 3D Studio, and Designer 3D models can also be loaded into those CAD packages which will accept the ACIS form of data file (extension *.sat). However, as with loading Designer files into AutoCAD for Windows, all parametric details will be lost.

Designer parts can be interchanged between Designer drawings with the aid of the **Part Out...** and **Part In...** commands (Fig. 9.20). This means that if a drawing of a Part is already on file, it can be loaded into another Designer drawing, saving time in having to reconstruct the Part. When **Part Out** or **Part In** are called, the AutoCAD **Open Drawing File** dialogue appears from which a selection of the required drawing file can be made.

AME (Advanced Modelling Extension) 3D data will not load into Designer 1.

Questions

1. What is the purpose of rendering CAD constructed 3D models?
2. Can a Designer 3D model be rendered in AutoCAD for Windows?
3. Can a Designer 3D model be rendered with the **Render** command system of AutoCAD Release 12 for DOS?
4. A Designer 3D model is constructed as a wireframe. Can this then be rendered?
5. What is the purpose of the Designer command **admesh**?

Exercises

The reader is advised to reload any of 3D models constructed in answering exercises from previous chapters and render them. If AutoVision is not available, reasonably good renderings can be obtained with the aid of the AutoCAD **Render** command system. Two more advanced Designer models are given below for the reader to not only have further practise in the constructing of Designer models, but also in their rendering.

1. Figure 9.21 is a rendering of the electronic probe dimensioned in the orthographic projection (Fig. 9.22). The materials for the rendering were – Handle Blue Plastic; Probe – Gold. Construct a Designer 3D model to the dimensions given in Fig. 9.22 and render the model.

Fig. 9.21 Exercise 1. The rendering

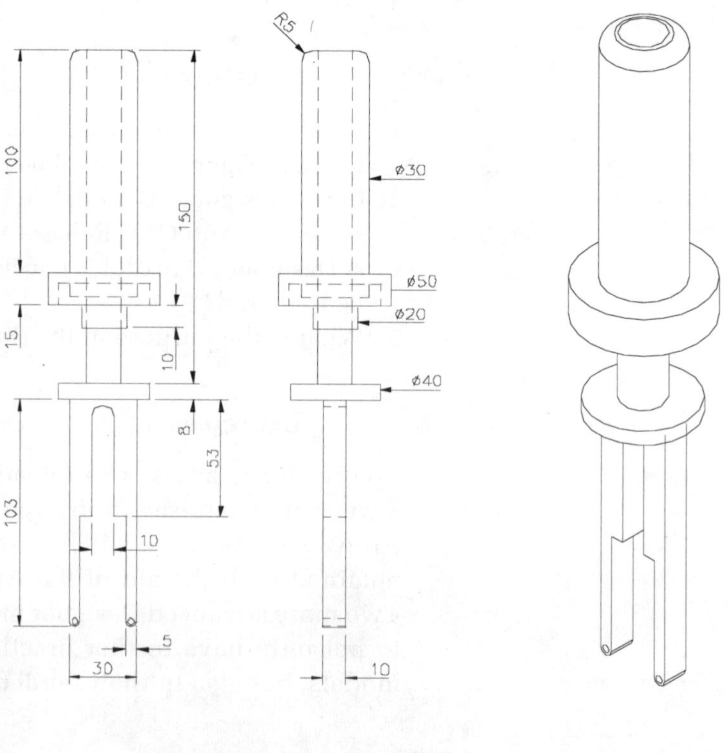

Fig. 9.22 Exercise 1. Orthographic projection and isometric view

2. Figure 9.23 is a dimensioned Designer orthographic projection of a clip. A rendering of the clip is given in Fig. 9.24 and an isometric view in Fig. 9.25.

   Construct a Designer 3D model of the clip and render your model. The rendering in Fig. 9.24 was in the material Brass Gifmap.

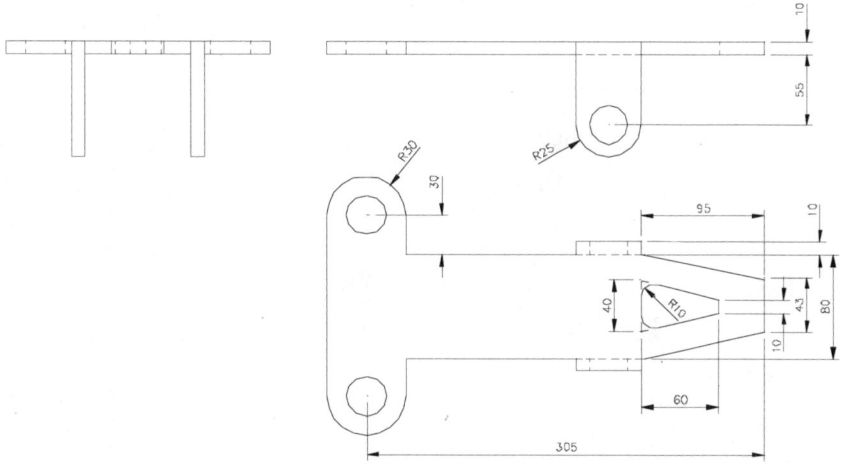

Fig. 9.23 Exercise 2. Orthographic projection

Fig. 9.24 Exercise 2. Rendering

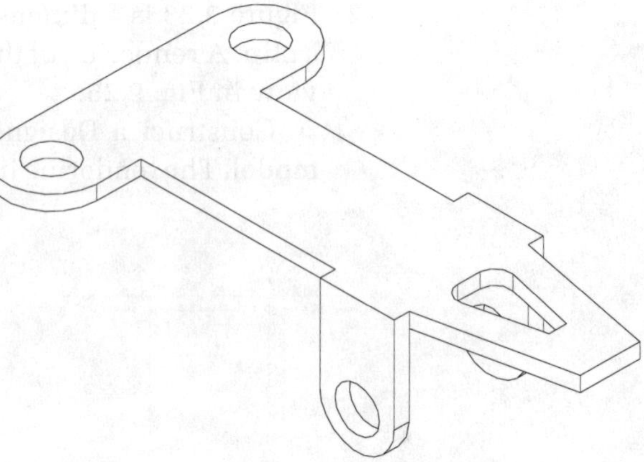

Fig. 9.25 Exercise 2. Isometric view

CHAPTER 10

Release 1.2 for AutoCAD 13

Introduction

So far in this book, we have been dealing with Autodesk Designer Release 1.1, a version which replaced Release 1.0. Designer Release 1.1 will only work in the MS-DOS version of AutoCAD Release 12.

In this chapter we will introduce Autodesk Designer Release 1.2, which works in AutoCAD Release 13 – either in the MS-DOS or in the Windows environments for that AutoCAD release. Although there are some enhancements in Designer Release 1.2 compared with Release 1.1, basically the methods of operating the software are very similar. The major difference is that in addition to being able to construct 3D models by either by *entering* Designer command at the keyboard or/and selecting them from the **Designer** pull-down menu, commands can also be selected in the Windows version of Release 13 from Designer toolbars.

Because we have been dealing with the MS-DOS version of AutoCAD Release 12 in previous chapters, all references to the use of Designer Release 1.2 will be confined to the Windows version of AutoCAD Release 13.

The AutoCAD Release 13 window with Designer 1.2 loaded

It is assumed that the Designer software files have been loaded into the computer so that on startup of AutoCAD 13, the Designer files will automatically load. The usual method of starting AutoCAD Release 13 for Windows is to *double-click* on the AutoCAD R13 icon in the Windows **Program Manager** (Fig. 10.1). After a few seconds, the AutoCAD Release 13 window appears (Fig. 10.2).

Left-click on **Designer** in the menu bar and the **Designer** pull-down menu appears (Fig. 10.2). Note its similarity to that of the pull-down menu in the DOS version of AutoCAD Release 12.

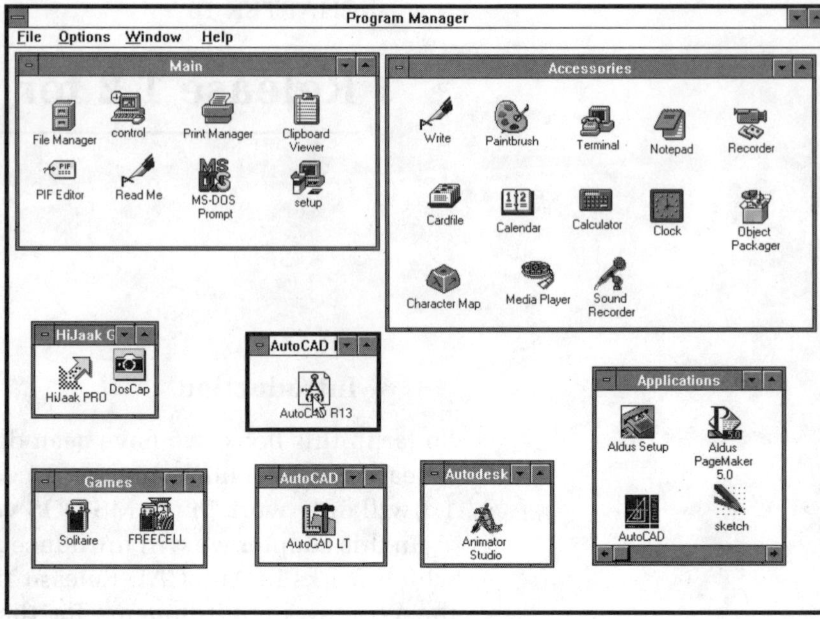

Fig. 10.1 To startup AutoCAD Release 13 for Windows *double-click* on the R13 icon in the **Program Manager**

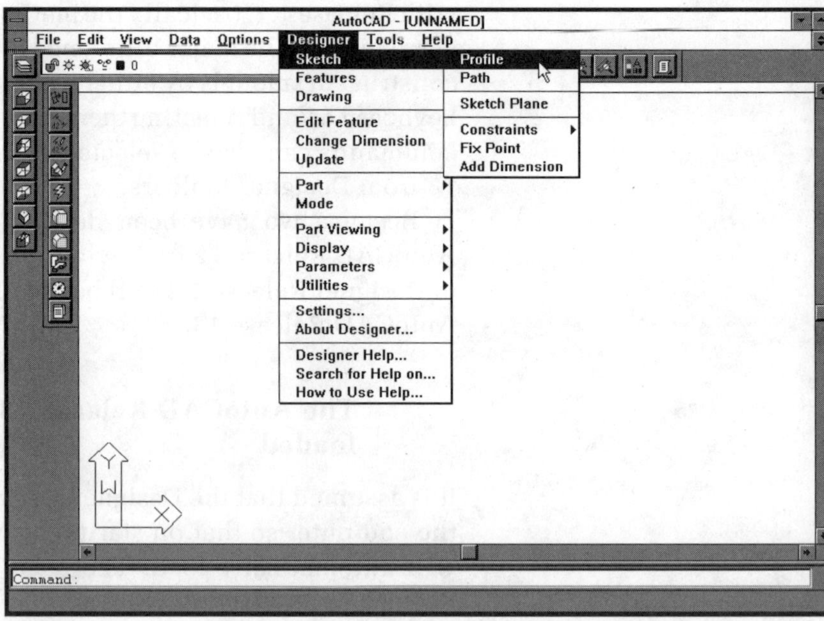

Fig. 10.2 The AutoCAD Release 13 window, showing the **Designer** pull-down menu

In addition two Designer toolbars appear. These may be as shown in Fig. 10.2 (at the left-hand side of the window), or elsewhere on the screen. These two toolbars contain icons representing the tools. (This is the term used for describing commands in AutoCAD Release 13). The names of the tools are shown in Fig. 10.3.

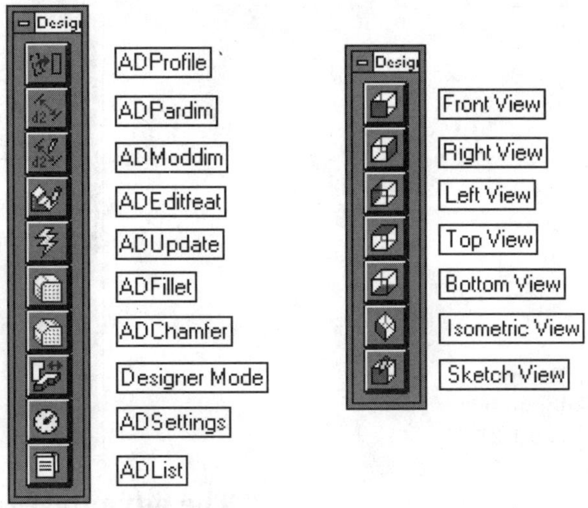

Fig. 10.3 The two Designer toolbars showing the names of the tools represented by the icons

Tool tips

If you choose to select Designer tools from the **Designer** toolbars, this is done by moving the mouse cursor onto a tool icon. As the cursor moves onto the icon a tool tip showing the tool name appears in a box. An example of choosing **adprofile** from the Designer Main toolbar is shown in Fig. 10.4. Compare this with selecting **Profile** from the **Designer** pull-down menu as shown in Fig. 10.2, or *entering* the tool name **adprofile** at the Command Line. No matter which of the three methods of calling the command (tool) is chosen, the Command Line prompts are the same, although when selecting from a toolbar or from the pull-down menu, the name appears automatically at the Command Line preceded by a dash, as in the following example:

Command:_adprofile
Select objects for sketch:

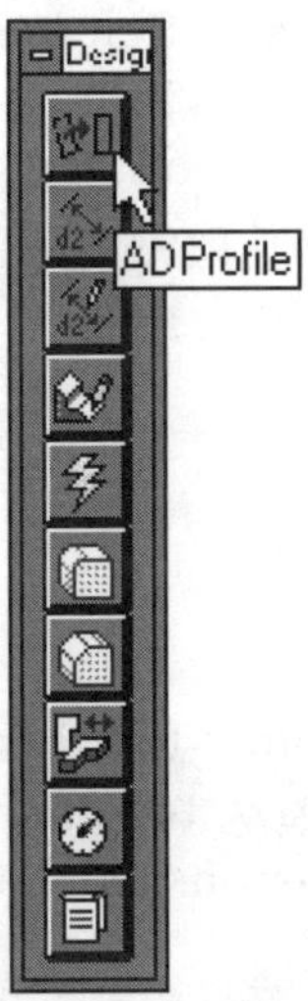

Fig. 10.4 The tool tip for **adprofile** tool from the Designer main toolbar

The Release 13 dialogue boxes

The contents of the Designer Release 1.2 dialogue boxes are similar to those in Release 1.1, although their appearance is slightly different. As an example, let us take the **Designer Extrusion** dialogue box (Fig. 10.5). Its contents are the same as shown for the Release 1.1 boxes in earlier chapters, but its appearance differs. In all the dialogue boxes, settings in check boxes and in the settings boxes are the same as for the previous release.

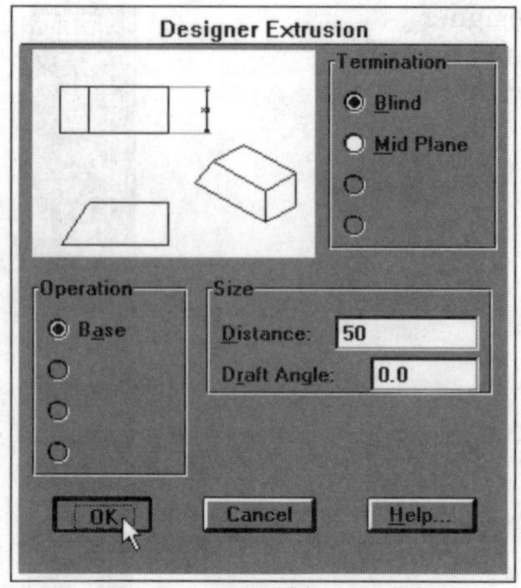

Fig. 10.5 The **Designer Extrusion** dialogue box for Designer Release 1.2

The advantages of using Release 1.2

From the above, it will be clear that if you can construct 3D models in Release 1.1 and from them produce orthographic projections, you will have no problems with the same working practices in Release 1.2. However, there is one advantage in using 1.2 in the Windows version of AutoCAD R13, which is to be able to link or embed parts of a Designer drawing into documents produced by word processor or desktop publishing packages. This will be explained in later pages.

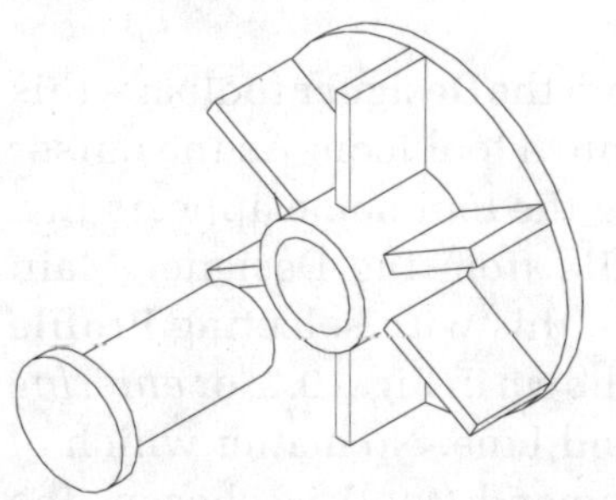

Fig. 10.6 First example. An isometric view of the model

Examples of Release 1.2 Designer drawings

First example

Figure 10.6 is a Designer isometric view of the model for this example. The stages in its construction are given below, together with a series of illustrations (Figs 10.7 to 10.15). Dimensions can be taken from the orthographic projection (Fig. 10.14).

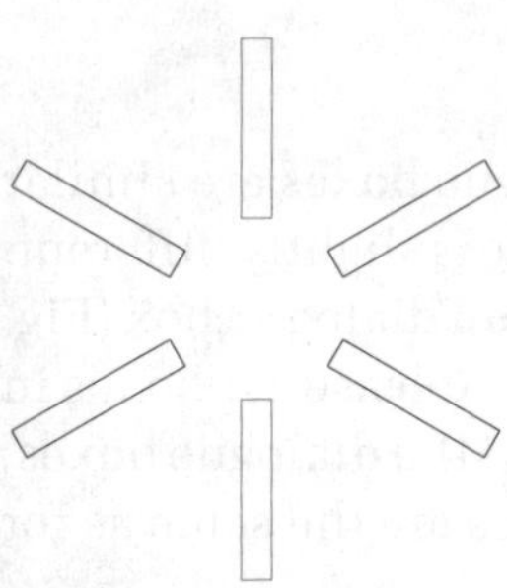

Fig. 10.7 The polar array for the six vanes

1. Commence by drawing the array for the sketch profiles for the vanes shown in Fig. 10.7 using AutoCAD command **Array (Polar)**. The sketch profiles for the Designer part which includes the vanes (Part 0) are all constructed on the same sketch plane – the WCS. However to ensure that the various parts all belong to Part 0, each of the six parts of the polar array must be separately sketch profiled and extruded with the extrusion **Join** in action. The easiest way to construct this is to construct the polar array, then call the isometric option of the **adpartview** command and **adprofile** each vane of the polar array in turn, followed by **adextrude** (**Join**) each sketch profile (50 units). This produces the 3D model (Fig. 10.8).

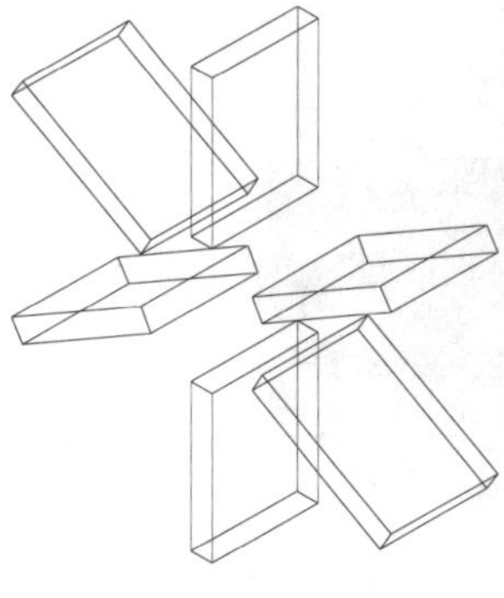

Fig. 10.8 The six vanes after **adprofile** and **adextrude**

2. Call **adpartview** and accept the default **Sketch** option. Draw a circle for the cylinder which connects the six vanes and **adprofile** the circle followed by **adextrude Join** 70 units resulting in the model (Fig. 10.9).
3. Go back to the sketch plane with the aid of **adpartview** and draw another circle for the base of Part 1. **Adprofile** and **adextrude Join** (by 10 units). Note that the **Flip** must be in the opposite direction to the first cylinder of Part 0.
4. Call **adhole** and make a **Through Drilled** hole (Fig. 10.10) through the model to complete Part 0 (Fig. 10.11).
5. With the aid of **adworkpln** place a work plane at the top of the cylinder. Offset another work plane 50 from this first work plane. Use the **Designer work plane** Parameters **Planar Parallel** and **Offset** (Fig. 10.12) for this second work plane. The two work planes are shown in Fig. 10.13.

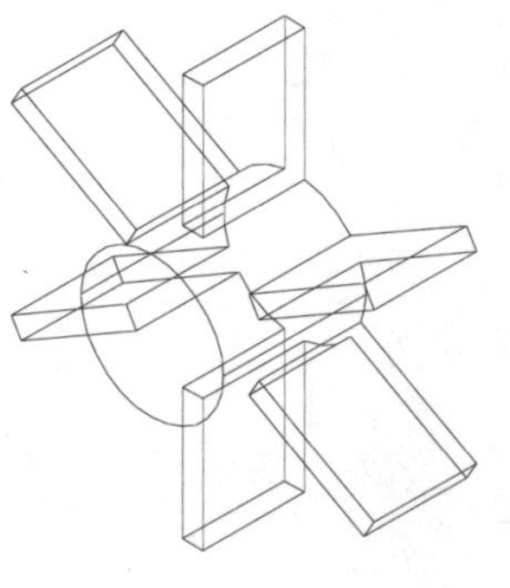

Fig. 10.9 Adding the cylinder to the vanes

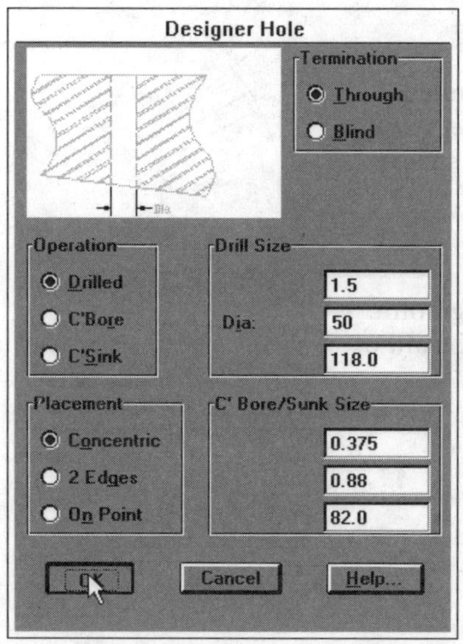

Fig. 10.10 The **Designer Hole** dialogue box

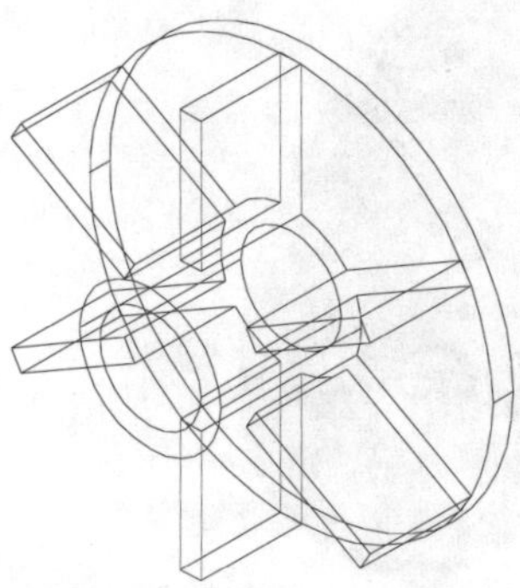

Fig. 10.11 The completed Part 0

6. With **adskpln** place the sketch plane on the **Offset** sketch plane and with **adpartview** place the sketch plane in the **Sketch** option position.
7. Call **adnewpart** to start constructing Part 1. This is constructed on two sketch planes, the first based on the **Offset** work plane, the second based at the end of the 50 diameter cylinder of Part 1 (Fig. 10.13).
8. With **adview** make up the orthographic projection (Fig. 10.14). The isometric view shown in Fig. 10.6 can also be added with **adview**.
9. Call **admesh** and add surface meshes (0.5). The meshed model can

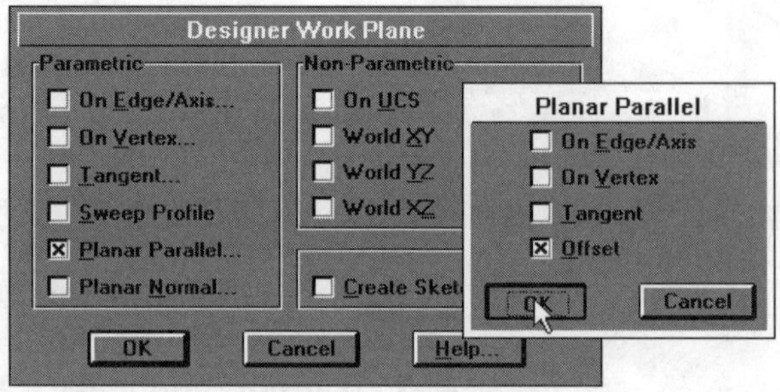

Fig. 10.12 Setting parameters for an **Offset** work plane

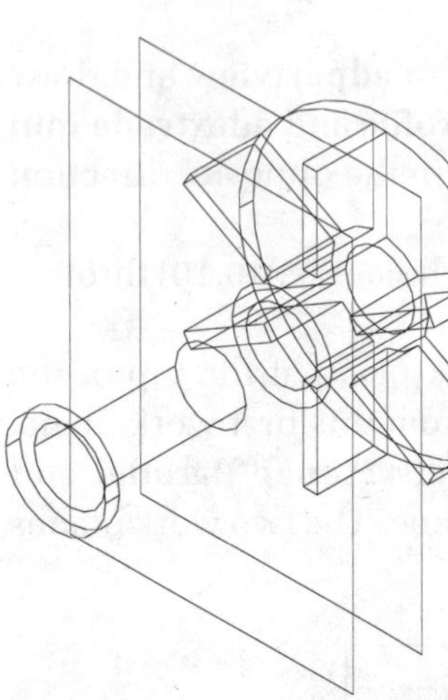

then be rendered as shown in Fig. 10.15. This rendering was made with the aid of the AutoCAD Release 13 **Render** commands.

Fig. 10.13 Part 1 included with Part 0. The **Offset** work plane is shown in this view

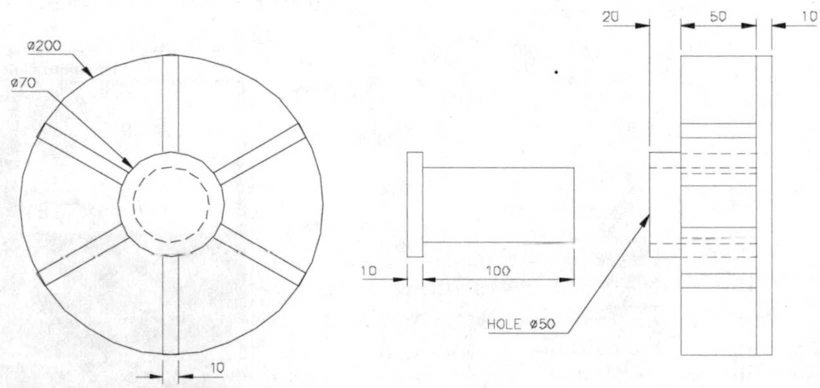

Fig., 10.14 The orthographic view obtained with the aid of **adview**

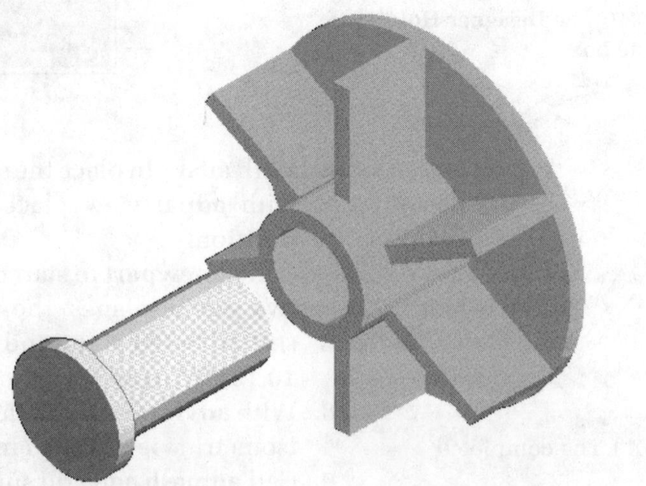

Fig. 10.15 The rendered model of the first example

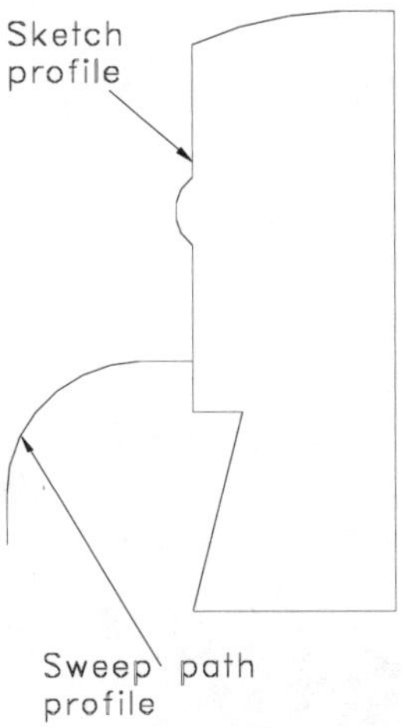

Fig. 10.16 The sketch and path profiles for the second example

Second example

This second example is included here to show the use of a Designer Sweep and a revolved solid as constructed in AutoCAD Release 13.

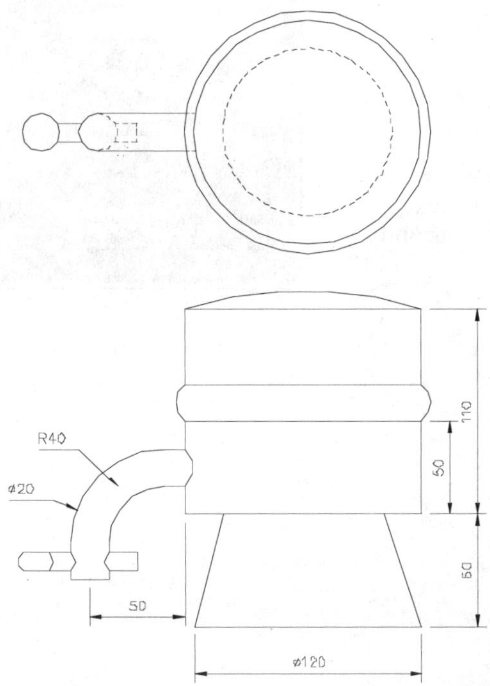

Fig. 10.17 The Designer orthographic projection of the second example

Only a few details of its construction are given, on the assumption that, by now, the reader is reasonably conversant with designer methods of construction.

The path and sketch profiles on which the construction was based are shown in Fig. 10.16. Details of dimensions are shown in Fig. 10.17. The construction was drawn in an A3 size screen (limits 600,420).

Figure 10.18 shows the work planes and work axes used in the construction.

Adrevolve with settings as shown in Fig. 10.19. Note the **Full** button shows that a 360° revolution is required.

Figure 10.20 is an AutoVision rendering of the finished model.

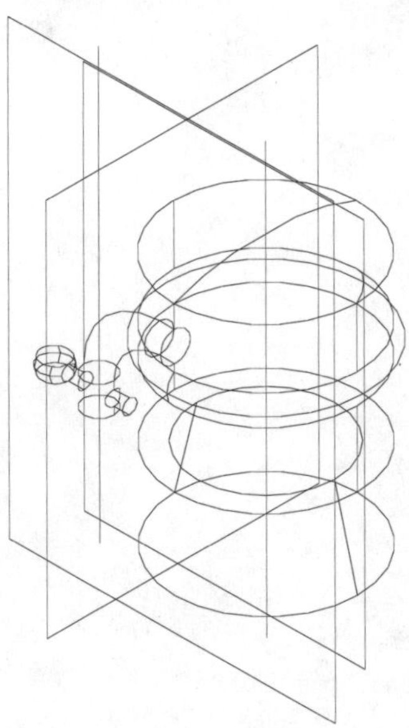

Fig. 10.18 Work planes and work axes of the example

Third example

This third example is only included here to show that it is not only engineering parts which can be constructed as solid models in Designer. Figure 10.21 is an AutoVision rendering (material white

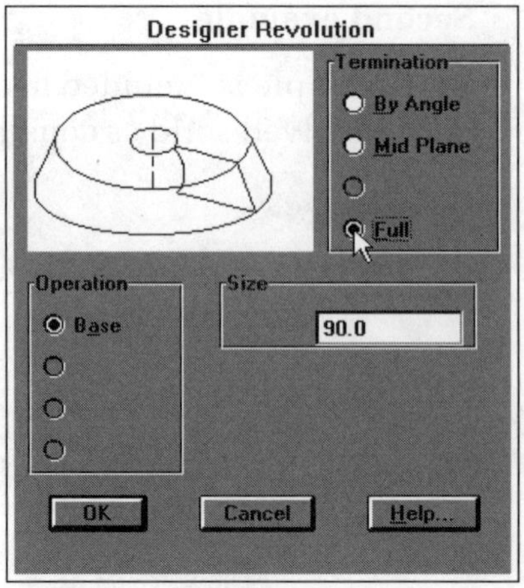

Fig. 10.19 The **Designer Revolution** dialogue box with settings for the second example

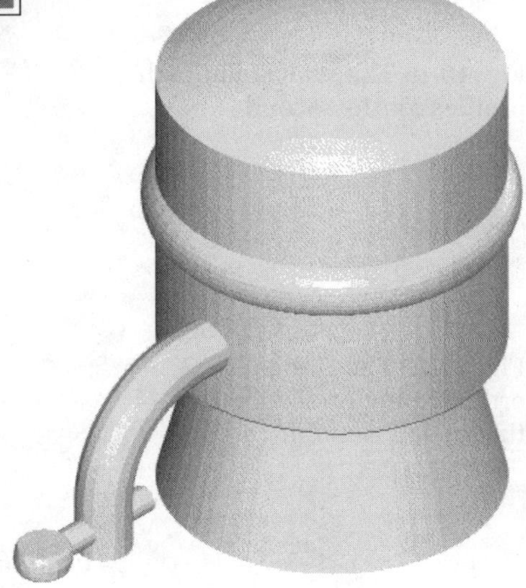

Fig. 10.20 An AutoVision rendering in cream plastic of the second example

Fig. 10.21 An AutoVision rendering of the third example

ash) of a simple garden table, the 3D model for which was constructed in Designer in AutoCAD Release 13. An **adhole** was cut into the circular top support rail using the settings shown in Fig. 10.22. Note the figure of 180 entered as the PT Angle to ensure that the base of the hole was at right angles to its sides. Figure 10.23 is the Designer two-view orthographic projection of the table.

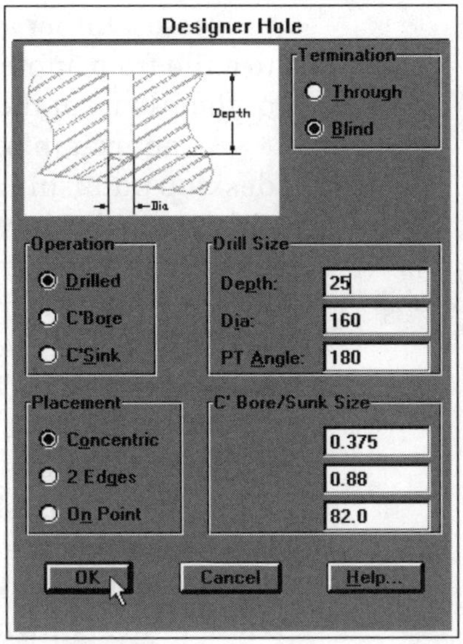

Fig. 10.22 The settings in the **Designer Hole** dialogue box for cutting the hole in the support rail for the third example

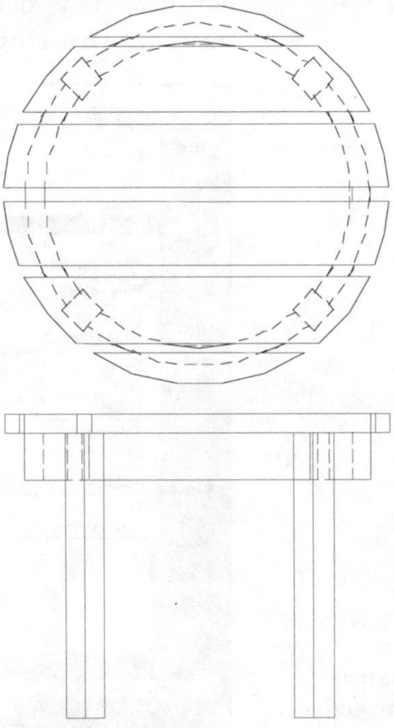

Fig. 10.23 The Designer two-view orthographic projection of the third example

Object Linking and Embedding

One big advantage of using applications which run in Windows is that graphics and text from one application can be placed into another. To a limited extent this facility can be used to place some parts of Designer drawings into manuscripts composed in applications such as desktop publishing or word-processing programs. This process is called Object Linking and Embedding. It is really two processes. Either a drawing from an AutoCAD screen can be linked to a file from another application, or it can be embedded in the data of the file from the other application.

As an example, when a drawing is linked from AutoCAD to a desktop publishing program such as Pagemaker 5.0, any subsequent changes in the drawing in AutoCAD is automatically reflected in the linked file in Pagemaker 5.0. If a drawing from AutoCAD is embedded in a file from Pagemaker 5.0, the drawing data then becomes part of the Pagemaker file data and changes subsequently made in the AutoCAD drawing do not affect the embedded drawing in Pagemaker.

Object Linking and Embedding takes place via the Windows Clipboard. Figures 10.24 to 10.26 show an example of two isometric views from a Designer orthographic projection being taken into Pagemaker via the Clipboard.

The problem with orthographic drawings in Designer is that each view is in its own Model Space viewport, within a Paper Space window. This can be seen if Model Space is called while in the Designer **Drawing** window:

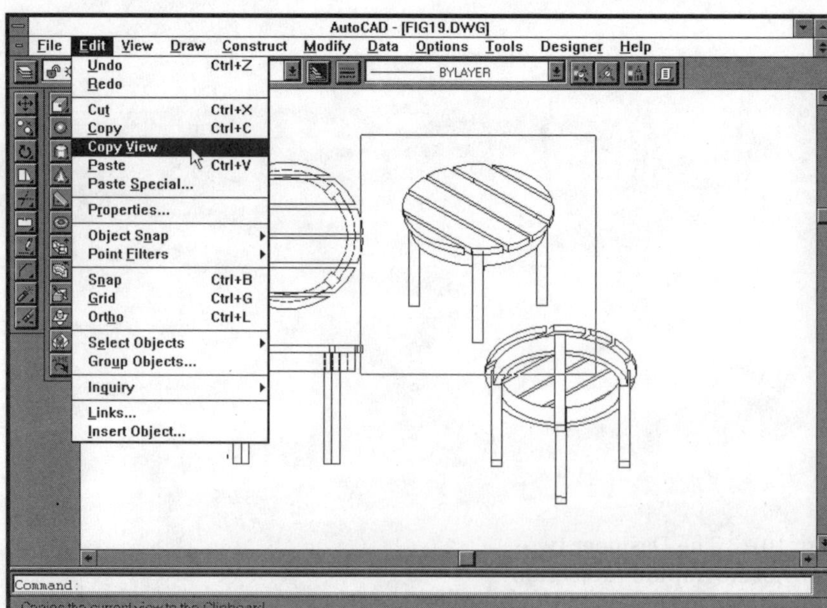

Fig. 10.24 After calling MSpace one of the MSpace viewports is seen to be active

Command: *enter* ms (MSpace) *right-click*
MSPACE
Command:

And one of the MSpace viewports will be seen as indicated in Fig. 10.24. Because this is the only viewport which is active, it is only the contents of that viewport which can be Object Linked or Embedded into another application. Check that each view is in its own MSpace viewport by moving the cursor over any view, followed by a *left-click*. It will be seen that the selected view is in its own viewport, quite distinct from any other view.

Left-click on **Edit** in the menu bar, followed by another *left-click* on **Copy View** in the **Edit** pull-down menu. The Drawing in the active MSpace viewport appears in the Clipboard. This is shown in Fig. 10.25.

If now one switches to the Pagemaker 5.0 window, by selecting **Paste Link** from the Pagemaker **Edit** pull-down menu the linked drawing can be pasted into the Pagemaker window. Figure 10.26 shows two such linked drawings from the AutoCAD Designer window shown in Figures 10.24 and 10.25.

If you wish to embed a Designer drawing into a document from another application, use the **Copy** command from the AutoCAD **Edit** menu. You will then be prompted to place a window around the drawing you wish to embed. After doing so, followed by a *right-click*, the drawing can be embedded into the other application.

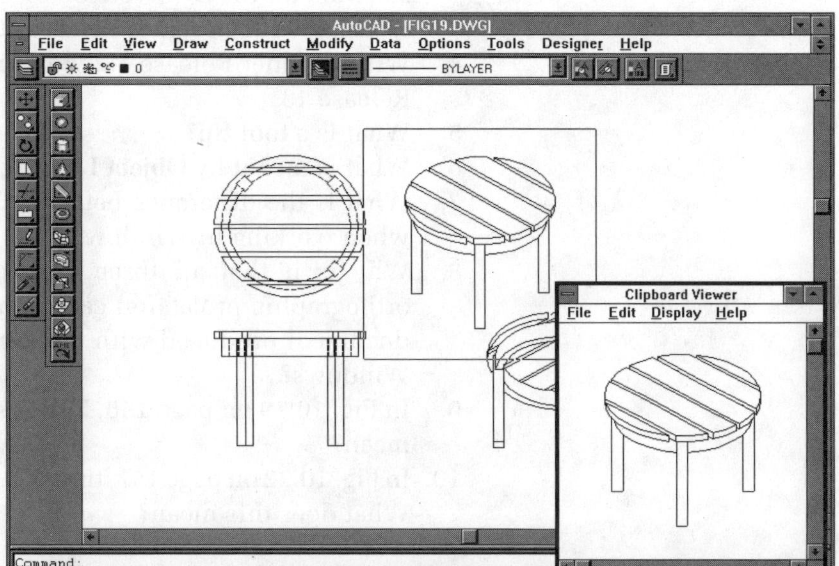

Fig. 10.25 The contents of the active viewport appear in the Windows Clipboard

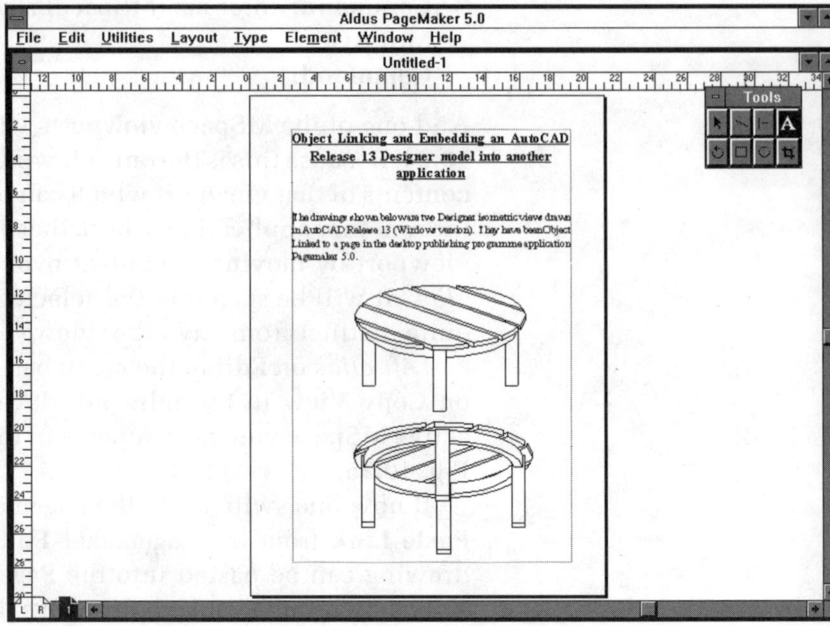

Fig. 10.26 Two of the isometric views shown in Fig. 10.23 Object Linked into a Pagemaker window

Questions

1. What is meant by the term **toolbar**?
2. What are the three methods of calling commands when working in AutoCAD Release 13?
3. Will the Designer commands which are used in Release 1.1 of the software for the DOS version of AutoCAD Release 12 work when working with Designer Release 1.2 in AutoCAD Release 13?
4. Will Designer Release 1.2 work in the DOS version of AutoCAD Release 13?
5. What is a **tool tip**?
6. What is meant by **Object Linking** when working in Windows?
7. What is the difference between Object Linking and Embedding when working in Windows?
8. Why is it that all three views of a Designer 1.2 three-view orthographic projection cannot be embedded at one time into a document produced with the **Write** word-processing package of Windows?
9. In Fig. 10.19 on page 156, **Full** is shown as active. What does this mean?
10. In Fig. 10.22 on page 157, the **PT Angle** box shows the number **180**. What does this mean?

Exercises

Only two exercises are given below. If you have AutoCAD Release 13 available on the computer at which you are working, not only can these two exercises be worked on your machine, but so also can any of the exercises taken from previous chapters.

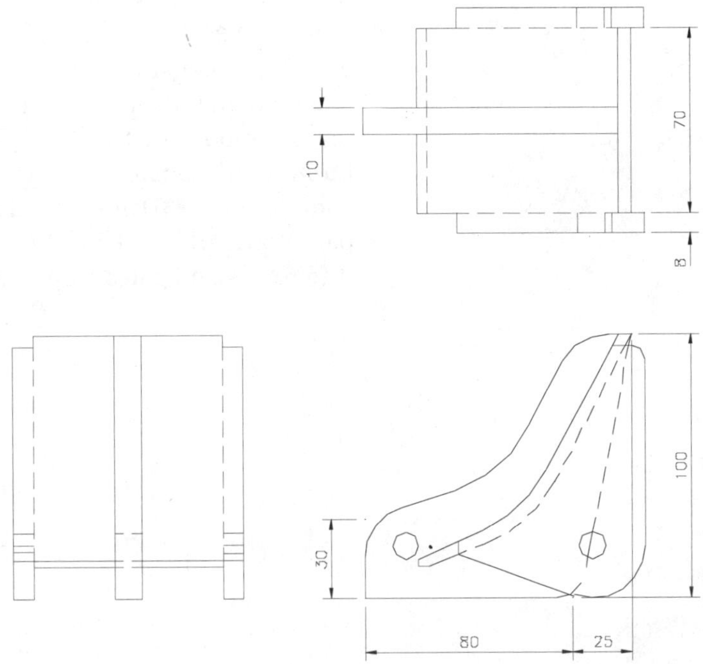

Fig. 10.27 Exercise 1. The Designer orthographic projection for the exercise

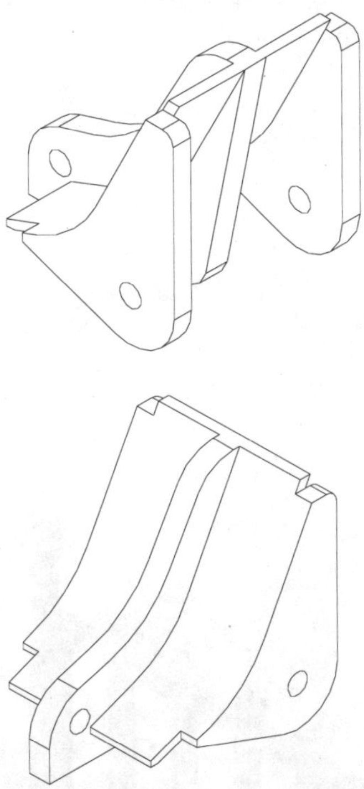

Fig. 10.28 Two Designer isometric views for Exercise 1

1. Figures 10.27 to 10.29 show details of the model of a spacing device for this exercise. Note that the orthographic projection does not

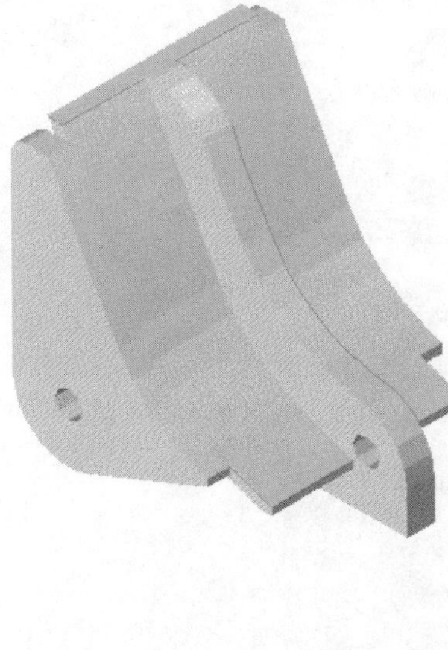

Fig. 10.29 A rendering of Exercise 1

carry many dimensions. The dimensions have been deliberately left from the views in order to avoid clustering them unnecessarily. Construct a Designer 3D model of the device. Sizes not included are left to your judgement, but should be included in the sketch profiles as they are produced in order that you can test the parametric functioning of your model. Include the orthographic projections and isometric views in your drawings.

2. Figure 10.30 is a Designer two-view orthographic projection of a gate. No dimensions are included with the drawing, sizes being left to your own judgement. Figure 10.31 is an AutoVision rendering of the 3D model of the gate. Construct a gate to a similar design. Include dimensions in your sketch profile. When you have completed the 3D model and the orthographic projection, edit sizes parametrically and produce several orthographic projections to different-sized gates from your original 3D model.

Fig. 10.30 A Designer first-angle orthographic projection of the gate

Fig. 10.31 A rendering of Exercise 2

CHAPTER 11

Designer commands

Introduction

Throughout this book all of the Designer commands have been 'called' by entering the full command name at the Command Line from the keyboard. The alternative of selecting the command names from the **Designer** pull-down menu has been illustrated for both Designer in AutoCAD Release 12 (DOS) and in AutoCAD Release 13 (Windows). A further method when working in AutoCAD Release 13 is by the selection of tool icons from the Designer toolbars. In practice the operator will choose the method most suited to his/her ways of working. For example, some operators may wish to enter some command names at the keyboard and select some from pull-down menus and perhaps use the tool icons at times.

The *acad.pgp* file

My own method of working is to amend the *acad.pgp* file found in the acad/support directory (Release 12 DOS) or in the acadr13\common\support directory (Release 13). Entries in this directory allow abbreviations for command names to be used in place of the full command name. My *acad.pgp* files include the following abbreviations for Designer command names:

AC ***ADCHAMFER**
AE ***ADEXTRUDE**
AH ***ADHOLE**
AF ***ADFILLET**
AP ***APROFILE**
APV ***ADPARTVIEW**
AR ***ADREVOLVE**
AV ***ADREVOLVE**
AW ***ADWORKPLN**

This means that I can call the Designer command **adview** by *entering* **av** at the Command Line, or **ae** for **adextrude** and so on. I also occasionally select command names from the **Designer** pull-down menu and if working in Release 13 (Windows) sometimes select tool icons from **Designer** toolbars.

Problems can arise if Designer command name abbreviations are included in the *acad.pgp* file. Each extra name uses some memory, so if memory on the computer in use is tight, it is best to avoid adding to *acad.pgp*. This is particularly so when working in the Windows version of Release 13 because a minimum of 16 Mbytes of memory is required for running AutoCAD with Designer.

Another problem is that if other operators use the computer at which you work with AutoCAD, you should not amend the *acad.pgp* file. Doing so may cause difficulties for others using the computer.

The Designer command *adworkpln*

I am starting with this command because you cannot expect to be able to construct Designer 3D models efficiently until you understand the various settings possible when using the command. A number of examples of setting work planes have already been included in previous chapters. Six further examples are included here.

When the command is called, the **Designer work plane** dialogue box automatically appears. There are a large number of different settings possible in this dialogue box and in its associated dialogue boxes.

On Edge/Axis and On Edge/Axis

When **adworkpln** is called in the **Designer work plane** dialogue box, *left-click* in the **On Edge/Axis...** check box and when the **On Edge/ Axis** dialogue box appears *left-click* in the **On Edge/Axis** check box in this secondary dialogue box. Then *left-click* on the **OK** button of both dialogue boxes.

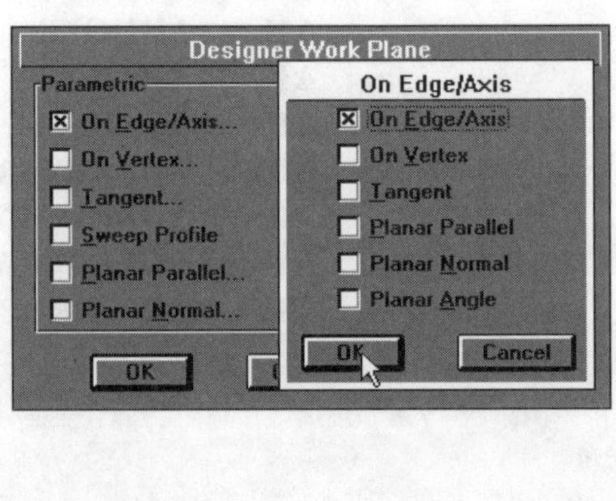

Fig. 11.1 **On Edge/Axis** and **On/Edge Axis...** in the **Designer work plane** dialogue box

At the Command Line, the default prompt will be:

<Select work axis or straight edge>:

On the model which has been constructed (Fig. 11.2) *left-click* on the edges shown. The work plane appears on screen. The right-hand drawing of Fig. 11.2 shows two holes cut by then selecting the work plane as the new sketch plane.

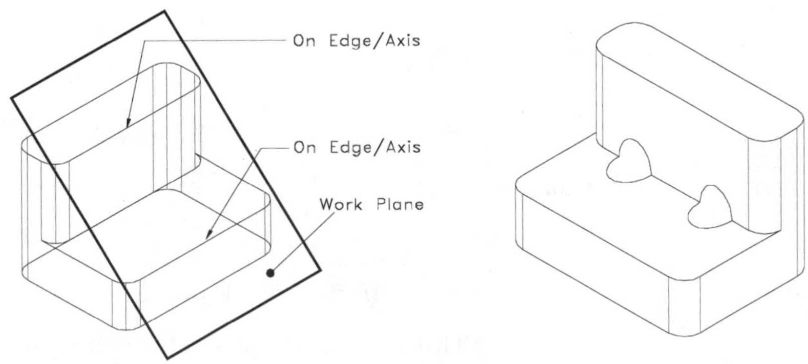

Fig. 11.2 An example of **On Edge/Axis** and **On Edge/Axis**

On Edge/Axis and Tangent

This second example (Fig. 11.4) utilises the **On Edge/Axis** and **Tangent** combination. When these two settings are made in the **Designer work plane** dialogue box (Fig. 11.3), the two Command Line options are:

Select cylindrical face:
<Select work axis or straight edge>:

Upon responding by *picking* the cylindrical face and the straight edge as shown in Fig. 11.4, the work plane appears as shown. The sloping square hole in the end of the 3D model produced by setting the sketch plane to the work plane is shown in the right-hand drawing of Fig. 11.4.

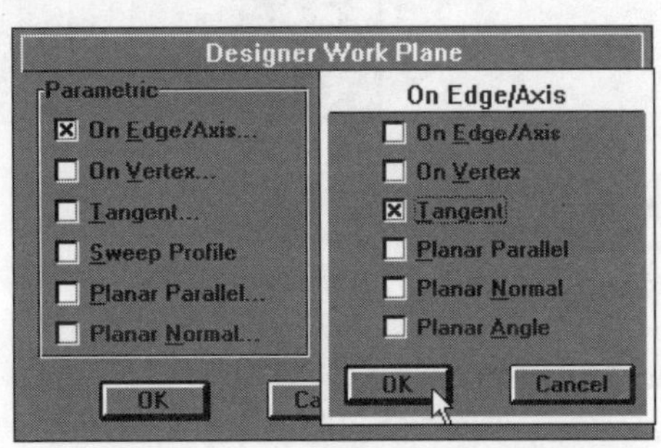

Fig. 11.3 **On Edge/Axis** and **Tangent** in the **Designer work plane** dialogue box

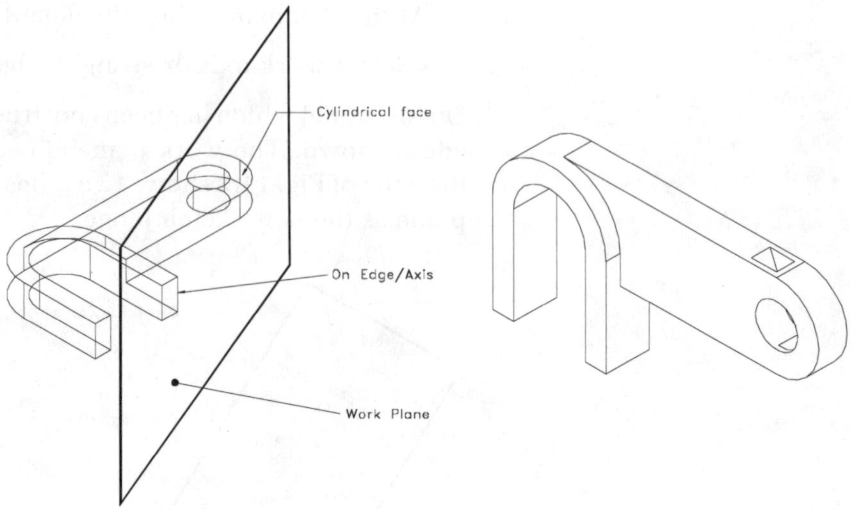

Fig. 11.4 An example of **On Edge Axis** and **Tangent**

Offset work plane

This example required the setting up of two work planes, the first in one pair of dialogue boxes, the second in another pair. Figure 11.5 shows the settings in the two **Designer work plane** dialogue boxes for this example.

Figure 11.6 shows the **offset** work plane in position. The right-hand drawing of Fig. 11.6 shows the keyway cut in the spindle after setting the sketch plane to the offset work plane and extruding a rectangular sketch profile from the sketch plane.

The options at the Command Line for the settings in the first of the two **Designer work plane** dialogue boxes are:

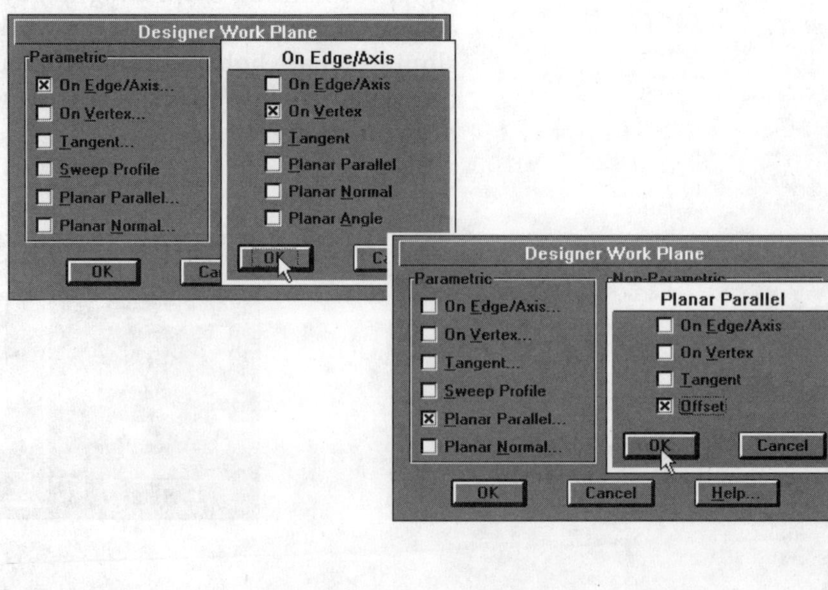

Fig. 11.5 Setting up an **Offset** work plane

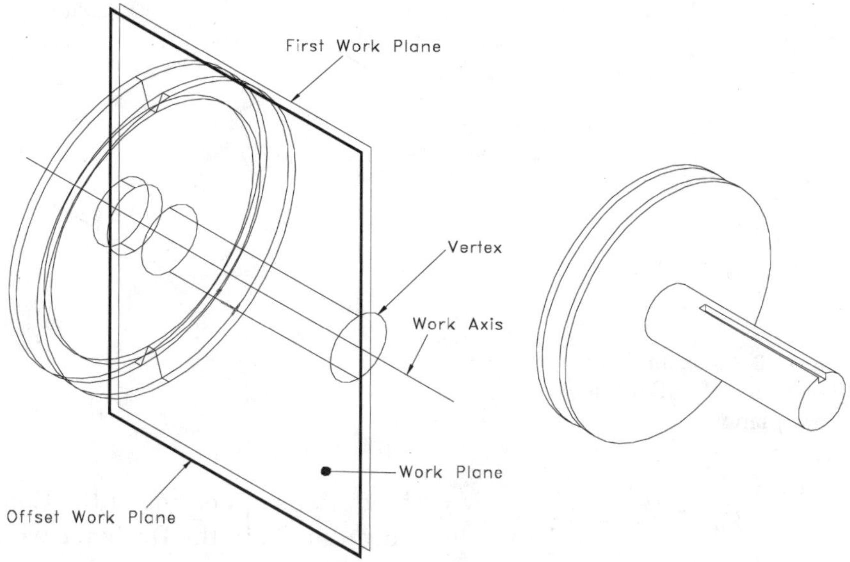

Fig. 11.6 An example of **Offset** work plane

<Select work axis or straight edge>:
Select vertex:

And in the second dialogue box:

Select work plane or planar face:
Offset <1>: *enter* require offset figure
Flip/<Accept>: according to the direction of the arrows appearing at the corners of the offset work plane

On Vertex and Planar Parallel

Figure 11.7 shows the settings in the **Designer work plane** dialogue box for placing a parallel work plane at the vertex of a planar face. Figure 11.8 shows the work plane appearing at the top of the 3D model and, to the right of this, the resulting 3D model after using the work plane as a sketch plane and using **adextrude (Cut)** to cut a groove in the upper part of the model.

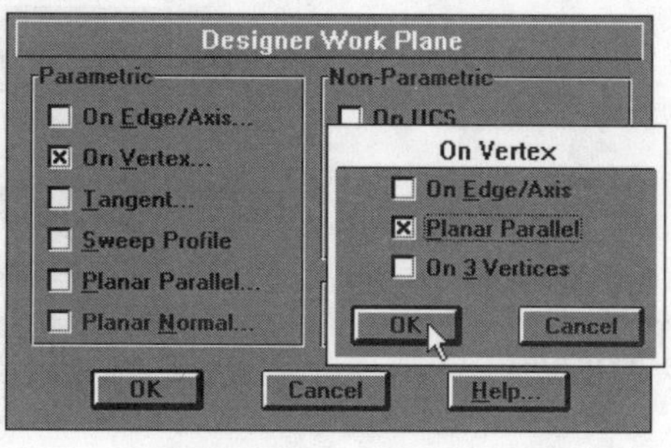

Fig. 11.7 An example of **On Vertex** and **Planar Parallel**

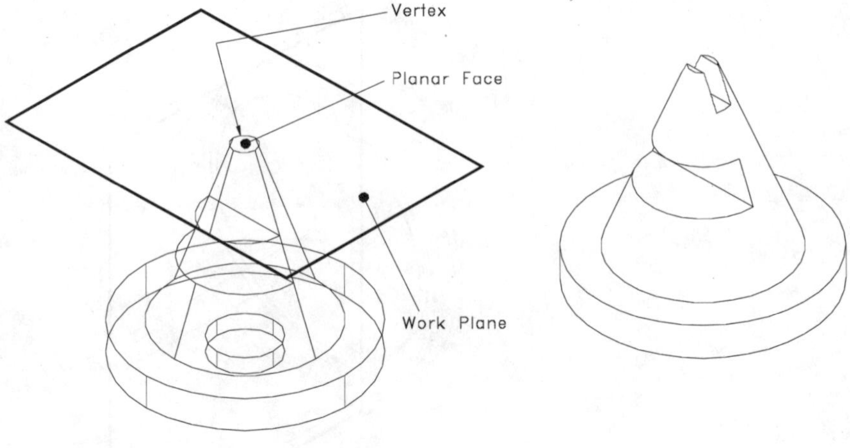

Fig. 11.8 An example of **Vertex** and **Parallel Plane** work plane

The options appearing at the Command Line when the settings have been made in the **Designer work plane** dialogue box are:

Select vertex:
Select parallel plane:

When the vertex and parallel plane have been *picked* as indicated in Fig. 11.8, the work plane appears.

On Edge/Axis and Planar Angle

Figure 11.9 shows the settings in the **Designer work plane** dialogue box for this example and Fig. 11.10 the results of using the work plane produced as a sketch plane to add a leg at an angle to an existing leg in a 3D model. In order to add the second leg a second work plane was added with the aid of the **Offset** settings shown in previous examples.

When the necessary check boxes have been set in the dialogue boxes, the default Command Line options are:

<Select work axis or straight edge>: *pick*
<Select work plane or planar face>: *pick*

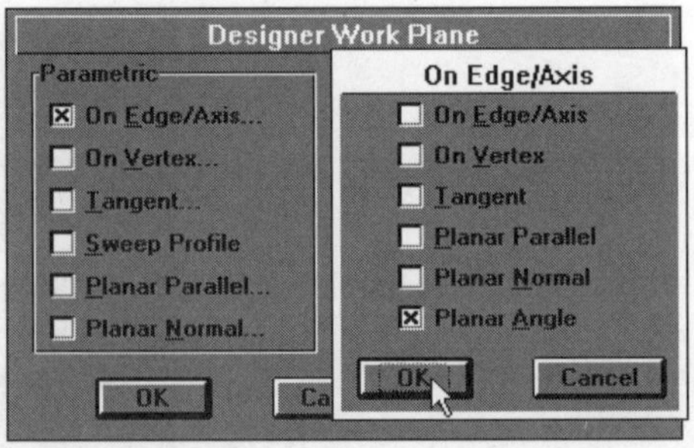

Fig. 11.9 An example of settings for **On Edge/Axis** and **Planar Angle**

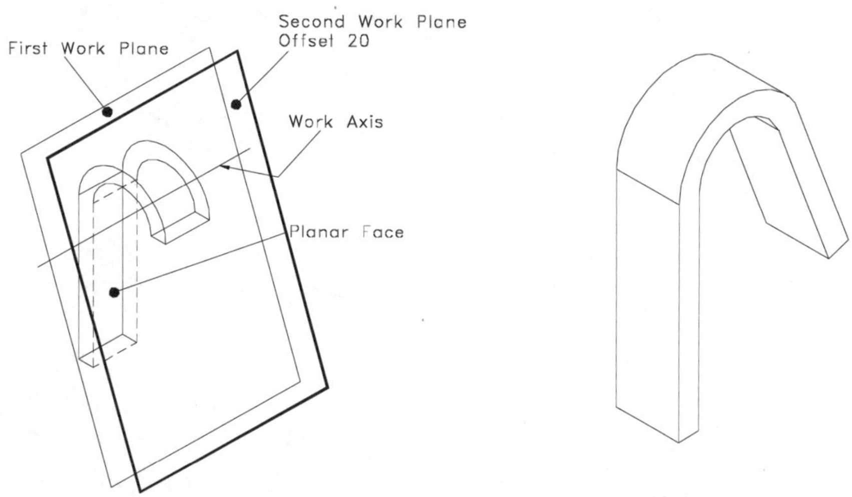

Fig. 11.10 An example of **On Edge/Axis** and **Parallel Angle** work plane

Next/<Accept>: *right-click* if correct face highlights
Angle in degrees <45>: *enter* required angle
Flip/<Accept>: *right-click* if arrows pointing in right direction

On Edge/Axis and Planar Parallel

In this example two groups of settings were made in **Designer work plane** dialogue box as shown in Fig. 11.11. The use of the **Planar Normal** work plane to use as a sketch plane for cutting a hole into the end of the smaller boss of the 3D model is shown in the right-hand drawing of Fig. 11.12.

When the first work plane settings have been made, the Command Line default options are:

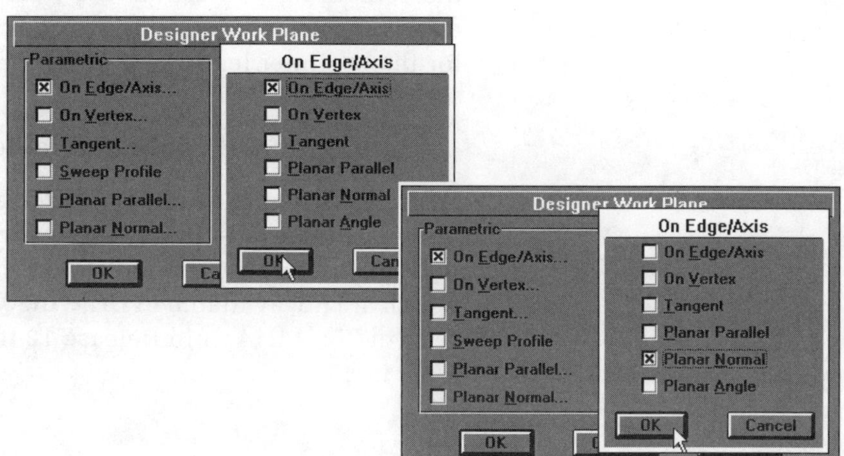

Fig. 11.11 Setting up an **Planar Normal** work plane

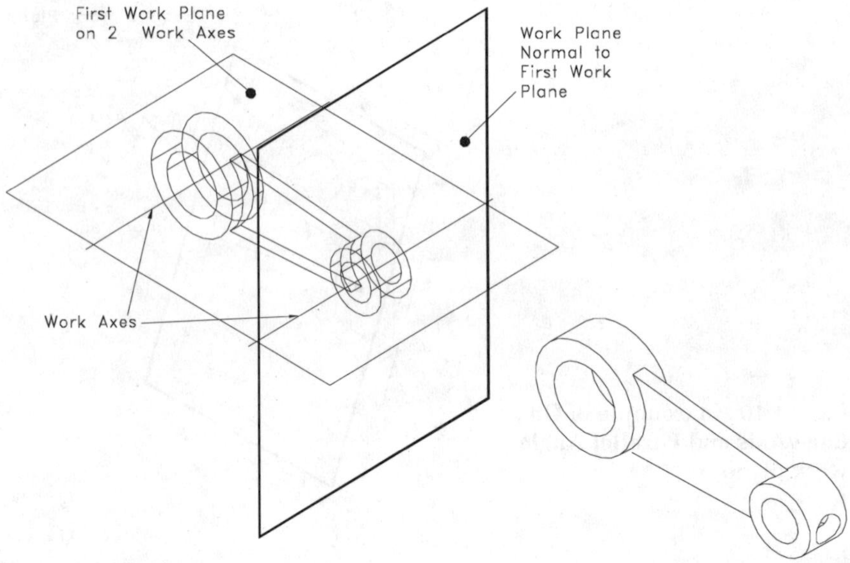

Fig. 11.12 An example of **Parallel Normal** work plane

<Select work axis or straight edge>:
Select work axis or straight edge:

And for setting the **Planar Normal** work plane:

<Select work axis or straight edge>:
Select work plane or planar face:

Other Designer commands

Most of the Designer commands have already been described and their uses illustrated in the previous chapters of this book. Some of the remaining commands are described in the following pages; others are beyond the scope of a book such as this, which is designed for the beginner learning how to use Designer.

Commands only available in Drawing Mode

While in **Drawing Mode**, with Designer orthographic views in the drawing editor *left-click* on **Designer** in the menu bar. The **Designer** pull-down menu appears and if working in Release 13 those commands which are not available in **Drawing Mode** are 'greyed out', as can be seen in Fig. 11.14. If in Release 12 the 'greying out' does not occur (Fig. 11.13).

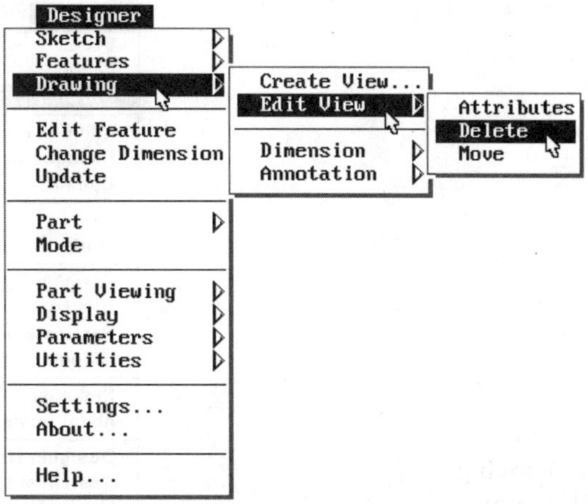

Fig. 11.13 Selecting **Drawing/ Delete** from the **Designer** pull-down menu

The command *addelview*

This is the command shown as selected in Fig. 11.13. When the command is selected, any view in the **Drawing Mode** editor can be deleted by placing the screen cursor onto a view followed by a *left-click*. The view instantly disappears, unless it is the parent view when the operator is asked whether he/she wants just that view deleted or the view and its related views.

The command *admoveview*

Figure 11.13. Select **Move** from the **Edit View** sub-menu. Place the cursor under mouse control onto the view to be moved and drag the view to its required new position. If it is the parent view that is selected, views related to it move as well. Other views can be moved independently.

The command *adrefdim*

Call **adrefdim** or select **Ref Dim** from the menu (Fig. 11.14) and by selecting any entity in a view in the **Drawing Mode** editor, a dimension can be added to the view. The dimension figure comes up automatically based upon the actual size of the entity (and related to its scale). An example is given in Fig. 11.15. Dimensions can be deleted from a view with the aid of **addelref** (**Delete Ref Dim** in the menu).

From the same sub-menu in Fig. 11.14, dimensions can be moved, frozen or thawed. The commands **adfrzdim** and **adthawdim** have been referred to in earlier pages.

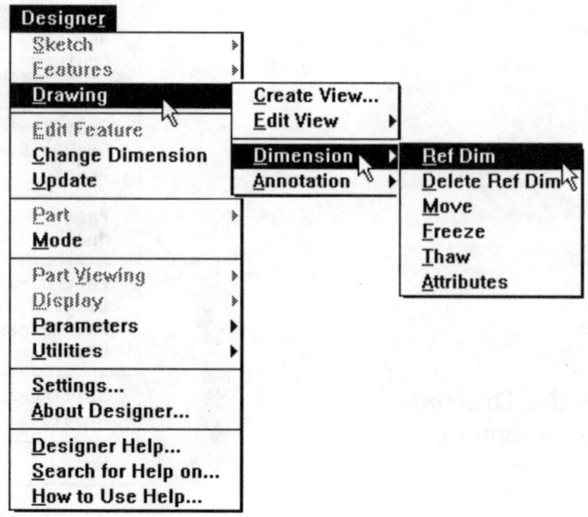

Fig. 11.14 The **Drawing/ Dimension** sub-menu

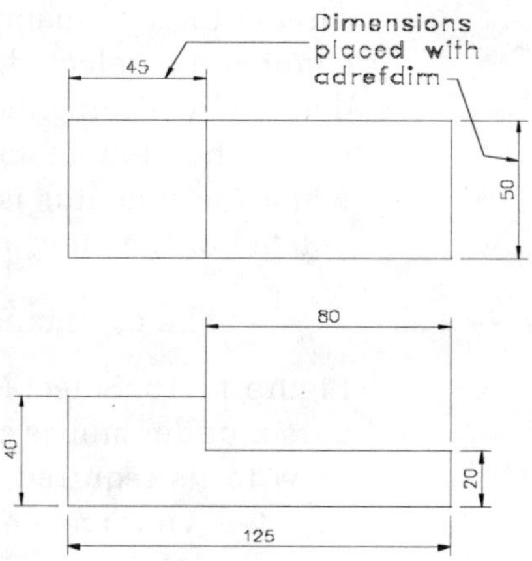

Fig. 11.15 An example of dimensions added with **adrefdim**

The command *addimatt*

When the command **Attributes** is selected from the sub-menu in Fig. 11.14, and a view selected, the dialogue box **Base Drawing View Attributes** appears (Fig. 11.16). An example of the use of **addimatt** is given in Fig. 11.17.

The commands in the Annotation sub-menu

These commands deal with adding notes to views when in **Drawing Mode**. Notes can be created (**Create**), deleted, moved, added or removed. Dimension leaders can be moved with **Move Leader**. A good example of an annotation is the addition of a **Hole Note** previously illustrated on page 129.

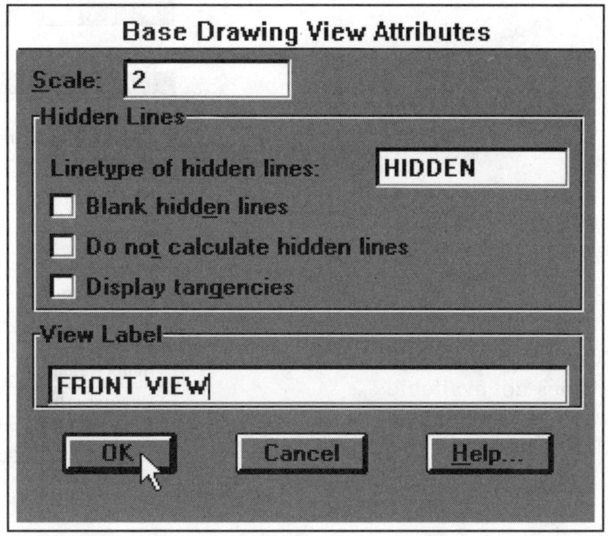

Fig. 11.16 The **Base Drawing View Attributes** dialogue box

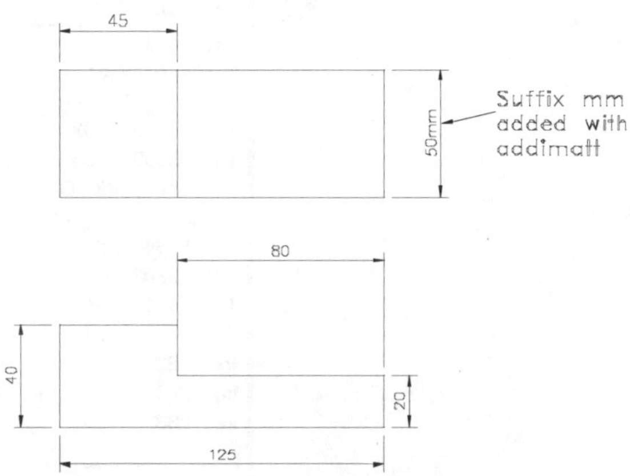

Fig. 11.17 A suffix (mm) added to a dimension with the aid of **addimatt**

The commands in the Utilities sub-menu

A few of the commands in this group (Fig. 11.20) are of interest to those learning to use Designer.

Mass Properties – *Left-click* on **Mass Properties** and the **Designer Mass Properties** information box appears (Fig. 11.19) related to the part selected when the command is called. This particular group of mass properties relate to the simple 3D model shown in Figs 11.15 and 11.17.

Show Active – informs the operator of which Part is active among several parts in a 3D model.

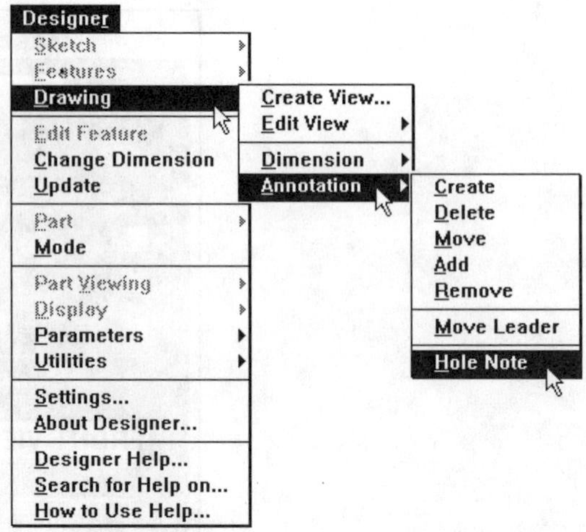

Fig. 11.18 The 'greying out' of command names not available when in **Drawing Mode** when in AutoCAD Release 13

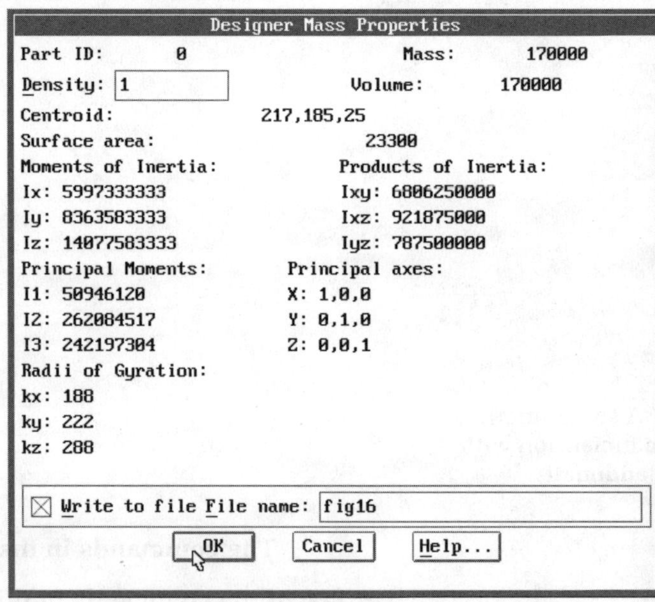

Fig. 11.19 An example of a **Designer Mass Properties** box

Transfer – Part Out allows a part from a Designer 3D model to be taken to its own file. That file containing the data of the part can be taken into another Designer drawing with **Part In**.

Transfer – SAT Out and **SAT In** allow the 3D data to be transferred to and from files in **.sat* format (ACIS files).

Transfer – AutoSurf/Out allows Designer 3D model data to be transferred to Autodesk AutoSurf, another 3D modelling and rendering software package that will work within AutoCAD (if loaded).

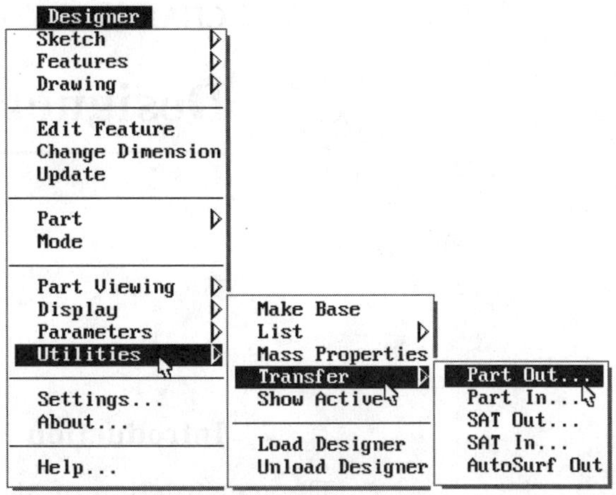

Fig. 11.20 The **Transfer** group of commands

Help

Help information boxes appear when **Help...** is called from the pull-down menu, by *entering* **help** or a **?** at the Command Line. If in the middle of working in a command sequence, *entering* **help** brings up the **Help** information boxes.

CHAPTER 12

Designer system variables

Introduction

The construction of 3D models in Designer is controlled to some extent by the settings of Designer *system variables*. In this chapter only those settings for the variables most likely to be of interest to the reader will be explained.

The Designer Settings dialogue box

Most, but not all, of the system variables can be set in the **Designer Settings** dialogue box (Fig. 12.1) called by either *entering* **adsettings** at the Command Line, or by a *left-click* on **Settings...** in the **Designer** pull-down menu. Some of the settings require check boxes to be **ON** or **OFF** (diagonals present or not present). Others may require the entry of figures. Some of the settings are made in dialogue boxes called from the **Designer Settings** dialogue box.

Settings can be made from the dialogue box as follows:

Rule Mode – if its box is checked, constraints are applied automatically. If unchecked, constraints are not applied. The variable can also be set from the Command Line:

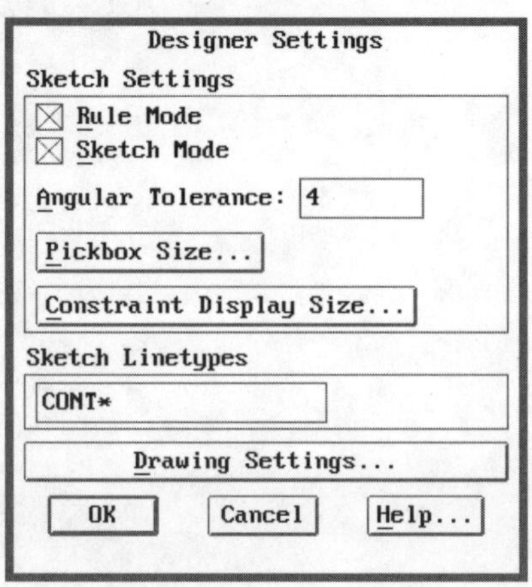

Fig. 12.1 The **Designer Settings** dialogue box

Command: *enter* adrulemode *right-click*
New value for ADRULEMODE (1=assume on, 0=off)<1>:

And either accept ON with a *right-click*, or *enter* 0 to turn OFF.

Figure 12.2 shows the constraints on a sketch profile with **adrulemode** set **ON** and Fig. 12.3 with **adrulemode** set **OFF**. If it is **OFF**, the parametricity of the 3D model is mostly destroyed (Fig. 12.4). However, if the parametric function of Designer is not required when constructing a 3D model, this may not matter.

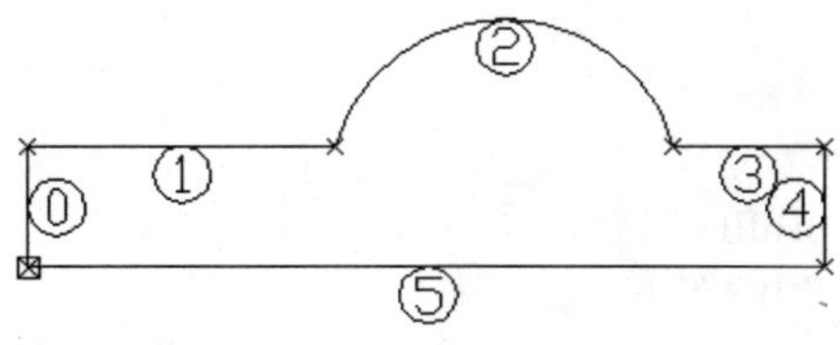

Fig. 12.2 A sketch profile showing constraints with **adrulemode** OFF

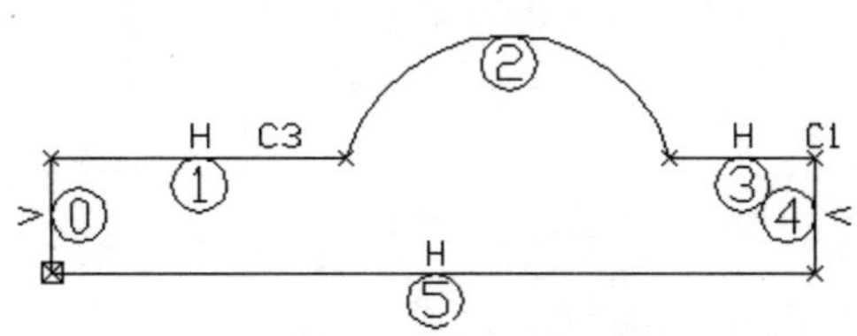

Fig. 12.3 The same sketch profile showing constraints with **adrulemode** ON

Sketch Mode – if its box is checked, poorly constructed outlines for sketch profiles are automatically 'cleaned up', any entities out of vertical, horizontal, perpendicular, etc., being restrained to vertical, horizontal, perpendicular, etc., within the limits of the **Pickbox Size** (see later) – Fig. 12.6. If the check box is unchecked, the

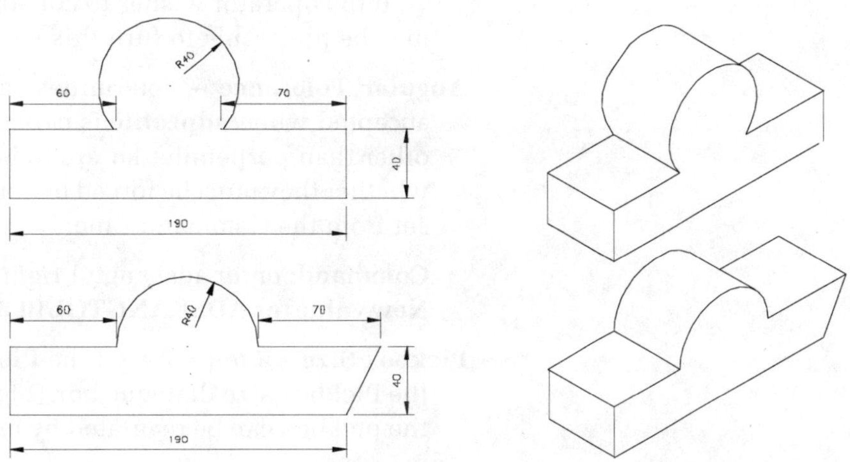

Fig. 12.4 3D models showing the reults of using **adeditfeat** to change one dimension when **adrulemode** is ON (top drawings) and OFF (bottom drawings)

outline is accepted as the required sketch profile (Fig. 12.5). This variable can also be set from the Command Line:

Command: *enter* adskmode *right-click*
New value for ADSKMODE (1=sketch, 0=precise)<1>:

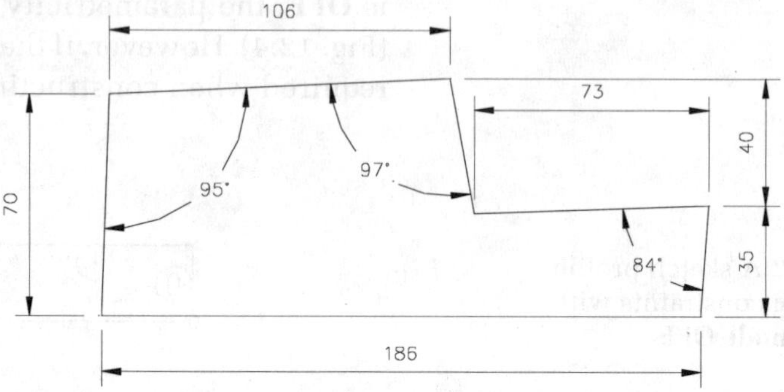

Fig. 12.5 A sketch profile dimensioned with **adpardim** with **adskmode** OFF

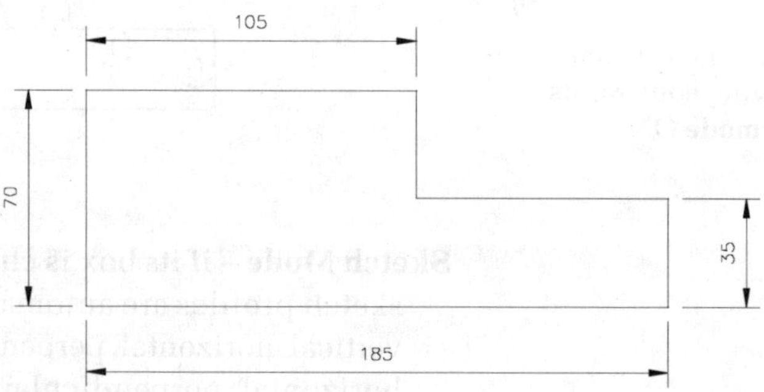

Fig. 12.6 The same sketch profile as in Fig. 12.5 with **adskmode** ON

And either accept with a *right-click* or *enter* 0 to turn OFF.

If the operator wishes to construct precise Sketch outlines, it may be preferable to turn this setting OFF.

Angular Tolerance – determines the limits of angles which are accepted when **adprofile** is called as to whether lines at angles other than perpendicular are to be regarded as being precise or whether they must be forced to horizontal or vertical. Can also be set from the Command Line:

Command: *enter* adskangtol *right-click*
New value for ADSKANGTOL (0.001 to 10): *enter* required figure

Pickbox Size – a *left-click* on the **Pickbox Size...** button, brings up the **Pickbox size** dialogue box (Fig. 12.7), from which the size of the pickbox can be regulated by moving the slider. This variable

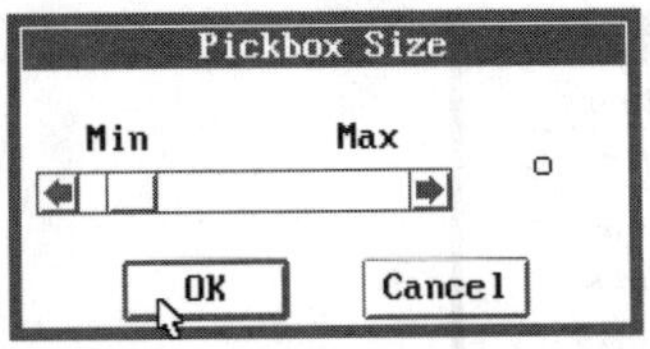

Fig. 12.7 The **Pickbox Size** dialogue box

can also be set from the Command Line. Note that this is an AutoCAD variable, not a Designer one:

Command: *enter* pickbox *right-click*
New value for pickbox <3>:

And either accept with a *right-click*, or *enter* another figure.

In Designer, pickbox size is not only important in that, when picking a point on a drawing, the point must lie within the limits of the box size, but also, as indicated above, controls the outline of the sketch profile when **adskmode** is ON.

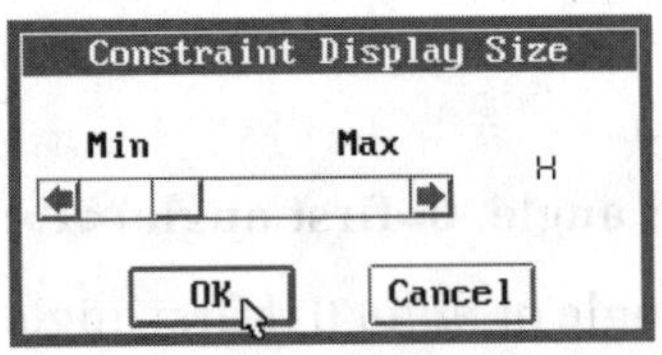

Fig. 12.8 Setting the size of the constraints in the **Constraint Display Size** dialogue box

Constraint Display Size – a *left-click* on the **Constraint Display Size...** button brings up the **Constraint Display Size** dialogue box (Fig. 12.8). The variable may also be set from the Command Line:

Command: *enter* adcondspsz *right-click*
New value for ADCONDsPSZ (1-19) <5>:

And either accept the 5 with a *right-click*, or *enter* another figure.

Figure 12.9 shows the constraints on a sketch profile with the size set to 3 and Fig. 12.10 with the setting at 5.

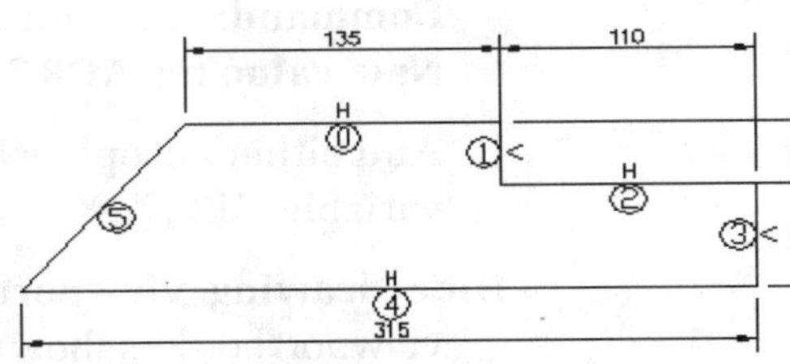

Fig. 12.9 A sketch profile with constraints 3 high

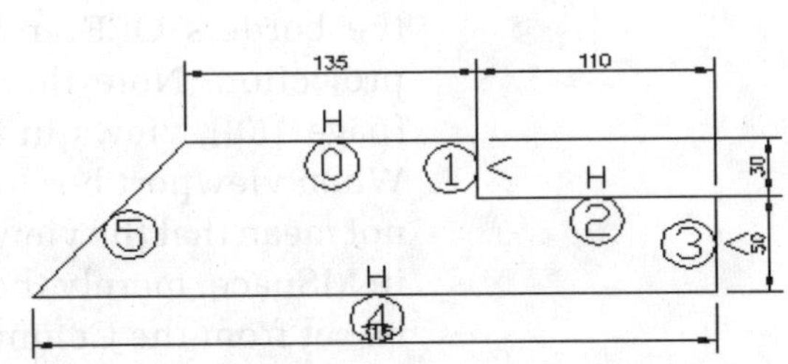

Fig. 12.10 A sketch profile with constraints 5 high

Drawing Variables

A *left-click* on the **Drawing Settings...** button, brings up the relevant dialogue box (Fig. 12.11), from which a number of variables can be set.

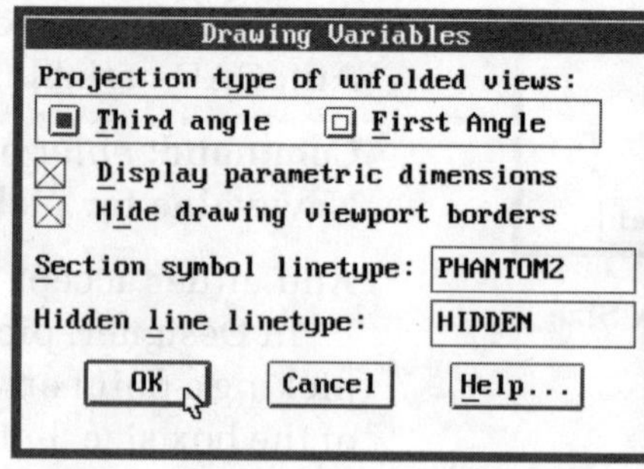

Fig. 12.11 The **Drawing Variables** dialogue box

Third Angle or **First Angle** – either *left-click* in the desired box or from the Command Line:

Command: *enter* adprojtype *right-click*
New value for ADPROJTYPE (1=third angle, 0=first angle)<1>:

And either *right-click* to accept third angle or *enter* 0 if first angle projection is required.

Display parametric dimensions – if OFF (check box clear), parametric dimensions do not show in the orthographic projection when **adview** is called. If ON the dimensions do show in the orthographic views. This variable can also be set at the Command Line:

Command: *enter* adreusedim *right-click*
New value for ADREUSEDIM (1=yes, 0=no)<1>:

And either accept ON with a *right-click*, or *enter* 0 to switch the variable OFF.

Hide drawing viewport borders – if the check box is set ON, viewport borders show in the **Drawing Mode** orthographic projection. If OFF (default) they do not show. Figures 12.12 and 12.13 show the borders OFF and ON in a simple Designer orthographic projection. Note that, as has been stated earlier in this book (page 158), views in **Drawing Mode** are in MSpace viewports. When viewport borders are showing with **adborder** ON, it does not mean that the views showing in the **Drawing Mode** screen are in MSpace, merely that the borders show. This variable can also be set from the Command Line:

Command: *enter* adborder *right-click*
New value for ADBORDER (1=hide, 0=show):

And either accept **hide** with a *right-click* or *enter* 0 if it is wished to show the viewport borders.

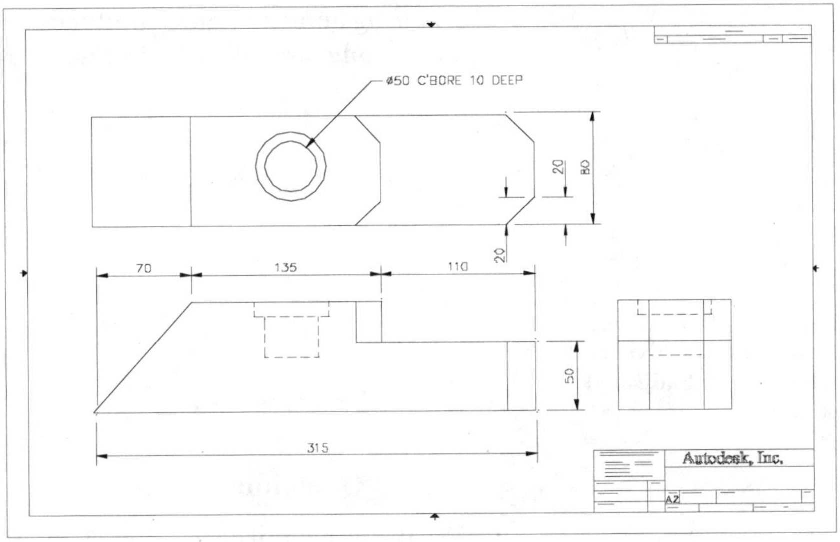

Fig. 12.12 **Drawing Mode** with **adborder** OFF

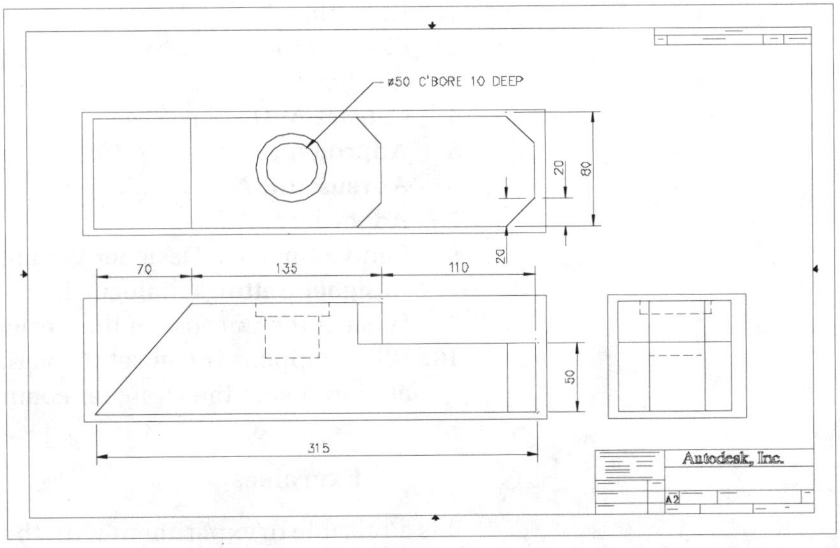

Fig. 12.13 **Drawing Mode** with **adborder** ON

The two other boxes within the **Designer Settings** dialogue box allow linetypes to be set, as shown in Fig. 12.11.

One other Designer variable which the reader should experiment with is **adisocyl**. This sets the number of lines used in isometric drawings in the **Part Mode** of Designer. This variable is set from the Command Line:

Command: *enter* adisocyl *right-click*
New value for ADISOCYL (0 to 100) <2>:

Entering another figure produces a result in isometric drawings in **Part Mode**, as indicated in Fig. 12.14.

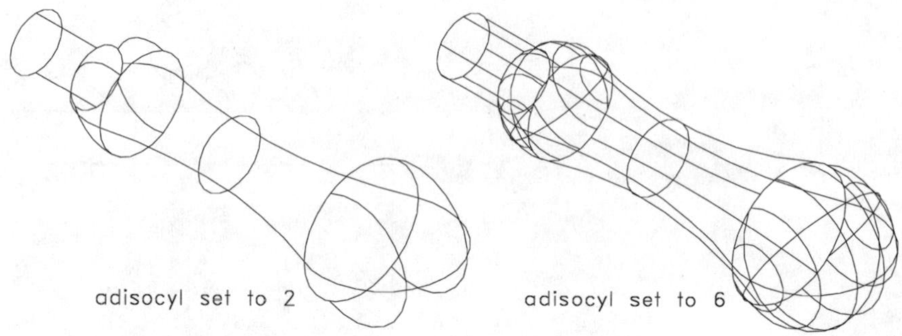

Fig. 12.14 Two views of a **Designer adrevolve** model with different **adisocyl** settings

Questions

What is the purpose of each of the following Designer system variables:

1. Rule Mode?
2. Sketch Mode
3. Pickbox?
4. Constraint Display Size?
5. **Adprojtype**?
6. **Adreusedim**?
7. **Adborder**?
8. Can you name a Designer variable which cannot be set from the **Designer Settings** dialogue box?
9. What is the purpose of the Designer variable **adisocyl**?
10. What happens if you set the variable **adrulemode** OFF and then attempt using the Designer command **adeditfeat**?

Exercises

It is advisable to experiment with the Designer system variables, but when you do so, make certain that you leave the computer with the settings as they were when you started experimenting. If you change the settings and leave them changed, the next operator to use the computer may find difficulties with his/her work. This does not matter if you are the only person to use the computer.

As examples of experimentation:

1. The 3D model (Fig. 12.14) is an **adrevolve** forming a handle of the type fitted to files. Working to any suitable sizes, construct a solid of revolution of a similar form, after first setting **adisocyl** to the

figure 12. Then, undo your drawing back to the sketch profile with repeated use of the AutoCAD command **undo** (abbreviation is usually u). Then reset **adisocyl** to, say, 4 and **adrevolve** the sketch profile again.

2. Set the Designer variable **adborder** to 0 (that is to show borders). Then construct the Designer drawing shown in Fig. 12.12 and from it produce orthographic views in the **Drawing Mode** editor. Then reset **adborder** back to 1 and call **adupdate**. What happens?
3. Experiment with the various settings of the variable **adcondspsz** to check what happens to a sketch profile when setting the figure to, say, 2, then 6, then 18, etc. when **adshowcon** is called and the **All** prompt selected. Each time you do this, construct a new sketch profile **after** setting the variable.
4. One variable you should experiment with is **adrulemode** by setting it first OFF then ON. After each setting build up a simple Designer 3D model from a dimensioned sketch profile and try amending dimensions with **adeditfeat**.

CHAPTER 13

Parametric models

Introduction

This final chapter describes three simple models with dimensions which are in parametric form with equations linked to one main dimension. The first example is an extrusion, the second a solid of revolution and the third a sweep.

First example – an extrusion

The first example is a Designer 3D model of a gib key.

1. The outline for the sketch was drawn, it was then changed to a sketch profile with **adprofile** and before dimensions were added, the Designer command **addimdsp** was called to set parametric dimensions:

   Command: *enter* addimdsp *right-click*
   Parameters/Equations/<Numeric>: *enter* p *right-click*
   Command:

   And all dimensions change to parametric form as in Fig. 13.1.
2. The sketch profile was then extruded through 10 units (**adextrude**).
3. **Adview** was called and a single base view placed in **Drawing Mode** (Fig. 13.2).
4. With the model in the isometric view of **adpartview**, the Designer command **adeditfeat** was called to change all dimensions into equations linked to dimension d0 (which is 125):

   Command: *enter* adeditfeat *right-click*
   Sketch/<Select feature>: *pick* the model
   Select dimension to change: *pick* dimension d1
   New value for dimension <25>: *enter* =d0/5 *right-click*
   Select dimension to change: *pick* dimension d2
   New value for dimension <5>: *enter* =d0/25 *right-click*
   Select dimension to change: *pick* dimension d3
   New value for dimension <40>: *enter* =d0/8.33 *right-click*

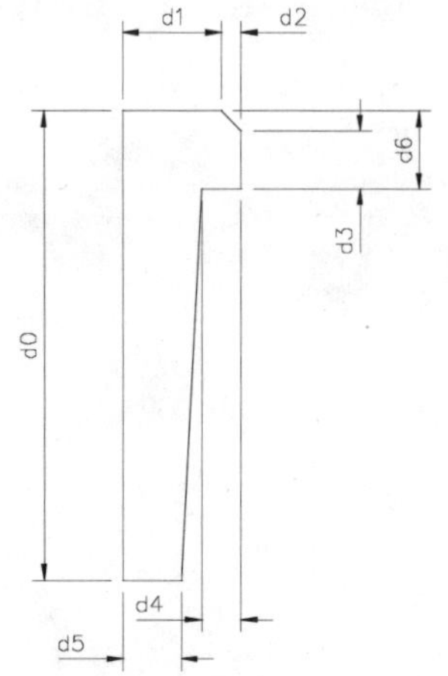

Fig. 13.1 First example. The sketch profile with parametric dimensions

Continue in this manner until all dimensions have been linked by an equation to the dimension d0. The resulting complete set should be:

d0 = 125
d1 = d0/5
d2 = d0/25
d3 = d0/8.33
d4 = d0/12.5
d5 = d0/8.33
d6 = d0/6.25
d7 = d0/12.5
Command:

5. Call **adupdate** to update the changes to parametric dimensioning.
6. Call **adview** and place a single **Base** view in the **Drawing Mode** screen (Fig. 13.2).
7. Call **admode** to get back into the **Part** screen.

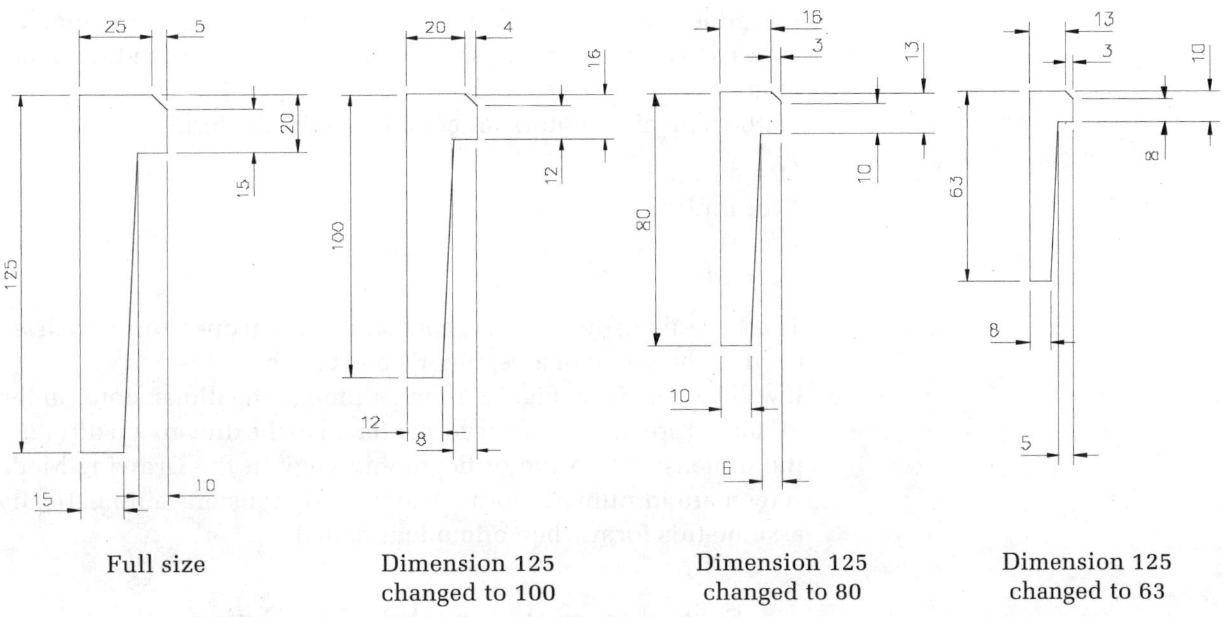

Fig. 13.2 First example. The original full-scale drawing of the gib key, together with changes to the basic dimension d0 from 125 to 100, to 80 and to 63

8. Call **adeditfeat** again:

   Command: *enter* adeditfeat *right-click*
   Sketch/<Select feature>: *pick* the model
   Select dimension to change: *pick* dimension d1
   New value for dimension <125>: *enter* 100 *right-click*
   Select dimension to change: *right-click*
   Command:

9. Call **adupdate** to update the changes made.
10. Place this updated view into a **Base** view in the **Drawing Mode** screen with **admode.**

    Continue in this manner changing the basic d0 dimension of 125 into 100, 80, and 63 as shown in the series of views in Fig. 13.2.

Notes

1. Remember to ensure that ALL dimensions are linked to a single dimension. Failure to do so will result in a warning appearing at the Command Line when you attempt to update.
2. All dimensions require an equation linked to the base dimension.
3. **Adupdate** must be called before using **adview** to obtain orthographic views. If you forget to do so, a warning appears at the Command Line.
4. Mathematical operators for equations take the form:

   / for divide
   * for multiply
   – for subtract
   + for add

5. There are also a number of other mathematical operators which are beyond the scope of a beginner's book such as this.
6. It will be seen from Fig. 13.2 that, although the dimensions on the 3D model are in parametric form related to the dimension d0 (125), the dimensions on the orthographic view in the **Drawing Mode** screen are in numeric form. The view dimensions automatically assume this form when **admode** is called.

Second example – a solid of revolution

This example was constructed following the same methods as for the first example, except that the 3D model was produced by **adrevolve** from the sketch profile illustrated in Fig. 13.3. The stages were (in abbreviated form):

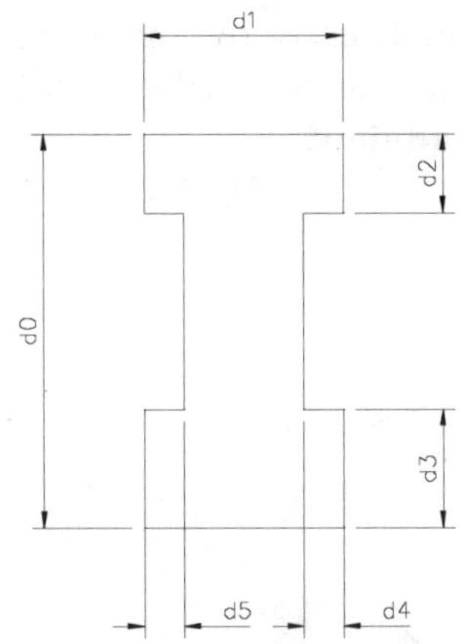

Fig. 13.3 Second example. The sketch profile with its parametric dimensions

1. Draw the sketch outline. Call **adprofile** and change it into a sketch profile.
2. With **adpardim** dimension the sketch profile until it is fully dimensioned/constrained.
3. With **addimdsp** set the dimensions to be in parametric form. This is the form in which they appear in Fig. 13.3.
4. With **adrevolve** change the sketch profile into a **Full** solid of revolution.
5. With **adeditfeat** set equations for the dimensions. These should be:

   d0 = 100
   d1 = d0/2
   d2 = d0*.2
   d3 = d0*.3
   d4 = d0*.1
   d5 = d0*.1

6. With **adupdate**, update the amendments.
7. Call **admode** and produce a **Base** view. From the base view produce an **Ortho** view (Fig. 13.4).

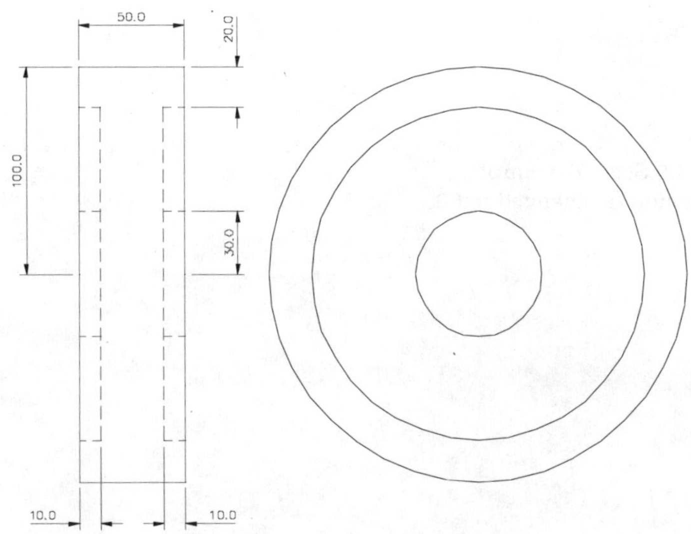

Fig. 13.4 Second example. Before modifying dimensions

8. With **adeditfeat** change dimensions parametrically by changing the 100 dimension (d0), first to 80 (Fig. 13.5), then to 60 (Fig. 13.6), followed in each case with **adupdate** and **adview**.

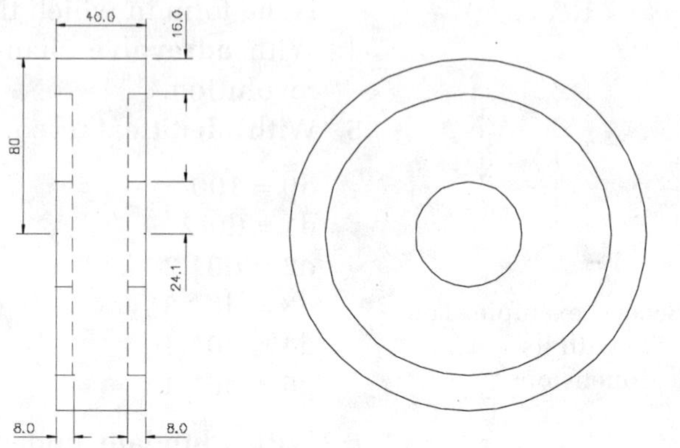

Fig. 13.5 Second example. Dimension d0 changed to 80

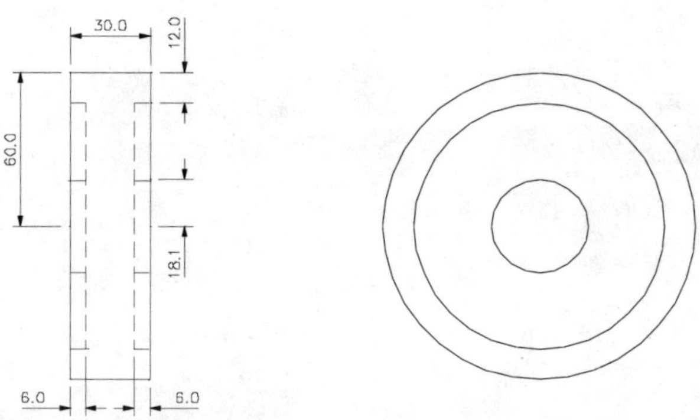

Fig. 13.6 Second example. Dimension d0 changed to 60

Third example – a sweep

The same procedures were followed for this example as for the first two. Note, however, that when the dimensions are scaled below a certain level, the results may not be as desired. This is evident from the result of amending the d0 dimension to 30 (Fig. 13.9). Although the drawing retained its parametric functions, the results were not at all what was intended.

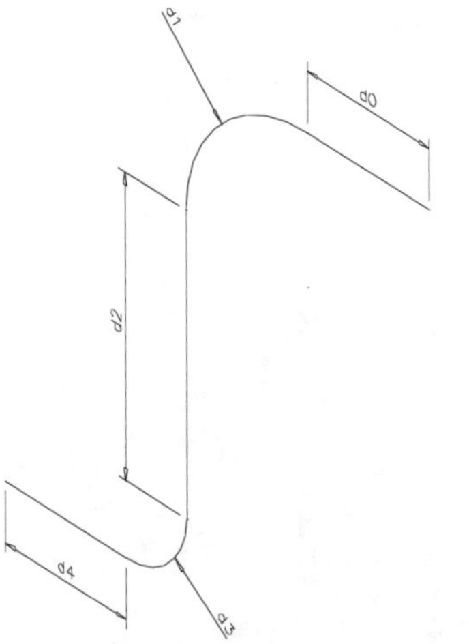

Fig. 13.7 Third example. Path profile for the sweep, showing parametric dimensions

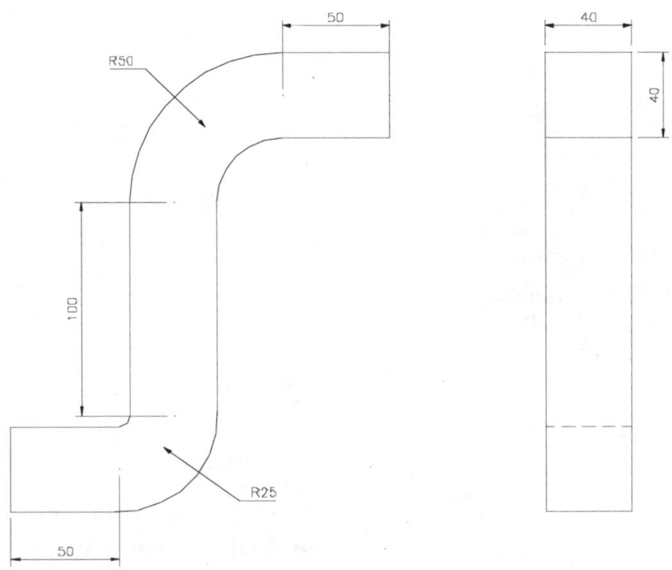

Fig. 13.8 Third example. A two-view orthographic projection from the original 3D model

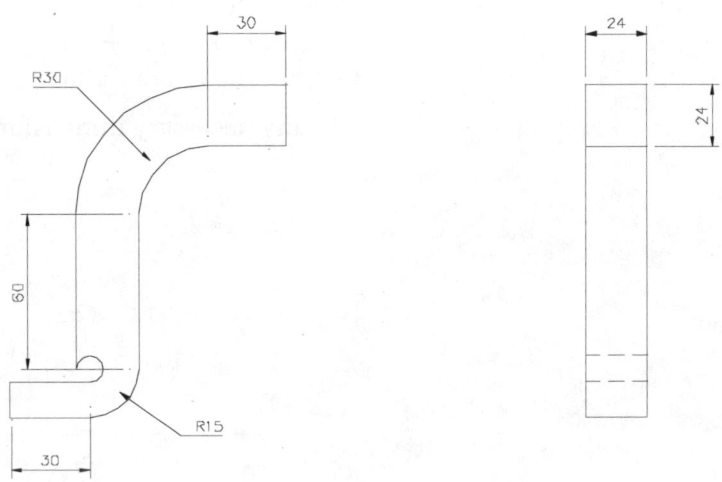

Fig. 13.9 Third example. After amending the dimension d0 to 30

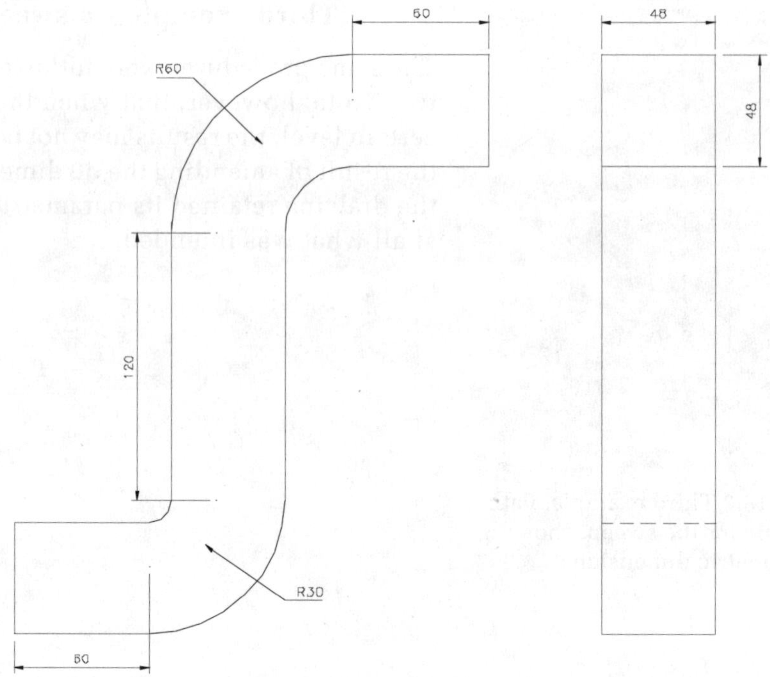

Fig. 13.10 Third example. After amending the d0 dimension to 60

Exercises

1. Construct a 3D Designer model of the feature shown in Fig. 13.11. Include dimensions in your sketch profile with **adpardim**. Using parametric dimensions, produce three two-view third-angle orthographic projections as follows:

   1 – with the height = 50
   2 – with the height = 35
   3 – with the height = 25

   Add any necessary dimensions to your views with **adrefdim**.

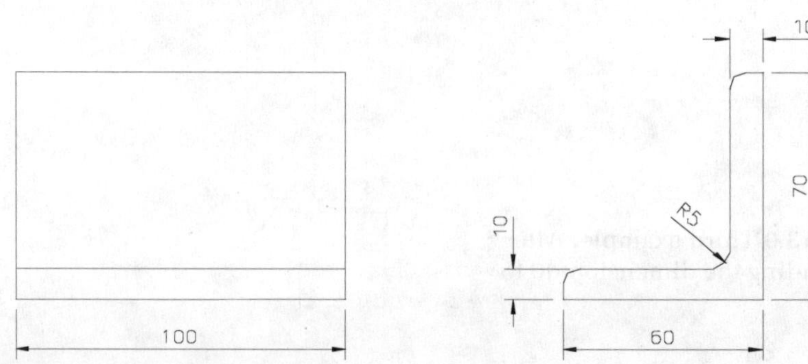

Fig. 13.11 Exercise 1

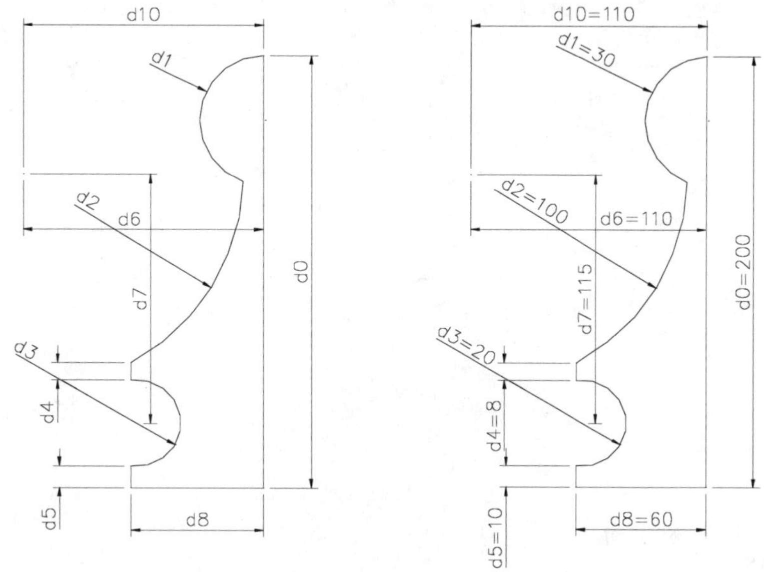

Fig. 13.12 Exercise 2. The sketch profile with **Parametric** and with **Equation** dimensions

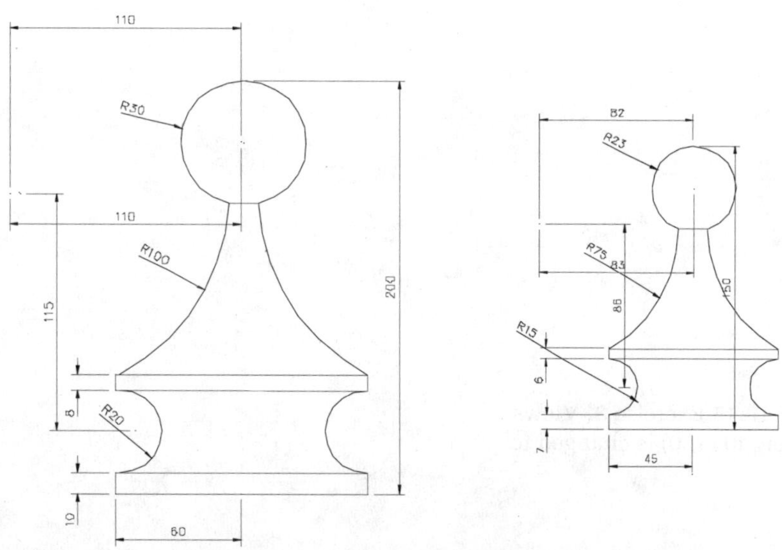

Fig. 13.13 Exercise 2. The two parametric orthographic projections

2. Figure 13.12 shows two copies of the sketch profile for this exercise. The second shows dimensions after calling **addimdsp**:

   Command: *enter* addimdsp *right-click*
   Parameters/Equations/<Numeric>: *enter* e *right-click*
   Command:

   Draw the sketch profile; with **adrevolve** turn it into a solid of revolution and with **adeditfeat** produce the second view of Fig. 13.13.

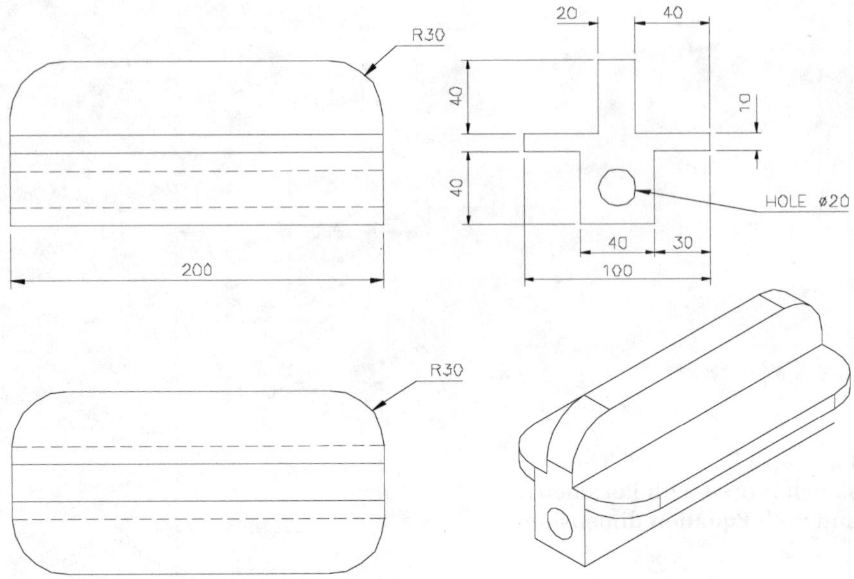

Fig. 13.14 Exercise 3. Full-size views

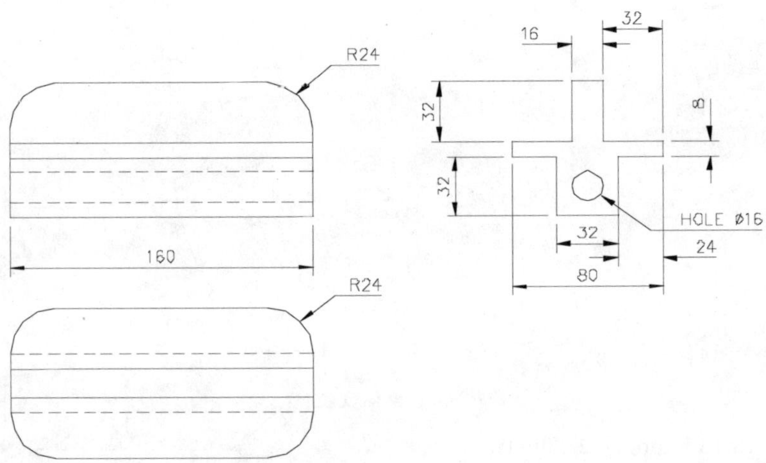

Fig. 13.15 Exercise 3. Views when d0 (100) is changed to 80

3. Figures 13.14 and 13.15 show two orthographic projections and an isometric view of a slider. Construct a Designer 3D model to the dimensions given in Fig. 13.14, ensure that dimensions on the sketch profile are parametric and produce both sets of orthographic views given in Figs 13.14 and 13.15.

   Note that the hole and the fillets must be selected as a Designer hole and fillets in response to prompts when **adeditfeat** is called. The hole parameter must also be set in the **Designer Hole** dialogue box.

Further exercises

The remaining exercises in this chapter are not intended to be of a parametric type. They are included here to give the reader further practise involving rather more complicated Designer models.

4. Figure 13.16 is an AutoVision rendering of a lever from a machine. Figure 13.17 is a Designer isometric view of the lever and Fig. 13.18 a Designer third-angle orthographic projection of the lever. Working to the information given in the three illustrations construct a Designer 3D model of the lever, add the orthographic and isometric views, and if you have access to a rendering program, render your model.

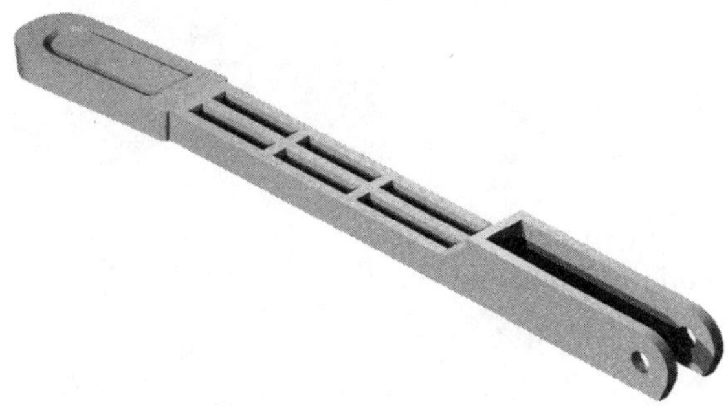

Fig. 13.16 Exercise 4. A rendering of the model

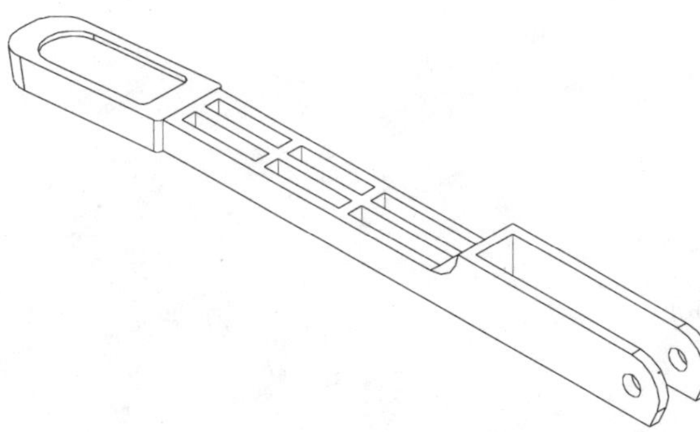

Fig. 13.17 Exercise 4. An isometric view of the model

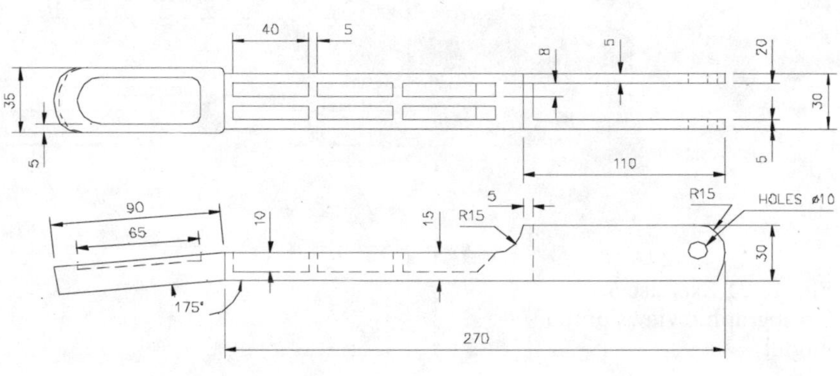

Fig. 13.18 Exercise 4. Orthographic views of the model

5. Figure 13.19 is a rendering of a slider from the machine which includes the lever for Exercise 4. Figure 13.20 is a Designer isometric view and Fig. 13.21 gives Designer orthographic views of the slider.

   Construct a Designer 3D model from the information given in the three illustrations, and add the isometric and orthographic views.

   If you have access to a rendering software package, render your 3D model.

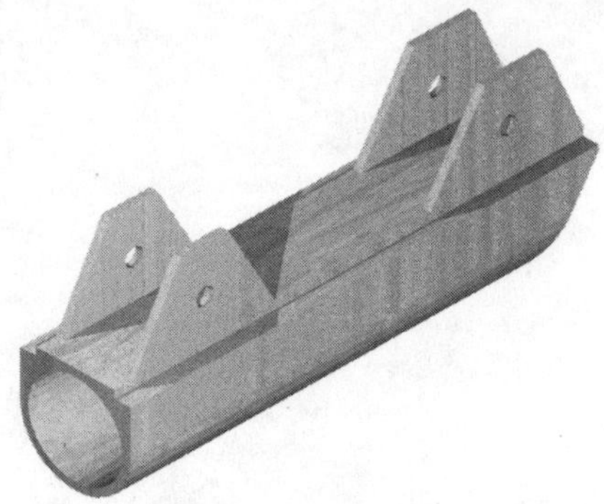

Fig. 13.19 Exercise 5. A rendering of the model

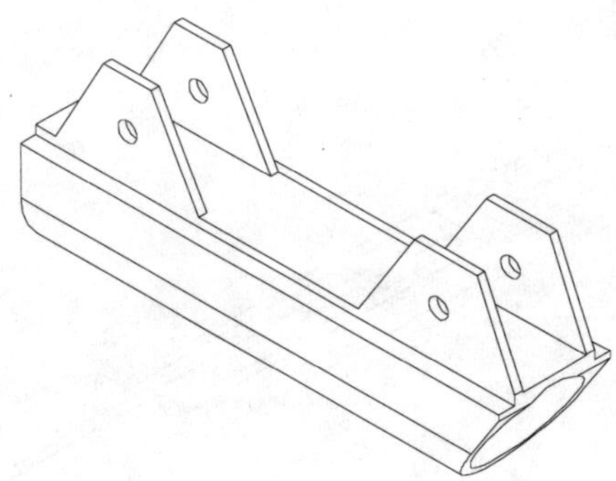

Fig. 13.20 Exercise 5. An isometric view of the model

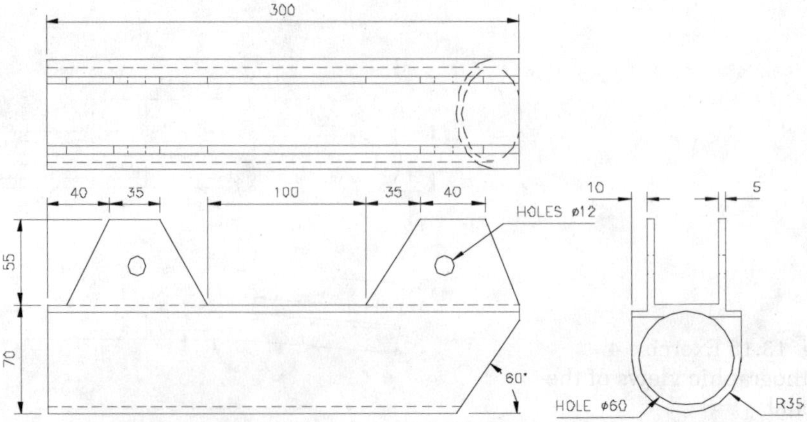

Fig. 13.21 Exercise 5. Orthographic views of the model

Index